Lockout

Lockout

Why America Keeps Getting
Immigration Wrong When Our Prosperity
Depends on Getting It Right

⌐◦⌐

Michele Wucker

New York

Designed by Trish Wilkinson
Set in 11.5-point Goudy by the Perseus Books Group

Library of Congress Cataloging-in-Publication Data

Wucker, Michele, 1969–
     Lockout : why America keeps getting immigration wrong when our
prosperity depends on getting it right.
        p.   cm.
     Includes bibliographical references and index.
     ISBN-13: 978-1-58648-356-2 (hardcover : alk. paper)
     ISBN-10: 1-58648-356-0 (hardcover : alk. paper)   1. United
States—Emigration and immigration—Government policy.
2. Immigrants—Government policy—United States. I. Title: Lock out.
II. Title.
JV6483.W83 2006
325.73—dc22   2006007259

10 9 8 7 6 5 4 3 2 1

Contents

Acknowledgments

I would like to thank the World Policy Institute at the New School and my colleagues there, especially Belinda Cooper, Ian Cuthbertson, and Mira Kamdar of the Program on Citizenship and Security, for providing a supportive, engaging environment in which to write this book. I am grateful to Yamil Avivi, Christina Kiel, Kate Maloff, Aninka Martek, Andrea Schierbaum, and Julio Schuback for research assistance. Karl Meyer and Linda Wrigley helped to develop some of the ideas here for articles in *World Policy Journal*. Thanks also to Radiah Dove, Silvana Paternostro, Bill Hartung, Ben Pauker, and Stephen Schlesinger and to Aristide Zolberg at the International Center for Migration, Ethnicity, and Citizenship.

Some of the reporting for this book also appeared in very different form in publications including *The American Prospect*, *Tikkun*, *Worth*, and *Harper's*.

So many friends, family members, and mentors have been important to seeing this book through that I know I would leave out important people if I attempted to mention them all. Instead, I will try to list those who have been most directly involved in the book: Anne Kornhauser, Michael Pettis, Katie Orenstein, Lucia Suarez, Ian Bremmer, Peter Marber, Jon Anderson, David Buchmann, David Callahan, Rajiv Khanna, Cyrus Mehta, Susan Benesch, Maria Perignon, Scott Fitzgerald, Lenora Suki,

Katie Thomson, and Amy Waldman, for providing feedback and encouragement; Linda Chen, Emily Schwartz Greco, Tommy Greco, Frank Smyth, and Florence and Tanya Dinerstein for their friendship and for hosting me on research trips; and Jessie Klein, Mary D'Ambrosio, Jean Leong, and Melissa Rawlins Hanley, for unflagging enthusiasm and affirmation. Cheryl Wertz and Bryan Pu-Folkes at New Immigrant Community Empowerment provided ongoing inspiration through their commitment to collaboration among immigrants and "established" Americans. Ron Hayduk, my colleague at the Immigrant Voting Project, also provided helpful background information on the history of immigrant political participation.

I also would like to thank those people, too many to mention individually, who took time to sit down with me to talk about the issues in this book and to provide me with additional leads and contacts.

Special thanks to my agent, Andrew Stuart, for believing in a book that did not fit neatly into any preconceived package, as did Clive Priddle and Peter Osnos at PublicAffairs. Carol Smith and John Guardiano did a wonderful job shepherding the book through production and copyediting.

The many Dominicans and Haitians whom I met because of my first book, *Why the Cocks Fight*, cannot begin to know how important their stories were in inspiring this book. Finally, thanks to my family for providing the kernel of this story and for supporting my decision to write it.

Preface

I am a typical mongrel American whose ancestors came from Germany, Central Europe, and Belgium during three very distinct periods: the 1848 exodus of German reformers, the Great Wave of immigration at the beginning of the twentieth century, and the end of World War II. As it has been for many Americans, immigration is a pillar of our family story. When I was a little girl learning how to read in the Midwest, my mother taped note cards with French translations into my books. My favorite was *Are You My Mother?* (*Êtes-vous ma mère?*). I loved how the *teuf-teuf* explained to the little *oiseau* that a steam shovel couldn't possibly be a little bird's mother. I didn't come to understand until years later that the hand-lettered cards in my books represented my mother's own quiet rebellion; she was reclaiming the language that had been forced out of her childhood. From age two, she'd lived in Milwaukee, where her GI father had brought her and his Belgian wife from Brussels after the end of World War II. There they encountered my great-grandmother—a fierce woman whose own grandfather had come to America from Germany a century earlier—who turned an icy shoulder to her daughter-in-law for being a foreigner. My mother had to speak only English "because it wasn't polite to speak a foreign language in front of people who didn't know it." But my great-grandmother effortlessly operated on a double standard: she spoke German. Although her family had been in America

for a hundred years—generations!—she had not given up the old language, even after two World Wars in which the old country was on the wrong side. My mother later insisted I learn French and call my Belgian grandmother "Bobonne," because the English word "Grandma," by which my dour great-grandmother was known, evoked such painful memories of a harsh welcome to America. My mother did not receive her family's blessing to speak French until she started college and convinced them that there were good job prospects for translators.

My mother's insistence that I start learning a foreign language early was the best thing she could have done for me. The ability to speak another language has been the deciding factor that has won me nearly every job I've ever had. In 1990, my resume and packet of clips found its way onto the city editor's desk at the *Milwaukee Sentinel* just days after the city's Hispanic leaders complained to the paper that it was not doing a good job of covering the community's burgeoning Hispanic community. With a firm command of Spanish after living in the Dominican Republic, where I had worked for a small newspaper, I began writing about Milwaukee's Mexicans, Puerto Ricans, and Central Americans. A year later, when I moved to New York City, I wrote about Central Americans, Dominicans, and Haitians, whose lives all seemed to be split between two countries.

In San Miguel, El Salvador, just at the end of the country's twelve-year civil war, I stayed with the family of a Salvadoran immigrant who was living in Queens so she could make enough money to support her two young sons. They had stayed behind with their grandmother in her home, which had a well but no running water. The eight-year-old was fascinated and confused about his mother's adopted New York City. "But when you get to the top of the skyscrapers, how do you get back down?" he wanted to know. In Washington Heights, a heavily Dominican neighborhood in Manhattan, I reported on political rallies for candidates for the presidency of the Dominican Republic, a country whose political parties raised roughly half of their campaign funds from the hundreds of thousands of Dominicans living in New York City. I interviewed a Dominican congressman who represented the province of

Santiago and all of the "absent Dominicans" from New York, Boston, Miami, Toronto, and other cities around North America. There was no formal such seat in the Dominican Congress, so the *dominicanos ausentes* held primaries here, and the winning candidate then had to return to the Dominican Republic to win another primary in his home province. As I write this, Dominican President Leonel Fernández, who grew up on New York City's Upper West Side, has been actively promoting the idea of creating formal offices. He argues that the absent Dominicans, who send home money on which the economy depends heavily, should be represented not only in their home country's national legislative body but also in municipal offices to reflect the fact that hometown associations in the United States fund many important public works in the Dominican Republic and therefore deserve a say in how money is spent.

This is a very different model of becoming American from the one I learned in school. To be American—at least the way I had come to understand it—meant leaving your old country behind. As I would come to understand later, this entrenched belief had become a central theme in the growing tensions over the newest wave of immigrants. To many Americans who, like me, had learned that you couldn't be American and something else too, today's immigrants' interest in their countries of birth represented a profound change. Perhaps because of my mother, I found this change exciting; yet many others were threatened by it.

The example of the Dominicans prompted me to try to learn more about my heritage on my father's side. I had always thought we were "German." How surprised I was to discover that our family was not German but had, in fact, come from what is now southeastern Austria, and when they arrived in America in the early twentieth century they spoke not only German but also the Croatian language of their ancestors who had come to the Burgenland 300 or more years earlier. As I dug into our history, I discovered other information that contradicted my expectations. Though my father still remembered that it was all but impossible to get his grandfather, Vincent, to talk about the old country, it turned out that my great-grandmother, Maria, had gone back to the Burgenland not once but three times. And more than seven decades after our

family supposedly "left everything behind," my grandfather's cousin still exchanged letters with members of the family in Austria, we dined out mostly at Milwaukee's many traditional German-style restaurants, and my grandmother still said "eggs" with a soft German "k" instead of a "g".

As I talked with friends and acquaintances about their family histories, I learned that so many had similar stories about their grandparents and great-grandparents. What was striking was not just how "American" they were, but how much they chose to retain from their ethnic pasts. A few years ago, my friend Mary, whose grandparents had come to Long Island from Italy, was able to get an Italian passport, which she now carries in addition to her American one. Certainly, the Italian document has significant sentimental value for Mary, who could pass for the classic Italian mother who serves fabulous dinners to her friends and family and is never convinced that they've eaten enough. But the passport also has practical and economic benefits. For one thing, she could work in the European Union if she wanted to. For another, as any frequent traveler abroad can attest, there are countries where the last passport you want to have to show is an American one.

Further research continually upset my expectations. In fact, the immigrants of the Great Wave and earlier had *not* given up their homelands. Until the First World War, for example, there were far more German-language than English-language printing presses in America (and how many Americans are aware that the Founding Fathers considered German as a possible national language instead of English?). Far fewer people stayed here than Americans had been led to believe. The historian Mark Wyman, in his book *Round-Trip to America: The Immigrants Return to Europe*, cites U.S. and European government statistics that suggest that during the Great Wave period, more than one-third of all immigrants—most of them European—went back to their home countries. For Italians, the rate from the 1880s through 1920s was 50 percent, and even higher during the turbulent years of 1902 to 1923. Those who stayed remained active participants in their homeland culture; they established vibrant ethnic societies, local media, and cultural organizations. Many of them, whether they stayed in America or went back to

their countries of birth, became involved in fighting for change in their homelands, where they sought to implant American ideals of democracy.

In the early 1920s, the American nativist movement that had been growing over a half century finally succeeded in dramatically cutting back immigration and intimidating immigrants into trying to obscure their foreign origins. Conventional wisdom today is that the Great Wave immigrants assimilated faster because America closed its doors and thus eased demographic pressure, because they were all European and thus could blend in easily, and because they accepted the covenant that they would give up their heritage.

Whenever people hear that I write about immigration, particularly integration and assimilation among today's immigrants, they inevitably launch into mini-lectures about how things were different when our ancestors came here. Speaking with an authority that no doubt goes all the way back to the same kind of grade school lessons that I absorbed, they tell me that until recently, immigrants came to America to stay. People who came from Europe during the Great Wave or even before—my cocktail-party companions will insist—knew that they had to Americanize, assimilate, learn English, and forget about going back home.

But if that were true, I wonder, why did my own family's story, as American as could be, contradict it? Why do we continue to celebrate St. Patrick's Day and learn in kindergarten about all of the foreign words—including "kindergarten" itself—that came from immigrants? Why are so many of America's favorite foods the creation of immigrants who blended their own traditions with American preferences to create entirely new foods like pizza and fortune cookies? Ersatz as they may be, these ethnic markers are not the evidence of a generation of immigrants that harbored no fondness for their old cultures and customs.

During the course of writing my first book, *Why the Cocks Fight: Dominicans, Haitians, and the Struggle for Hispaniola*, a social history of two nations on one island and the resulting tensions related to immigration and a shared border, I saw clearly that culture and our attitudes toward it are malleable. When I arrived in the Dominican Republic in 1998 to study the impact of cultural differences with Haiti, everyone told me

that the two countries had problems with each other because Haitian culture and history were so different. I soon came to believe that something very close to the opposite was true: that they had much in common, and people seemed to complain about cultural differences only when economic and political turbulence left them feeling powerless. Politicians then invoked race and culture, exploiting the emotional power of these themes, as a way to shift attention away from their failure to address the root causes of poverty and instability. If that meant distorting history and its lessons to suit their own ends, ignoring similarities and exaggerating differences, then that is what they did. My work in the Dominican Republic and Haiti also convinced me that it is impossible to understand the politics of culture and ethnicity without looking at the underlying economic situation, which often shows why people are at odds with each other. Arguments over cultural differences thus often are symptoms of economic and the related political problems. Battles over identity, in turn, have profound effects on the economic future of the ethnic groups who are tagged as "inferior" and on the fortunes of those who exploit their plight. Although Hispaniola's circumstances of two countries sharing one island were unusual, the exploitation of culture and history for economic and political ends are universal. Parallels exist all around the world, from Germany and its Turkish immigrants to France and its North African population to the United States and the Mexicans along the border in the Southwest.

Looking at the United States, I now see a very different picture from the one that conventional wisdom portrays of the lessons we should learn from the wave of immigration a century ago. Just as historical memory has all but erased the story of the ties that the Great Wave immigrants had to homeland and heritage, the mistakes and consequences of the time have largely been forgotten. Now, just as back then, the age-old scapegoating of foreigners seems like a way to distract a nation from its failings. The creation of an us-versus-them worldview and of isolationism then has lasted until today, leaving this country unprepared for a globalized economy in which we should by all rights have a huge advantage. The social systems that acted as bridges to help immigrants assimilate were dismantled and

generations alienated as a consequence of a system that made immigrants embarrassed about their origins. The false idea that white Americans had no ethnic traits was an illusion that helped lead to the culture wars of the late twentieth century. Overall, the events of a century ago became mythologized such that Americans are now unprepared to come to terms with today's new wave of immigration. The economic consequences are no less vivid: isolationism led to trade wars, which in turn were a principal cause of the Great Depression. The resulting vacuum in international leadership and cooperation became one of the factors that contributed to World War II.

America's dilemma today is very much like the one we faced a century ago: massive demographic change, economic transformation, geopolitical crisis, and a realignment of global powers. In some ways, the stakes are much higher. Unlike a century ago, when we were just emerging as a global power, the United States has been at the top of the heap for many decades. Globalization has brought the rest of the world much closer, not only as a market for American goods but as a competitor. The U.S. economy is shifting to services and knowledge-based fields as manufacturing jobs are migrating to countries with lower labor costs. This trend has intensified income disparities and social upheaval for many Americans. English may be the language of globalization, but those who excel in the global economy cannot rely on English alone. Understanding other cultures has become a necessary business skill, and we depend on immigration to fill out our workforce, from rocket scientists to busboys. At the same time, global terrorism has made Americans feel unsafe within our own borders, all too soon after the end of the Cold War gave us an unprecedented sense of security.

So, in many ways, at the opening of the twenty-first century, we have come back to the questions that confronted America at the beginning of the twentieth. If we continue to embrace the wrong lessons from that time, we are more likely to make the same mistakes that have cost us before. We faced similar choices a century ago, during the turbulence of the 1880–1920 Great Wave of immigration and the First World War, when the fear of the stranger overwhelmed America's confidence in our ability

to create one nation out of many peoples. We slammed the gates shut, only to reopen them four decades later, after Hitler's atrocities showed the horrible consequences of singling out any group of people for exclusion, after European exiles who had found refuge here helped us win the war in Europe, and after our own civil rights movement reinvigorated America's stated commitment to promoting freedom and equality. Reopening the gates also created a new wave of immigration even greater than the one that had preceded it, even as new global economic forces once again caused profound economic and social changes that accentuated the demographic wave that was changing America. Just as happened a century ago, attacks on immigrants and warnings of a cultural threat reflect the fear that we cannot live up to the ideals on which our nation was founded.

Instead of recognizing our role as leaders of the world, we are talking about putting up fences to shut it out—not just figuratively but literally, in the form of the nearly 700 miles of twelve-foot-tall fencing along the U.S.-Mexican border, at a cost of $2.2 billion, that the House of Representatives approved in December 2005. We have hobbled our immigration bureaucracy so that many of the world's best and brightest are giving up in frustration instead of being able to put their skills to use to the benefit of the U.S. and world economies.

We have failed to understand and act on America's greatest strength: our ability to bring together people from disparate cultures and create a new society by combining their strengths and shedding their weaknesses. In 2005 we witnessed the tragic bombing of London's subway by alienated second-generation Muslim youths, followed by ethnically tinged riots in the suburbs of Paris. It was clear to commentators of every nationality that those incidents of violence were the direct result of failures to integrate immigrant and minority youths into the mainstream economy and society. For a moment, despite all of the hand-wringing that Americans have done in recent years over whether our melting pot is still working, the American model of creating pathways of opportunity looked relatively successful. Even as France was coming to realize the mistakes that it had made in shutting its immigrants out of a permanent place in society,

America seemingly was forgetting what we had done right. Several weeks after the riots, the House of Representatives passed a jarringly short-sighted bill that would make felons out of the millions of undocumented immigrants in this country, penalize Americans for not cooperating in efforts to marginalize these people further, and, of course, build that fence along the border. Even though polls consistently showed that a solid majority of Americans favored allowing undocumented immigrants to apply for legal status instead of deporting them, Congress was pandering to the small but vocal contingent that believed it could gain politically by demonizing immigrants, all in the name of protecting America.

Once again, culture and national character are not just abstract concepts. The way America interprets them, applies them to the policies we develop, and communicates our expectations to the newest immigrants has significant and lasting consequences for our social stability and prosperity. This book is about how our misconceptions about how earlier generations became American have affected the choices this nation has made about immigration so far, what they mean for the decisions we must make today, and what the consequences might be.

— 1 —

The Governator
and the Wetback

In April 2005, on one of the first spring days when it was warm enough to do so, Li Liu sat with me on the steps of the amphitheater at the foot of the Stata Center for Computer, Information, and Intelligence Sciences at the Massachusetts Institute of Technology. The building's raucous angles and curves and mix of metal, brick, and bright colors had been architect Frank Gehry's way of expressing the university's goal for the center: "to create spaces in which the mind would be free, where walls could be moved, rooms reconfigured, and students and faculty alike could benefit from the best and most stimulating work environment." It is a fitting metaphor for the conditions that helped America promote and foster innovation and excellence, attract millions of people here from other nations, and become the world's greatest economic and political power.

Li, an advanced doctoral student in nuclear engineering, is a classic example of the caliber of people America has attracted to contribute to the body of knowledge that our country generates. She studies the properties of supercooled water, which remains liquid at temperatures far below freezing. For scientists, this elusive "fourth state"—in addition to the known forms of gas (water vapor), liquid (water), and solid (ice)—is

tantalizing for the possibilities of what it might tell us about how the universe works. To supercool water, Li has been creating tightly confined conditions by enclosing water in silica cells only 14 angstroms in diameter and then cooling it to temperatures below water's normal freezing point. Her work involves real-life concepts from the realm of science fiction, involving not only technical and scientific sophistication but also abstract ideas so complex that many people could not even begin to imagine they even existed.

The potential discoveries that await Li, however, are not the only reason I have sought her out. Unfortunately, because Li works in the nuclear engineering department and the neutron scattering technology she uses was originally developed in conjunction with nuclear plants, she is of particular interest to antiterrorism investigators, although her research has nothing to do with nuclear fission and fusion. In the context of a "war on terror," her story—of bureaucratic frustration that put her scientific quest on hold—is one of far too many.

A few days earlier, I had e-mailed MIT's Chinese Student Association asking about students' visa experiences, and within hours I had appointments with a half dozen graduate students who call themselves "checkees," referring to the security checks that turned their lives upside down. Frustrated as much by the inability to pursue the work about which they were so passionate as they were by the inconvenience of being stranded in China and of their finances and professional lives being put at risk, these graduate students were a study in the way the world's most talented people hold affection and admiration for America despite the obstacles that increasingly are rising in their way.

Before she went home to China to visit her family in the summer of 2002, Li had heard about the risk of "getting checked" and stranded, but nobody expected that any delay would be more than a month. So she returned to China in July and dutifully reported to the U.S. consulate in Chengdu—a day's bus ride from her family's home—to apply for a new visa. They forgot to give her back her passport after she showed it to them, and they lost her I-20, the form certifying that she was an enrolled student in the United States. She had to contact MIT for another one. The

delays continued even after MIT sent a new form, and she kept calling the consulate but couldn't get an answer. Back in the United States, her husband—a graduate student in chemistry at Northeastern University—kept calling the U.S. help line number the consulate had given, but got the same answer over and over: your wife is not in our system. When Li's name finally showed up in the database, her visa status was listed as declined. Nearly in tears, Li's husband finally reached a supervisor, who helped figure out that her file had been lost, so she had to send it in again. Li did so and still kept waiting, calling to check every couple of weeks as she had been told to do, but again to no response.

Finally, she decided to try to get a job while she waited for her visa, but right then the SARS (severe acute respiratory syndrome) epidemic hit. Her small hometown was spared, but she could not travel to any place big enough to have an appropriate job for her to do. Her visa finally came through, after nearly a year of excruciating waiting. The SARS epidemic was still going on, which made her trip back to MIT—and her welcome—difficult. "They kept taking my temperature: when I arrived at the airport, when I got to the gate, before I got on the plane," she recalled. Her boss insisted that she wait out the two-week incubation period before meeting with him to catch up and get back on track with her research. He wants his team of graduate students to travel abroad with him to present their research at a conference, but she's not sure that she wants to risk getting stranded in another country.

Like many other foreign students—and especially those from China—Li was caught in the security trap that followed the September 11, 2001, terrorist attacks on the World Trade Center and the Pentagon. At U.S. consulates around the world, the vice-consuls who processed visa applications were terrified that they would inadvertently let the next successful terrorist into the United States. (This fear only intensified when, six months after the 9/11 attacks, the State Department approved student visas for two of the hijackers who had applied to flight schools.) New rules vastly increased the amount of paperwork and required interviews and security checks, which also reduced the amount of time consular staff had available to evaluate the paperwork needed for the tens of millions of

short-term visitors who enter the United States each year—tourists, students, guest workers, scholars, diplomats, and their family members, for a total of 179 million visits in 2004. The result sucked in Li Liu and many others like her, at a great cost not only to the hapless individuals affected but also to our country. It wasted a tremendous amount of energy and resources and deprived us of the efforts of the world's best and brightest to contribute to a body of knowledge that would ultimately advance American innovation and technological leadership.

These are the people whose skills are essential to maintaining American economic competitiveness. In the last quarter century, science and engineering jobs have grown four times faster than the general economy. By some estimates, more than half of the growth of the U.S. economy over the last half century has been the product of technological advances. The Industrial Research Institute reports that by far the biggest problem facing leading technology firms in 2004 was how to grow their business through innovation, a task that depends on their ability to convene the world's best and brightest. At the same time, our own universities are failing to meet today's demand for science and engineering students, partly because not enough Americans are pursuing technical careers even as the demand for those skills is rising. Meanwhile, American-born scientists and scholars are aging; their retirement will make the shortage even more acute.

In other words, without foreign-born scientists, there is no way that the U.S. economy will find enough skilled workers. The consequences will be twofold. First, many jobs will move to countries that can provide the supply of skilled labor that companies need. Second, and more alarming, the inability to attract these workers—at the same time that America is failing to train enough homegrown talent—will deprive American research centers of their lifeblood. Many of the world's best and brightest may no longer congregate in the country that long has been the center of scientific and technological innovation and an incubator of ideas. As a result, many possible breakthroughs will be delayed—or might not occur at all, and we won't even know what the world may have lost.

The checkees have been surprisingly patient and understanding about the frustration and humiliation they have suffered in order to study and work in America. But how long will they be willing to keep doing so? For every Li, who persists in the face of adversity, how many others will give up or not even try in the first place?

Li's story—and those of the many talented, hardworking foreigners like her—illustrates the paradox that is America today: an open society built on the ideas and hard work of immigrants, the wealthiest place in the world, the promoter of free markets and competition—yet also a country whose bureaucratic barriers can rival that of the communist bureaucracies we derided during the Cold War, a country that has risked crippling higher education and businesses by making it difficult for foreign scholars and scientists to come here, and a country where there is a rising clamor to shut the borders to keep out foreign people and goods and ostensibly to "keep in" technology and jobs. One of the most powerful elements of America's identity is that we are a nation of immigrants, yet there are few themes on which we have been as ambivalent as on immigration. The result is a mishmash of contradictory and ineffective immigration policies that work against our best interests and that today threaten our social cohesion and our economic well-being.

America's immigration laws have been called "second only to the Internal Revenue Code in complexity" and have been compared unfavorably to the labyrinth of King Minos in Crete. Filing deadlines change arbitrarily, certain nationalities are favored one day and not the next, and exceptions appear and disappear. A Colombian colleague of mine was ecstatic after she received a letter telling her that her green card was ready. But when she called to schedule a time to pick it up, the officer told her that the laws had changed and her green card approval had been revoked. Immigration lawyers tell me many stories that are similar and often far worse. There are countless cases of people who face deportation because retroactive changes in laws and the government's failure to notify them or their lawyers ended up making them "illegal" even though they had made every effort to follow the law—and even believed for good reason that they were complying with it.

Technically, foreign students are not "immigrants." When they pass through immigration control at our airports and border crossing stations, they enter the United States on "nonimmigrant" visas, as do those who come here on business, temporary guest worker programs, or tourist visas. Yet many students—and other "nonimmigrants"—eventually do stay here permanently, making up a vital part of this country's professional and scholarly class. In truth, it is almost impossible to tell when someone arrives whether they will just pass some time here and move on, or stay. And so the travails of anyone born in another country who comes here, no matter how long they may or may not be likely to stay, are enmeshed in an increasingly contentious argument about immigration to America: whom and how many to let in and for how long, whom to keep out, what to require of newcomers, and how to measure how well they are fitting in.

People like Li Liu come to America, lured not only by our record of economic leadership but also—perhaps even more so—by the sense of possibility that our national pride in individual freedom has created. American values of liberty, equality, and opportunity are not just nice ideals; they are an economic asset, part of the culture that has drawn the world's best and brightest here and made America into the world's center of innovation and progress.

Yet instead of capitalizing on our greatest asset, we have begun to lock out the people we need most. Sometimes it has been because of distrust and political expediency, but just as often the culprit is our long-term neglect of both our immigration system and the root causes of the political and social tensions over immigration. Instead of addressing long-term problems like the need to provide resources and a legal framework that would help us to better integrate immigrants, to streamline and strengthen our immigration bureaucracy and enforcement laws, and to provide the education that Americans need to compete in a global economy that puts a premium on knowledge, we have been implementing short-term measures that may sound good to a frightened public but in fact are making things worse.

In many cases, hastily conceived policies have effects that are the opposite of those they were intended to have. Universities have been complain-

ing bitterly about rules imposed in 2001 by a provision of the USA Patriot
Act, supposedly to protect Americans from bioterrorism, that prevent certain foreign nationals from handling, being in a room with, or even being
told research results involving pathogens that might potentially be used as
bioweapons. As Robert C. Richardson, a Nobel laureate in physics at Cornell University, complained to the *New York Times Magazine*, the effect has
not been to make America safer, but instead to make it less so: "So what is
the situation now? We went from thirty-eight people who could work on
select agents to two. We've got a lot less people working on interventions
to vaccinate the public against smallpox, West Nile virus, anthrax and any
of thirty other scourges."

In other cases, the world's best and brightest have been treated so badly
that the image of America as the place to convene to circulate ideas and
recognize accomplishment has been damaged. In 2004, U.S. authorities
detained Ian McEwan, the author of the bestselling novel *Atonement* and
winner of the Booker Prize for literature, for more than twenty-four hours
in Vancouver. His passport was stamped "Refused Admittance," which
will make it harder in the future for him to travel to the United States and
possibly other countries as well. "Homeland Security is making America
safe from British novelists," McEwan declared in typical dry British humor. (The issue apparently was whether the considerable speaking fees he
would receive on the trip required him to get work authorization before
entering the country.) The same year, South African J.M. Coetzee, the
2003 winner of the Nobel Prize in Literature, declined an invitation to a
ceremony in his honor at the University of Texas, where he had studied as
a graduate student, because he did not want to deal with the red tape and
hassle of applying for a visa in post-9/11 America.

Visa delays have cost companies tens of billions of dollars since 9/11.
Academic and business conferences are being moved to other countries,
at a tremendous cost to our culture of scholarship and innovation. Between 2001 and 2003, the number of student visas granted fell by 80,000,
or 27 percent, and the number of skilled workers admitted to the United
States fell by 60,000, also 27 percent—the result of our refusing more applications and of fewer people applying to come here. The United States

is now among the countries with the highest barriers to legal immigration, alongside Russia, Italy, Spain, Japan, Venezuela, and Brazil.

No longer can we take for granted that this country is the destination of choice for the world's best and brightest. Noting that the number of Asians coming to study computer science in the United States has fallen by 35 percent in the past few years alone, Microsoft chairman Bill Gates has warned that the United States may lose its status as the IQ magnet of the world. This is the fault not only of a chilled immigration climate but also of other countries' having embraced a competitive ethos on which America no longer has a monopoly. The management guru Peter Drucker praised New Delhi's medical school as now among the world's best, and Indian universities are turning out technical graduates who are as good as any around the globe. Analysts at the Educational Testing Service (ETS), which administers many of the tests required for university admissions in the United States, declared in 2004 that the "bubble has burst on foreign student enrollments," as the number of international students registering for the Graduate Record Exam (GRE) dropped precipitously among Chinese, Taiwanese, and Indian students.

At the same time, massive demographic change, a collapsed immigration bureaucracy, a changing global economy, and fear of terrorism have driven tensions over immigration in the United States to the highest level in a century. Critics warn that today's immigrants and their circumstances are profoundly different from those who came here during the Great Wave of immigration a century ago and that as a result, instead of assimilating, they will Balkanize America. Other critics, in turn, are too apt to condemn worries about social cohesion as mere racism and too likely to reject the suggestion that America might benefit from modestly moderating the overall level of immigration. Even if both sides were to agree to lower the number of immigrants who come to this country, agreeing on how—or even if it is possible—to actually do so is another matter entirely. Americans of all stripes are worried about those who come here illegally—a population that represents roughly one-third of all immigrants today. But it is not proving easy to find the right combination of enforcement and legal-

ization policies to make sure that the immigrants we need can come here legally even as we maintain secure borders.

We are at an impasse. If we fail to deal with our broken immigration policies now, we face serious economic and social consequences. But we will not solve anything if we limit the terms of the debate to a question of less or more immigration or simply resort to epithets. Emotion and anger must be replaced by knowledge and pragmatism. The questions we should be addressing are whether policies intended to achieve one end instead result in the exact opposite; whether some of the problems blamed on immigration actually have other causes; and how we treat immigrants when they arrive here, what we expect of them, and what they might expect of us.

～•～

During his tenure as Federal Reserve Board chairman, Alan Greenspan made the case often that the U.S. economy needs immigration of both skilled and unskilled workers. "As we are creating an ever more complex, sophisticated, accelerating economy, the necessity to have the ability to bring in resources and people from abroad to keep it functioning in the most effective manner increasingly strikes me as relevant policy," he testified to the U.S. Senate in 2000. During the 1990s, he frequently praised immigration for keeping inflation in check and thus enabling the Fed to keep interest rates low and in turn create the longest stretch of peacetime prosperity in memory. The low wages that kept inflation tame were, of course, a bane as well as a boon, since immigration of low-skilled workers was thought to hurt the job prospects of America's least educated and lowest-paid workers, and resentment soon grew over society's poorest members having to pay a heavy price for everyone else's prosperity.

There should be no doubt that immigration is a pillar of the U.S. economy as a whole. A 1995 survey polled a group of economists that included Nobel Prize winners, former members of the President's Council of Economic Advisers, and past presidents of the American Economic

Association. When asked, "On balance, what effect has twentieth-century immigration had on the nation's economic growth?" an overwhelming 81 percent of respondents answered "favorable," with the remaining 19 percent replying "slightly favorable." Not a single one believed that immigration hurt America's economy.

Many Americans think of immigrants as doing "the jobs that Americans won't do"—the jobs that occupy most of the long-running U.S. argument over whether immigration is too high, too low, or at just about the right level. Certainly, these jobs—farming, construction, services—are so important to the day-to-day functioning of our economy that even Americans who believe that immigration is too high recognize that we depend on low-skilled immigrant workers. Immigrants make up a large percentage of employees in agriculture (37 percent), services (23 percent), and home maintenance work, such as landscaping and housecleaning (42 percent). Overall, however, this work is not representative of the jobs immigrants do.

Few Americans realize how much we depend on the immigrants at the other end of the socioeconomic spectrum: the engineers, scientists, entrepreneurs, and scholars who drive the knowledge economy. Immigrants make up only 20 percent of low-wage workers but represent 50 percent of research and development workers and 25 percent of doctors and nurses. About a quarter of foreign-born workers are managers and professionals; one-fifth are in technical, sales, and administrative support, and another fifth are in service occupations; 18 percent work as operators, fabricators, and laborers. Only 4 percent work in stereotypical fields like farming, forestry, and fishing.

Despite the stereotype of the immigrant as a low-skilled and poorly educated worker, the vast majority of foreign-born workers have completed high school, and 45 percent of foreign workers have attended or completed college—a rate higher than among American workers. To be sure, 30 percent of foreign-born workers here have not completed high school, compared with just 7 percent of those born in this country.

Although they are spread across occupations, immigrants nevertheless are overrepresented among low-skilled workers, underrepresented among

those with high school and some college education, and overrepresented among the highest-skilled population. They represent only a small number relative to the total foreign-born population, yet the lowest-skilled immigrants are at the center of a growing controversy over how warm a welcome America should give immigrants. Although Americans are likely to agree that low-skilled immigrants, legal and illegal, make essential contributions to our economy, these immigrants are also the ones who attract the most profound resentment. They represent the other half of America's immigration mythology: the tired, the poor, the huddled masses yearning to breathe free. America's attitudes toward unskilled immigrants have come to define the national immigration debate and shape policies toward all the noncitizens on whom the U.S. economy depends— and thus the fate of the huddled masses will profoundly affect our future ability to attract the best and the brightest as well.

﹏•﹏

On a clear late-summer day in the town of Babylon, a crowd gathered in front of American Legion Post 94 on an otherwise quiet Long Island street an hour's train ride from New York City. With pale yellow wood siding and white trim, the building could have come straight out of *Leave It to Beaver* had it not been for the graffiti freshly painted on it the night before. Several grim-faced men stood on the front steps, monitoring everyone who approached and letting in select groups, two or three at a time, of people whose main distinguishing feature was that they were so nondescript: the kind of typical white Americans you might see at the supermarket or the hardware store. They were members of the Minutemen Civil Defense Corps, the group that organized a month-long volunteer patrol of the U.S.-Mexico border in April 2005, and they had called this September meeting on Long Island to organize a similar vigil along the U.S.-Canada border in October 2005. The Minutemen had attracted attention not only for their border patrol efforts, but also for the white-supremacist groups that had embraced their work. The Minutemen tried to portray themselves as law-abiding, concerned

citizens, but it was hard to live down America's sad history of crimes committed when individuals have taken the law into their own hands. Nor did widely circulated photographs of Nazi flags being waved at a Minutemen rally help their cause. President George W. Bush and Secretary of State Condoleezza Rice had called the Minutemen vigilantes, a term that still rankled members of the group.

Long Island was far from the Canadian and Mexican borders, but it was nonetheless a major battleground in an intensifying war over illegal immigration. A few weeks earlier, Suffolk County Executive Steve Levy had ordered the expulsion of immigrants living in an overcrowded house, responding to residents' understandable complaints over building code violations but leaving the residents with no place at all to live. The new controversy stirred up emotions that were still raw from a fight that took place after a brutal attack in 2000 on Mexican day laborers in Farmingville, a once bucolic town of 15,000. The attack, portrayed movingly in the documentary film *Farmingville*, polarized residents, some of whom saw illegal immigration as the main problem and deportation as the only solution, and others who felt that the blame fell on unscrupulous employers and landlords. Residents fought tooth and nail over a proposal to provide a central place where day laborers could seek work instead of congregating on streets and curbs. National pro- and anti-immigration groups had adopted Farmingville as a cause, drawing the town into a high-stakes struggle that was a proxy for national issues.

Eventually the Minutemen joined the fray. Not surprisingly, many of the Long Islanders who had opposed the day laborer center were among the forty or so people who showed up that September afternoon. The Minutemen stationed on the American Legion hall steps warily eyed a growing delegation of protesters on the sidewalk. Both sides were armed with digital cameras and video recorders, photographing each other. As the protesters marched back and forth on the sidewalk, a man who sympathized with the Minutemen stood in their midst, audio-recording the whole thing.

The protesters were a hodgepodge: families of liberal Jewish New Yorkers; serious-faced Mexican and Central American men and women;

greasy-haired teenagers dressed in black with pierced noses and eyebrows; and white middle-class Long Islanders. Holding a saucepan and a wooden spoon, a frightened-looking boy who was about six years old walked beside his mother, caught between the shouting protesters and Minutemen. A poster reading "Stop the Hate," clearly a veteran of many marches, waved above the protesters' heads next to an anarchist flag and several prints of a Native American chief declaring "Deport Illegal Immigrants"—clearly suggesting that the immigrants whose presence the Minutemen were protesting had as much right to be here as the white Minutemen who held their own "Deport Illegal Immigrants" signs. "No Human Being Is Illegal!" read another placard.

"Are you Native American?" one of the protesters screamed. "If you're not, then you're an immigrant too. We're all immigrants." A wiry Minuteman with sun-leathered skin and a nervous, angry energy screamed back at them, "Illegal means illegal! Do you know what the word illegal means?" The protesters tried out various chants against Nazis, fascists, racists, and homophobes. "Racists Go Home!" they yelled. A heavyset middle-aged woman sitting on the steps hollered back, "I *am* home!" Both sides mirrored the increasingly polarized tone of a national debate. To the protesters, the Minutemen were Nazis, vigilantes, fascists, racists. Too many of the Minutemen, for their part, had taken the stance that anyone who wasn't with them was against them: if you didn't agree with their methods, then you were against protecting America.

At the foot of the steps of the American Legion hall, an argument broke out as several newspaper reporters—many of them from Hispanic media—protested loudly that they were not being allowed in to what had been billed as a public meeting. Reporters from two local television stations were allowed in, but no one else from the media (except for a Long Island newspaper reporter who pretended not to be one). Later, when a television reporter from Univision tried to get in, she was refused. "It's too bad my wife isn't here," said the gatekeeper. "She's from Venezuela and she's very upset by illegal immigration." The reporter stiffened at his condescension. "Sir, I was born in Puerto Rico and you should know that I am an American citizen," she said. The gatekeeper told her he'd send someone out to be

interviewed, but after the reporter descended the steps, he made no move to do so. If the Minutemen hoped to control damage to their image by barring reporters from their meeting, they had succeeded in doing exactly the opposite through their unsubtle choices of which media representatives to let in and through the question they left in everyone's mind: If they were indeed the law-abiding citizens they claimed to be, what did they have to hide?

During the course of the afternoon, it became clear that there was no such thing as a typical Minuteman. There was, of course, Chris Simcox, the group's thin, tense-lipped founder, wound up with nervous energy, who had moved to Arizona from California and bought a local newspaper, which he used as a mouthpiece for his campaign. There were the angry men dressed in varying combinations of red, white, and blue. There were the Farmingville residents who complained about overcrowded homes, public urination, the illegal status of day laborers, and the government's failure to do anything about illegal immigration.

A Minuteman in a cowboy hat and boots was a Pennsylvania native who had made Arizona his home for more than a decade and become fed up with rising petty crime and the complaints of ranchers whose land the migrants were crossing indiscriminately. As I asked questions to try to understand where he was coming from—and he asked questions of his own to try to get a sense of how I might portray him—I was pleasantly surprised that he seemed open to information that contradicted his assumptions. When I told him about a recent study suggesting that there were many times more people who wanted to learn English in New York than there were classroom spaces for, he said he was glad to hear that. We disagreed, of course, on how to address the problem of illegal immigration. He was confident that it was possible to secure the Mexican border—after all, the Minutemen had succeeded in closing down part of it in April, he said. But, I pointed out, that was only twenty miles. To secure more than 2,000 miles would require more than 50,000 people, not just for one month but for a very long time. And that wouldn't solve the problem of making sure that the American economy had the workers it needed.

We agreed to disagree on the border issue, but he agreed wholeheart-
edly when I said I thought a big problem was the unscrupulous employers
who used immigrants' illegal status to abuse them—some employers even
call immigration authorities on themselves to clear out workers who
complained about violations of labor and safety laws. It was that type of
employer that dragged down wages and made American workers far less
attractive than illegal immigrants to employers. Why hire someone at
higher wages who was not afraid of being deported if he stood up for his
rights? By making it impossible for honest businesses to find legal immigrant workers, and by not imposing any meaningful financial or other
kinds of penalties on abusive employers, our lawmakers had been making
the problem worse.

The Minuteman in the cowboy hat nodded. "I feel for them. I really
do," he said. "The illegal immigrants are caught in the middle, and so are
the American people." Our conversation was interrupted as the group on
the sidewalk degenerated into a series of catch-all slogans. As they in-
veighed against President Bush and the war in Iraq, the Minuteman
shook his head. "You know, I actually agree with those protesters on a lot
of things."

‿•‿

We Americans view ourselves as the most tolerant nation in the world,
able to create *e pluribus unum*, one out of many. "The nature of this
country is one that is good-hearted and our people are compassionate,"
President Bush declared in 2004 after he relaunched a plan to give guest
worker status to undocumented immigrants who have been working
hard in American jobs. Most of us would agree. We cannot separate our
identity and our future from the question of whom to welcome to America and how to welcome them. The fear is that losing control of who is
American means losing control of America. But our demographics are
only part of our destiny. What has made America great has been our
ability to shape that destiny as one nation made of many peoples.

When I told a friend who heads research at a respected New York think tank that I was writing about the growing pressures to close the doors to immigrants, he raised an eyebrow. But America is one of the most open countries in the world, he said, noting the president's guest worker proposal, the size of the foreign-born population, and our open society.

He is right. After all, roughly a million immigrants come here each year, more by far than to any other country in the world; America hosts one out of five immigrants worldwide. One in eight people in this country were born elsewhere, the highest level in a century. About half a million newcomers take the Oath of Citizenship each year to become naturalized Americans. The stars of the 2004 Democratic and Republican national conventions both came with stories of the immigrant's American Dream: Arnold Schwarzenegger, the Austrian immigrant turned movie star and California governor, and Barack Obama, the son of an American mother and a Kenyan father who had emigrated to America. We like to be inspired by our apparent openness to immigrants. We are even talking about amending the Constitution to allow a foreign-born president—inspired, of course, by the ultimate American Dream success story of an Austrian bodybuilder who became a movie superstar, married into American political royalty, and won a landslide election to become governor of California.

"In my book, anyone who comes here and gives an honest day's work for an honest day's pay is not only putting himself closer to the American Dream, he's helping the rest of us get there too," the Australian-born media mogul, Rupert Murdoch, wrote in the *Wall Street Journal*. "Frankly it doesn't bother me in the least that millions of people are attracted to our shores. What we should worry about is the day they no longer find these shores attractive. In an era when too many of our pundits declare that the American Dream is a fraud, it is America's immigrants who remind us—by dint of their success—that the Dream is alive, and well within reach of anyone willing to work for it."

Yet even as the Governator's electoral triumph in 2003 inspired and reassured Americans, it was accompanied by the shadow of the other enduring image of immigration: the possibility of failure. Indeed, two years

after Schwarzenegger's election, the dramatic downturn in his own political fortunes only reinforced how tenuous the American Dream can be. Immigration brings out both the best and worst in America and Americans. It's as if a little angel and a little devil stand on each of Lady Liberty's shoulders. The angel wears no halo, white satin, or wings, but instead appears in the form of the naturalized American success story: the Schwarzenegger, the George Soros, the Henry Kissinger, the Madeleine Albright. The devil is missing his horns and there is no forked tail flicking back and forth beneath the hem of a sweeping red cape; instead, he is a bedraggled peasant emerging just this side of the Rio Grande, a Chinese industrial spy, and a turbaned terrorist, a set of images that often obscure reality.

Much as we celebrate the exceptional example, Americans all too readily condemn its counterpart: the immigrant whose luck and station in life will never correspond to the effort he puts into bettering himself and his family, and who can consider himself to have succeeded only because the circumstances he left behind were so horrific. The Governator thus has a counterpart, the Wetback. It's an ugly word that conveys the depth of rejection that American society as a whole has inflicted upon this group. The Wetback provides insurance against our own failings: we will not fall as low as the foreigner, and we will have an outsider to blame.

❤️

America is at a tipping point in our attitudes not only toward immigration but toward our country's role in the world. Today's mix of global interdependence with the threat of global terrorism and economic and demographic change has created a maelstrom of fears. Encompassing concerns about our borders, our cultural and national identity, and our ability to maintain unity, immigrants represent all of the touch-points of our collective insecurity. Any change that comes too rapidly creates anxiety in even the most tolerant of societies. The contradictory and uniquely American tendency to both demonize and romanticize the immigrant has only confused matters. Politicians and interest groups cynically invoke

both emotions, sending the country swinging wildly from one pole to the other and making it all the harder to see through the fog of rhetoric.

The terrorist attacks of September 11, carried out by foreigners who had come here under various immigrant and nonimmigrant visa categories (some of which had lapsed, making their continued presence illegal), merely catalyzed an immigration debate that had already been building for many years. With roughly a million immigrants arriving in the United States each year through the 1980s and 1990s, the foreign-born population was approaching 12 percent of the U.S. population, the highest proportion in a century. The sheer mass of people had long since overwhelmed our immigration bureaucracy, and as a result more and more immigrants—about one in three, by some estimates—have been coming here illegally. Many of the new immigrants, legal and illegal, come from Latin America and Asia and are not white, which adds a racial element to the massive demographic change taking place.

The ending in the 1950s and 1960s of race-based immigration bars, combined with growing diversity and racial acceptance, opened many doors for immigrants who did not happen to be born white. This change speaks worlds of Americans' ability to find common ground in differences, yet it also exposes the lingering prejudices that we have not yet overcome. Recessions and the loss of manufacturing jobs in recent decades have made Americans feel that their economic future is insecure even as they noticed that immigrants who looked different no longer occupy mainly the stereotypical jobs at the bottom of the ladder, the work that "Americans didn't want to do," but instead are solidly embedded in the American middle class. The racial and ethnic differences represented by recent immigration catalyze the volatility of the country's reaction to them.

2

Patriots

Collinsville, Illinois, just northeast of St. Louis, today is the home of the International Horseradish Festival and the world's largest ketchup bottle, but a century ago the town of 4,000 people centered its economy on a coal mine and a smelting plant. When the United States entered the Great War in Europe in April 1917, the nation's mines and munitions factories swung into full capacity supplying the Yanks and the Allies. War was a bonanza for Collinsville, and given the jobs and money it provided, Collinsville was especially hostile to any suggestion of disloyalty. In the first few months of 1918, locals held frequent "loyalty rallies" to warn anyone not enthusiastic enough in their support of the Allied cause; several men, including a Polish-born priest, had been tarred and feathered in nearby towns.

One of the newcomers who flocked to Collinsville in search of work was Robert Paul Prager, a 45-year-old German-born would-be miner. He had applied to become an American citizen, but because he had not yet received his naturalization papers, he dutifully registered with the government as an enemy alien. Nearly a year into the war, on the evening of April 4, 1918, Prager spoke out at a gathering in Maryville, a nearby mining town where he had done some work. Newspaper accounts of the time do not record his exact words; all they report is that whatever he said struck the locals as "disloyal utterances against the United States

and President Wilson." Whatever he said, it didn't help that Prager was known for being difficult, overenthusiastically trying to convert miners to socialism, frequently sparring with other union members, and turning minor matters into major disagreements. When the union's president called him a spy and a liar, Prager papered Maryville and Collinsville with handbills declaring his loyalty to America and accusing the union president of persecuting him. Not surprisingly, given such run-ins with its leadership, the local mining union had rejected his application to join, so Prager had found it nearly impossible to find work. The baker who had employed Prager for several months would later testify that Prager had "many peculiarities," including a hot temper; indeed, the baker had spent thirty-two days in jail after Prager complained to the police that the baker objected to Prager's display of the American flag.

After the meeting, Prager's fellow union members got to talking at a saloon where alcoholic spirits mixed too liberally with patriotic spirits. As Illinois Senator Lawrence Y. Sherman later put it, "It was a drunken mob masquerading in the garb of patriotism." In a liquor-stoked rage against Germans, they set out for the boarding house on Vandalia Street, Collinsville, where Prager lived. They found him there and dragged him out into the street. A crowd gathered as the drunken miners forced Prager to parade barefoot through the town, waving two small flags and every few steps kissing a giant American flag that the vigilantes had wrapped around him. Police rescued Prager from the crowd and took him to the jail in City Hall to protect him. There, he made a signed statement to police that his heart and soul were for the United States. Yet even as Prager convinced the officers of his loyalty, a crowd was gathering around City Hall, demanding that the police hand him over to them.

Collinsville's mayor, J.H. Siegel, appeared on the steps of the red-brick building to try to calm the crowd, which by this time had grown to more than 300 people. "We do not want a stigma marking Collinsville," he pleaded. "I implore you to go to your homes and discontinue this demonstration." This pacified them briefly. Just past 10 P.M., however, the frenzied mob rushed past a police cordon and swarmed into City

Hall, where they overpowered the four night officers guarding Prager and found his hiding place under a pile of scrap tiles in the basement.

They dragged him out and led him barefoot down the streets and along a road to a mile outside the town limits where an elm tree stood. There, as the clock struck midnight, Prager's captors let him write one last letter to his parents back in Germany:

> Dear Parents—I must this day, the 5th of April, 1918, die.
> Please pray for me, my dear parents. This is my last letter.
> Your dear son.
>   ROBERT PAUL PRAGER.

He then prayed in German on his knees for three minutes. A few minutes after midnight, Prager's captors pulled a noose around his neck and jerked him ten feet up in the air, hoisting and dropping him three times from the elm branch: one each for the red, the white, and the blue, as the ringleaders cried out to the mob—more than 300 strong, some vigilantes, some drunks, some good old boys looking for excitement, some onlookers afraid to watch but unable not to—who had gathered to see him hang. One witness said that Prager told the mob defiantly, "All right, boys, go ahead and kill me, but wrap me up in the flag when you bury me." When Prager was buried five days later, his coffin was draped with an American flag like the one that had been wrapped around him as his tormentors tried to humiliate him. Now, covered in flowers sent by dozens of anonymous mourners, the flag was an apology of sorts.

It was the first killing for disloyalty in the United States, and word quickly spread across the nation. Prominent politicians, including former presidents Theodore Roosevelt and William H. Taft, denounced it in the fiery language of the era. In Collinsville, many citizens were outraged and stood up to defend Prager's memory. Members of the International Order of Odd Fellows, one of the fraternal groups that were so popular at the time, wrote to the judge to refute rumors that he had failed to rise for the Pledge of Allegiance and to make sure that the judge knew that he had even tried to enlist in the Navy (which had turned him away because

he had one glass eye and could see none too well out of the eye that was left). The *New York Times* and the *Chicago Tribune* deplored the murder.

Nonetheless, there were those who openly approved of the mob's intention to root out disloyal elements. The *Washington Post* characterized the lynching as a fierce revolt by midwesterners who—unlike sophisticated northeasterners, of course—had been taken in by German lies but finally rose up in "a healthful and wholesome awakening." After all, the paper editorialized, "Enemy propaganda must be stopped, even if a few lynchings may occur." Congressmen, backed up by editorialists across the Midwest, intensified their efforts to pass antisedition laws "to punish men who eulogize the kaiser, German kultur or the German form of government."

For their part, the queasy Collinsville authorities tried to avoid arresting mob members, arguing that the murder had occurred outside of town limits and thus was none of their business. Only when the governor of Illinois threatened to impose martial law unless the murderers were brought to justice did they arrest and interrogate members of the lynch mob, who recounted in full detail how they had tormented Prager and marched him to his death. Most of the leaders were coal miners, joined by the saloon porter. Joseph Riegel, a 28-year-old honorably discharged U.S. Army soldier who now worked as a miner and shoe repairman, had even admitted that he took over leadership of the mob shortly after it dragged Prager from the jail—although he later recanted his confession. Riegel had been drinking in a saloon that officers had closed down, apparently in an attempt to calm the mood; the effort backfired by sending drunken men out of the bar and into the streets. The investigations and testimony went quickly; after three weeks, the jury was ready to give a verdict on June 8. Despite the confessions and the vast number of witnesses, it took the jury only minutes to acquit eleven of the accused perpetrators—at least four of whom were clearly participants in the crime and the others implicated to some degree.

"There was a peculiar coincidence at the trial," the *Edwardsville Intelligencer* wrote. "The Jackie Band was in Edwardsville for a patriotic demonstration. When a shower of rain came up the musicians were sent to the court house where it had been arranged to give a program." During

the court recess, the band struck up "The Star Spangled Banner." "The strains from the Jackie Band caused tears to flow down the cheeks of Riegel. He was still crying when he returned to the courtroom. As the jury came in with its verdict the band was at the head of a procession of draft boys and in passing the court house played 'Over There'."

Was the song a mere coincidence, a providential tribute to patriots who had been justly liberated for having defended their country from a seditious foreigner, or a tribute to a man who had been eager and willing to risk his life for his adopted country only to be murdered by Americans whose cause his bad eye had denied him the chance to defend? Was the verdict, as many citizens argued and appearances certainly suggested, a signal of public acceptance of mob rule? The prosecutor argued that it was not: that the government merely had failed to prove that events had happened the way it said they had. This was a rather odd statement, given that the participants had been so open about what they had done. Nevertheless, he insisted that justice had been carried out and that the affair was a warning that would prevent similar tragedies from happening in the future, or at least would guarantee justice if they did take place.

The lynching did not, of course, stop the hate crimes that continued against immigrants across the nation. What it did do was speed the passage by Congress in June 1918 of the Sedition Law, which muzzled free speech, supposedly in order to keep good citizens from having to take into their own hands the silencing of anyone who questioned any of President Woodrow Wilson's wartime policies—as they had done in the Prager lynching that helped politicians justify the Sedition Law.

It is plausible that Prager was lynched as much for being obnoxious as he was for being German or supposedly disloyal. Whatever the real reasons were for his death, they brought into sharp relief the peculiarities of the American character: a love of country and a belief that this is a tolerant and fair nation, coupled with an ability to compartmentalize incidents that contradict those beliefs. Crystallizing passions surging around a war that had drawn the United States back into the travails of an Old World from which Americans wanted to believe they had made a clean break, around the economic disruption that industrialization brought,

and around the social tensions created by economic changes combined with the massive arrivals of poor Europeans, the Prager lynching marked a turning point in American history. At a time when an adolescent nation had just become a player in its own right on the world stage, it suddenly lost confidence in the bold ideals that had brought it into being. What if the American project could not, after all, succeed in providing opportunities for those who fled Europe? And what would happen if, God forbid, the enduring passions of the Old World succeeded in pulling America apart? Not wanting to face those possibilities, the young nation set aside the defining values of individualism, freedom, equality, and the ability to find common purpose, and instead entered a period of distrust, fear, condemnation, and silence.

⌣•⌣

The First World War galvanized the struggle over immigration that had been going on practically since the first settlers arrived in America and had intensified in the decades leading up to the war. At its peak in 1910, the foreign-born population of 13.6 million represented 14.8 percent of the population of the United States. This huge demographic shift, a Great Wave of immigrants, threatened a fragile social order amid massive, destabilizing economic changes. As the United States shifted to an industrial, urban economy, jobs that once had required apprenticeships and training could now be done by machines that just about anyone could operate with minimal training. Skills that had once been valuable no longer were, but getting angry at a machine did not provide the same catharsis as blaming a human being.

Many of the immigrants who sought the new factory jobs were men seeking short-term or seasonal work, earning some quick cash and then returning to their home countries, as Mark Wyman has documented in his excellent book *Round-Trip to America: The Immigrants Return to Europe, 1880–1930*. For men who had no intention of staying, there was little reason to learn more English than they needed to get by on the job or to spend money on accommodations that were much more than a place

to sleep, no matter how crowded or filthy. "The desire for a short, profitable stay in America—with as few expenses as possible—combined with ethnic clustering in the slums and on railroad crews to isolate the immigrant. Though isolation has been common among newcomers in all lands in all eras, the situation was clearly worsened when immigrants arrived with plans already made that they would *not* become Americans," Wyman writes. Many Italians traveled to America in early spring for seasonal work and returned to Italy in late fall. An estimated 63 percent of the Italians who came to the United States from 1902 to 1923 returned to Italy; among Hungarians, 46.5 percent went back; 36.3 percent of Croatians and Slovenians; more than 48 percent of French; and 46 percent of Greeks.

Adding insult to injury, the immigrants who were coming to fill the factory jobs were no longer just the English, Scottish, Dutch, and Germans of the previous 150 years, but now included darker-skinned southern and eastern Europeans, many of whom brought with them budding socialist and anarchist ideologies. These workers looked, sounded, and smelled different; they were taking jobs that previously had belonged to skilled workers; and there were many, many of them. Wyman notes that in the iron and steel industries east of the Mississippi River in the first decade of the twentieth century, 58 percent of all workers were foreign born. In Pennsylvania, more than three-quarters of coal workers were foreigners, but not even 8 percent came from the British Isles or Germany, the traditional sources of immigration to the United States before that time. In the clothing industry, there were two foreign-born workers for every one born in the United States. In Chicago, Italians did 99 percent of road construction and repair. Perhaps cultural differences alone without the economic disruption, or vice versa, might not have provoked such turbulence, but the combination produced powerful social pressures that would test the ideals on which America had been founded.

Despite being a nation largely built by immigrants, the United States had always been ambivalent toward newcomers. America's Founding Fathers themselves had widely differing feelings—both among themselves and individually within their own minds. Benjamin Franklin in 1753

wrote that the German immigrants arriving in America were "the most stupid of their nation." Yet by the 1780s, he was urging European immigrants to come to America, extending to them the promise that citizenship and its accompanying rights were to be had easily. Thomas Jefferson warned of the dangers of indiscriminately promoting rapid immigration, yet his Republican party's support rested on immigrant votes, and he championed the rights of immigrants who had already arrived in the United States. Theodore Roosevelt, with his dramatic switches back and forth between sympathy and antipathy, exemplified America's seesawing perhaps better than anyone else. "As a jingo and an ardent immigration restrictionist in the 1890s, Roosevelt had upbraided immigrants who failed to break loose from every Old World Tie," wrote political scientist John Higham in *Strangers in the Land*. "Then, during the years of reform, the democratic and humanitarian strains in his character (encouraged by political expediency) brought him into sympathy with those who wanted to use the state in behalf of hyphenated minorities; in 1912 he championed a 'New Nationalism' that would bind the foreign-born closer to the rest of America by a broad federal welfare program. But with the scent of battle in his nostrils in 1915, he swung back to his earlier view of the hyphen as a menace rather than a challenge."

Overall, America remained a largely tolerant nation where politicians respected the large, silent majority even as they took care not to alienate any ethnic groups, and where the populace as a whole took pride in respect for freedom and equality—the "radical" concepts on which the nation had been founded. In 1835, in his classic book *Democracy in America*, French scholar Alexis de Tocqueville praised America's ability to form a society from so many disparate groups: "How does it happen that in the United States, where the inhabitants have only recently immigrated to the land which they now occupy, and brought neither customs nor traditions with them there; where they met one another for the first time with no previous acquaintance; where, in short, the instinctive love of country can scarcely exist; how does it happen that everyone takes as zealous an interest in the affairs of his township, his country, and the whole state as if they were his own? It is because everyone, in his sphere, takes an active

part in the government of society." Today, Tocqueville is still perhaps the most cited authority on America's democratic ideals and their ability to transform differences of custom and tradition into unity of purpose.

Nonetheless, a vocal nativist minority did exist, and it often included prominent public figures. Telegraph inventor Samuel Morse, in his widely read book *Foreign Conspiracy Against the Liberty of the United States: The Numbers of Brutus*, ironically published the same year as Tocqueville's book, derided "the evil of immigration" for bringing illiterate Roman Catholics to America. In the 1850s, the American Party—better known as the "Know-Nothings," the epithet that New York *Tribune* editor Horace Greeley gave them and they gleefully appropriated—ran on an anti-immigrant, anti-Catholic platform and won forty-eight seats in the 34th Congress, with another fifty-nine legislators sympathetic to their cause. (The Know-Nothings would lose their influence not long afterward, when the Civil War replaced the anti-immigrant, anti-Catholic cause with new reasons for hatred.)

By the end of the nineteenth century, a growing number of Americans were coming to resent the nations of the world that were assembling here. Immigration picked up in the early 1880s, escalating into the Great Wave that would feed the hungry factories of the new Industrial Age. From 1880 through 1920, millions of Italian, Greek, Slavic, Irish, and Jewish immigrants arrived in America, working in factories and living in the teeming slums that newspaperman Jacob Riis portrayed sympathetically in his famous book *How the Other Half Lives*. As the wave of newcomers grew, the established Americans of English and German stock began to resist.

American attitudes toward Chinese immigrants exemplified this tug-of-war among competing interests. Almost as soon as Chinese workers began arriving in the 1850s to build railroads across the West, California passed laws that imposed severe restrictions on Chinese immigrants. Nationwide needs prevailed over the state's, however. In 1868, the United States signed a treaty with China to help bring in more workers, whose numbers soon swelled to 250,000, or 4.4 percent of total immigration during the 1870s. A backlash against the "coolies" soon forced the government to

backtrack. In 1882, Congress passed, by large majorities, the Chinese Exclusion Act, which suspended Chinese immigration for the next twenty years and fueled a campaign to extend its provisions to all Asians. The act coincided with a growing movement to regulate immigration. The same year, Congress also passed an Immigration Act establishing a head tax on immigrants and barring convicts, lunatics, idiots, and persons likely to become public charges (prostitutes and criminals had already been barred under an 1875 law). In 1891, Congress created a bureaucracy to process the arrivals of new immigrants and authorized the deportation of illegal aliens.

Tensions over immigration at home were mirrored in fears over foreign powers' ambitions abroad. Immigration restrictionists pointed to Japan's victory over Russia in the 1904–1905 Russo-Japanese war as "evidence" of an expansionist Asian threat—no matter that the conflict had been an effort to rein in *Russian* expansionism (not to mention that it soon would prove to be an ironic counterpoint to U.S. and European efforts to the same end). By 1908, the Japanese Exclusion League boasted more than 100,000 members, many of them also belonging to affiliated labor unions, all united in an exclusionist cause that masqueraded as state loyalty. The minutes of one meeting of the Japanese and Korean Exclusion League declared: "As long as California is white man's country, it will remain one of the grandest and best states in the union, but the moment the Golden State is subjected to an unlimited Asiatic coolie invasion there will be no more California."

Such feelings by no means were confined to the West Coast. In Boston, Robert DeCourcey Ward and other Harvard alumni in 1894 founded the Immigration Restriction League, a lobbying group that would become an important force behind the laws that were passed in the early 1920s to sharply curtail immigration. Ward opposed immigration in part because, he argued while feigning compassion for "the Southern negro," it displaced freed slaves from the South. In effect, he had two grievances against the immigrants: not only were they overtaking his home state of Massachusetts, but they were forcing blacks to move north as well. "What the result will be for the negro," wrote Ward in a November 1905 essay in the *Atlantic*, "time alone can tell, but those

who have the welfare of the negro at the heart may well ask themselves whether the indiscriminate admission of hundreds of thousands of aliens will not inevitably force the majority of the colored race down." In targeting immigration, he had struck upon the perfect outlet for post–Civil War social pressures, which had racial, political, and economic roots.

In 1896, Massachusetts senator Henry Cabot Lodge sponsored a bill imposing a literacy requirement on prospective immigrants: they had to be able to read and write forty words in any language. Three Presidents— Rutherford B. Hayes, Grover Cleveland, and Woodrow Wilson—vetoed the literacy test. Indeed, with the nation's need for new workers in mind—not to mention the ethnic votes they had so assiduously courted—presidents refused to sign into law the vast majority of the twenty bills Congress passed between 1870 and 1922 to restrict immigration in various ways. The presidential vetoes pleased the business owners who relied on the immigrant labor supply, but they did nothing to address the fact that America was struggling with the uncertainties of a rapidly changing society. A broader but still modest reduction in immigration perhaps could have headed off some of the tragedies to come: the Prager lynching, the Palmer Raids, the drastic immigration laws of the 1920s, and America's ultimately unproductive inward turn.

By the turn of the century, the restrictionists were making headway in the court of public opinion. In 1903, Senator Lodge and the Immigration Restriction League successfully pushed an immigration act banning polygamists and anarchists. The much broader 1907 Immigration Act doubled the head tax on new immigrants to four dollars, and, giving a clear indication of what Congress thought overall of the would-be immigrants, expanded the categories of those to be excluded:

All idiots, imbeciles, feebleminded persons, epileptics, insane persons, and persons who have been insane within five years previous; persons who have had two or more attacks of insanity at any time previously; paupers; persons likely to become a public charge; persons afflicted with tuberculosis or with a loathsome and contagious disease; persons not comprehended within any of the foregoing excluded classes who are

found to be and are certified by the examining surgeon as being mentally or physically defective, such mental or physical defect being of a nature which may affect the ability of such alien to earn a living; persons who have been convicted of or admit having committed a felony or other crime or misdemeanor involving moral turpitude; polygamists, or persons who admit their belief in the practice of polygamy, anarchists, or persons who believe in or advocate the overthrow by force or violence of the Government of the United States, or of all government, or of all forms of law; or the assassination of public officials . . .

In the hands of the yellow press, the measures made for sensationalist copy, but they did not do much to limit immigration, since there was little reason for European peasant families to scrape together funds for the trip to America for anyone who was not likely to repay the invest-ment by sending home wages. All the new rules did was to add to the emotional tenor of the struggle over immigration.

The 1907 act also established a congressional commission, headed by Vermont's Republican senator William P. Dillingham, to investigate and make recommendations about how the nation should handle immi-gration policy—that is, how it should restrict Japanese and southern Eu-ropean immigration, since it had been convened in order to come to precisely that conclusion. The good commissioners' first order of busi-ness was to carry out "research" in Europe: Six of them promptly set out on a trip that, according to historian John M. Lund, "took on all the trappings of a grand tour," complete with an entourage of wives, family, secretaries, and staff members, with commissioners housed in private staterooms—an elegant setting for the commissioners who were dead-set on documenting the depravities, poverty, and other deficiencies of the European hordes clamoring to come to America.

"Instead of the tall, blond northwestern type of European, masses of people belonging to the east, central, and south European types are pour-ing into our country," Franz Boas, a Columbia University professor, wrote in a 1908 proposal to the commission to study the physical character-istics of 13,000 children of immigrants. "The question has justly been

raised, whether this change of physical type will influence the marvelous power of amalgamation that our nation has exhibited for so long . . . the development of modern anthropological methods makes it perfectly feasible to give a definite answer." Boas, himself a German-Jewish immigrant, slyly implied that his study would confirm that recent immigrants suffered from physical and mental deficiencies. How surprised, then, the committee members must have been when he submitted his findings in 1909. In his report, "Changes in Bodily Form of Descendants of Immigrants," Boas concluded that immigrant children's physical and mental characteristics quickly came to resemble those of Americans. Their race, in other words, had nothing to do with their potential for success in America. Boas's work would continue in this vein, and he would spend a large part of the rest of his life trying to discredit the argument that the new immigrants were inferior.

The Dillingham Commission's forty-two-volume report, released in 1911, confirmed that the mix of immigrants had indeed shifted to southern and eastern Europe and that the newcomers were settling in the urban Northeast instead of the rural Midwest, as earlier northern and western Europeans had done. It also cited research "proving" that immigration was the source of increased crime; of the mentally unfit and insane; of white-slave trafficking; and of the siphoning of American money to Europe via money sent by immigrants to their families back home. Most of the researchers employed methods guaranteed to portray immigrants in an unflattering light. In a survey study of charity, for example, researchers set out to prove that southern and eastern European immigrants were the most likely of all immigrants to receive charity. To ensure that their conclusions could not be otherwise, the researchers sent any questionnaires showing aid going to western or northern European immigrants back to their research subjects for "corrections."

In the end, the Dillingham Commission failed to convince Congress to act immediately on any of its recommendations. It had, however, spawned an industry of "scientific" arguments for the restriction of immigration on the basis of eugenics—an effort to breed better human beings and keep the races separate. By far the most prolific of the pseudoscientists of the

era was Madison Grant, a dapper, mustachioed lawyer and amateur naturalist. Born into a wealthy New York family in 1865, more than a century after his Scottish ancestors arrived in America, and educated at Yale and Columbia Universities, Grant argued tirelessly that the wave of southern and eastern European immigrants represented a profound racial and cultural threat to America. In his 1916 bestseller *The Passing of the Great Race*, he claimed to be defending America against a massive foreign incursion. "The new immigration, while it still included many strong elements from the north of Europe, contained a large and increasing number of the weak, the broken, and the mentally crippled of all races drawn from the lowest stratum of the Mediterranean basin and the Balkans, together with hordes of the wretched, submerged populations of the Polish Ghettos," Grant wrote. "With a pathetic and fatuous belief in the efficacy of American institutions and environment to reverse or obliterate immemorial hereditary tendencies, these newcomers were welcomed and given a share in our land and prosperity. The American taxed himself to sanitate and educate these poor helots." (Congress had instituted the first income tax three years earlier, in 1913, in part to finance schools; immigrants had to pay twice the tax that citizens did and were only allowed limited access to the services the taxes supported.)

Considering the dramatic social changes of the era, it was certainly reasonable to argue that immigration was too high. Many intellectuals and popular publications gave Grant's book a warm welcome. The *Saturday Evening Post* praised it profusely, as did many other periodicals, including *Science*, the journal of the American Association for the Advancement of Science. Grant used his popularity to encourage and promote like-minded authors, like Lothrop Stoddard, author of the 1920 diatribe *The Rising Tide of Color Against White World Supremacy*.

Nearly a century after the heyday of the eugenicists, Americans were still foretelling national ruin at the hands of hordes of immigrants of peoples of different colors and creeds. "Uncontrolled immigration threatens to de-

construct the nation we grew up in and convert America into a conglomeration of peoples with almost nothing in common—not history, heroes, language, culture, faith, or ancestors. Balkanization beckons," sometime presidential candidate Patrick Buchanan warned in *The Death of the West: How Dying Populations and Immigrant Invasions Imperil Our Country and Civilization*. Mostly written before the 9/11 attacks, the book became a bestseller when it was published in 2002, making apocalyptic predictions about the rise of "anti-Western" culture. Criticizing "political correctness" for silencing debate on immigration policy, Buchanan wrote: "Only 'nativists' or 'xenophobes' could question a policy by which the United States takes in more people of different colors, creeds, cultures, and civilizations than all other nations of the earth combined." Although his jab at the political correctness police was not entirely misplaced, Buchanan's rhetoric inflated the facts. In reality, the United States, though home to the largest number of the world's immigrants, is host to less than a quarter of the total number.

Also in 2002, columnist Michelle Malkin, who was born Michelle Maglalang, the daughter of Filipino immigrants, published *Invasion: How America Still Welcomes Terrorists, Criminals, and Other Foreign Menaces to Our Shores*. Later she would write that the United States was justified in interning more than 100,000 Japanese immigrants and Americans of Japanese ancestry during World War II and would be justified in doing the same today.

In 2004, Harvard political scientist Samuel Huntington, who won mainstream fame with his 1996 book *The Clash of Civilizations and the Remaking of World Order*, gave an academic imprimatur to the new culture warriors' doomsaying. *Who Are We? The Challenges to America's National Identity* similarly warned that America's national identity is at risk of decaying in the face of immigration and globalization. Because of the post-1965 immigration wave, he proclaimed that by 2000, "The Stars and Stripes were at half-mast and other flags flew higher on the flagpole of American identities." He attacked "transnational economic elites" and "globocrats" for their seeming indifference to national borders. Although a century ago criticism of immigrants focused mainly on the poor,

uneducated classes, in most other ways today's Cassandras are strikingly similar to those who preceded them.

⌣•⌣

On June 28, 1914, the nineteen-year-old Serbian nationalist Gavrilo Princip assassinated Archduke Franz Ferdinand, heir to the Austro-Hungarian throne, setting off a European military chain reaction. As hostilities in Europe escalated, the United States cast about, trying to decide whether to become directly involved with the affairs of the Old World in a conflict among the countries of origin of its most prominent ethnic groups. The Northeast's large Anglo population wanted to supply England with arms, credit, and food. For Americans of German and Austro-Hungarian origins, the choice was far more difficult because their homelands had been the first to declare war. Their effort focused not on convincing America to join Germany and Austro-Hungary but instead on keeping the United States neutral, since the only way that Germany could hope to win was if the Allies failed to win support. German Americans who sympathized with the motherland found kindred spirits in the Irish, who welcomed the chance to spit in the face of the British Empire. The dilemma that America now faced in balancing these interests soon would threaten to tear this country apart, and it created the now-entrenched notion that loyalty to any other nation was dangerous to the very existence of America.

For many immigrants on the eve of the First World War, it wasn't until they came to America that they had begun to think of themselves as loyal to a nation rather than to a regional leader or ethnic group. Firm national borders were so new—Germany, for example, had not unified as one nation until 1871—that passports were not required for travel abroad until after 1914, and had not even existed in much of Europe until then.

When the war began, the United States was home to more than 8 million first- and second-generation German immigrants and 3 million Austro-Hungarian immigrants and their children—in all, more than one in nine people with blood ties to the countries that the United States would eventually fight. Because Germany required its male citi-

zens to serve in the military, the men among the German-born population of 500,000 in America were technically reservists for the German military. A large potentially hostile population, including men whose land of birth could compel them to fight against America and our allies, was living on our own soil.

Although the vast majority of these new Americans were unquestionably loyal, that did not mean Germany and Austria-Hungary were not actively trying to convince them to rally to the cause of their homeland. Financing the publication of articles in the major German and Jewish (hence anti-Russia and anti-England) papers in America, Germany's propaganda war was heavy-handed and often offensive. In a Pulitzer Prize–winning analysis of the German American press, the *Milwaukee Journal* warned: "Day in and day out, the *Milwaukee Germania-Herald* has preached division along the lines of race and other war prejudices . . . It has virtually without exception opposed the government of the United States in every step that President Wilson has taken to protect American sovereignty and the rights of American citizens against the aggressions of Germany." The Austro-Hungarian embassy, meanwhile, warned that any of its subjects who worked in Allied factories in war-related industries should give up any hope of returning to their homeland, for they would be thrown in prison if they did so.

Rumors spread that German mill workers were grinding glass into flour and that meat packers similarly were lacing sausages and hot dogs with glass slivers. Ruffians stoned the delivery wagons of German American businesses; vandals threw yellow paint at German Americans' homes; immigrants were flogged, tarred and feathered, covered in yellow paint, and worse. Many German Americans were reported to have committed suicide after being accused of disloyalty. In Indiana, a mob locked a woman of German descent inside a lion cage and paraded her through town. Even loyal Americans were subject to such treatment merely for opposing the war, since at the beginning of the war neutrality implied support for Germany: in Baraboo, Wisconsin, home of the Barnum & Bailey circus, vigilantes jailed a 72-year-old Quaker grandmother in an abandoned lion cage because she was a pacifist. Such attacks shaped

Americans' complicated relationship with our immigrant past over the ensuing decades by showing that acknowledging pride in one's heritage too openly could be not just socially stigmatizing but actually dangerous for immigrants. Not surprisingly, immigrants wanted to protect their children from the suffering that a foreign accent or foreign sympathies could bring on.

In Milwaukee, America's most German city, every single street with a German-sounding name was rechristened in the name of loyalty. The City University of New York reduced by one credit every course in German. The German-language publishing industry, which at the turn of the century had boasted more newspapers than English-language ones, withered. Twenty-six states banned the use of the German language in schools; dozens of cities banned the use of German in public. Americans renamed German measles "liberty measles," dachshunds "liberty dogs," and sauerkraut "liberty cabbage"—much the way french fries were renamed "freedom fries" in the Congressional cafeteria in 2002 to protest French opposition to waging war on Iraq. From 1914 to 1918, sauerkraut consumption fell by 75 percent.

Anti-German sentiment even spread to the Prohibition movement, since America's beer industry was still largely the province of German-descended brewers, whose loyalty was suspect no matter how long ago their ancestors had arrived in America. The satirist H.L. Mencken, an avowed devotee of the beer hall, openly sneered at the teetotalers' cynical enlistment of wartime sentiment to win support for temperance. "Homo boobiens was scientifically roweled and run amok with the news that all the German brewers of the country were against the Eighteenth Amendment; he himself observed that all German sympathizers were made dreadful by dreams of German spies, he was willing to do anything to put them down, and one of the things he was willing to do was to swallow Prohibition," he wrote.

German Americans themselves were deeply torn over where to cast their loyalties. Hermann Hagedorn, a young writer who embraced America's cause despite the entreaties of his family back in Germany, lamented the nagging feeling of guilt that would not stop tormenting him: "Soberly

gratified though I might be at every German setback, every German victory set my Teutonic heart beating a little faster. Ambivalence is the word for it." Earlier German arrivals and their descendants sought to distinguish themselves from the newcomers—"the Prussians and the Prussianized," as novelist Owen Wister, himself of German ancestry, disparagingly put it. "Nothing that brought the South Germans brought them; they hadn't fled from horrible wars, they had run away from military service."

Many of the rumors that spread about German Americans were animated by nothing more than overblown hatred. There were nevertheless real reasons for concern. Although German spies were not nearly as ubiquitous as the anti-German school would have liked Americans to believe, they were active in the United States. The best-known today, Captain Franz von Rintelen, of the Imperial Navy, was plotting to convince Mexico to declare war on the United States; to buy up munitions works; and to sponsor strikes and sabotage in key American industries. Although most of Germany's sabotage efforts failed, those that succeeded were more than enough to inspire terror. For example, on July 30, 1916, four warehouses on Black Tom Pier in New York Harbor holding $25 million worth of armaments to be shipped to the Allies exploded, killing six people. Although the culprits were never identified, it was widely assumed that the Black Tom explosions were carried out by an alliance of German loyalists and Irish revolutionaries.

If any moderate sentiment toward Germany remained after that, it certainly disappeared in January 1917, when the notorious Zimmerman letter was made public. In the letter, the undersecretary for the German Foreign Ministry, Arthur Zimmerman, offered Mexico an alliance with Germany against the United States in the event that the United States failed to remain neutral: to "make war together, make peace together, generous financial support, and the understanding on our part that Mexico is to reconquer the lost territory in Texas, Arizona, and New Mexico." Germany had been supplying arms to the Mexican revolutionary Pancho Villa, whose guerrilla attacks in New Mexico were distracting the United States, which had to send an expedition to fight back the rebels. The Zimmerman letter not only confirmed what many Americans already believed about

the strength of German infiltration of North America, but it also brought the German threat much closer to home. Soon after the Zimmerman affair, Congress passed a literacy requirement for new immigrants and was able, for the first time, to override a presidential veto of the bill.

By now, the U.S. government had all but abandoned any efforts to contain public hysteria about Germans in America. In April 1917, President Wilson created the Committee on Public Information to shape public opinion on the war, both at home and abroad. Under the leadership of onetime muckraker George Creel, a former *Rocky Mountain News* editor, the new Committee on Public Information carried out a vigorous anti–German espionage campaign. "What we had to have was no mere surface unity, but a passionate belief in the justice of America's cause that should weld the people of the United States into one white-hot mass instinct with fraternity, devotion, courage, and deathless determination," he later wrote.

Creel's team arranged mass meetings, produced mass patriotic propaganda, and created the Four Minute Men—a group of 75,000 volunteer speakers, each of whom spoke for four minutes in support of the war for a total of 755,190 speeches. The four-minute limit, which was strictly enforced, had been designed to fit perfectly into the intermission of movies—and the movies themselves were often masterpieces of anti–German propaganda, depicting German soldiers as rapists and baby-killers. Many of the Four Minute Men dedicated themselves to the antiespionage campaign. One speaker warned: "Ladies and Gentlemen: I have just received the information that there is a German spy among us—a German spy watching *us*." Although he confined his remarks to German spies, not to German Americans in general, the underlying message was that one could never know who was a spy. In this case, he used his message not to exhort his audience to violence but rather to urge good deeds—buying Liberty Bonds: "Do not let the German spy hear and report that *you* are a slacker."

The Division of Civic and Educational Cooperation, a department of the Committee on Public Information, produced thirty-odd pamphlets, including titles like *The German Whisper* and *Conquest and Kultur*, and

movies like *Wolves of Kultur.* "Will it be any wonder if, after the war, the people of the world, when they recognize any human being as a German, will shrink aside so that they may not touch him as he passes, or stoop for stones to drive him from their path?" Professor Vernon Kellogue asked in one pamphlet. More rumors, some of them of government manufacture, spread: that the Germans had a factory to convert corpses to soap, that they were spearing babies on the tips of bayonets. Public libraries purged their stacks of materials that even remotely smacked of pro-German attitudes; one librarian even reported burning pro-German books that had been donated.

For their part, many German Americans, who were anxious to prove themselves loyal, joined the campaign, often with more fervor than Americans of other ethnic backgrounds. Some enlisted, like the captain in the largely German American 32nd Division, who declared: "These men will vote as they fight—for America." Many war heroes—like General of the Armies John J. Pershing and the legendary flying ace Captain Eddie Rickenbacker—bore German names and American hearts. But even such shows of patriotism did not spare loyal German Americans in the armed forces from attacks and hounding by officers and fellow enlistees who suspected them of spying for the enemy.

Other German Americans sent leaflets to Europe intended to help convince their former compatriots to surrender: "BROTHERS! We are American citizens of German descent. We know you and trust you. We beg you to trust us. The great German nation is the barbarian and the breaker of trust in the eyes of the world. You can recover your good reputation only if you overthrow this government, which has made German intelligence and German industry a danger to the world."

In some cases, German immigrants tried to be more American than the Americans—as Robert Prager had done during the dispute with his former employer over Prager's enthusiastic display of the Stars and Stripes. As George Viereck, publisher of the strident German-financed newspaper *The Fatherland*, put it, such German Americans "would deny the Holy Ghost if he were to approach them in German garb or with a Teutonic accent." In Bastrop County, Texas, two German Americans joined the

crowd that accompanied a deputy sheriff who would shoot and kill a local German farmer for failing to buy Liberty Bonds; the crowd then attacked and beat his widow.

In May 1918, Iowa Governor William L. Harding issued what was known as the Babel Proclamation, which banned the use of any language but English—or, as he put it, "American"—in any public gathering of two or more people. The ban even covered telephone conversations, as several grandmothers discovered when they were jailed for speaking German on the phone. Although the edict was aimed at the German language, it affected speakers of other foreign languages as well, like the Lutheran pastor who conducted a funeral service for a fallen soldier in Swedish so that the grandparents of the deceased could understand. After all, Governor Harding had said in public that God only heard prayers spoken in English.

H.L. Mencken later characterized such patriotism in a scathing essay, "The Star Spangled Men," in which he declared: "If the grand cordon or even the nickel-plated eagle of the third class were given to every patriot who bored a hole through the floor of his flat to get evidence against his neighbors . . . and to all who served as jurors or perjurers in cases against members and ex-members of the I.W.W. [Industrial Workers of the World] and to the German-American members of the League for German Democracy, and to all the Irish who snitched upon the Irish—if decorations were thrown about with any such lavishness, then there would be no nickel left for our bathrooms."

◡•◡

President Wilson found himself in the difficult position of managing an America that was deeply divided, often along ethnic lines, by opinions about where—or even whether—the country should cast its alliances. Although he is now known as an internationalist president, Wilson until 1912 had campaigned on a decidedly parochial platform, with sympathies for the nativist movement. He was prone to lecturing Americans about the dangers of old-country allegiances and had claimed that "the immigrants from Southern Italy, Hungary and Poland are the very lowest class of hu-

man beings, possessing neither intelligence nor initiative." By the time war broke out, he had toned down his rhetoric considerably, although his frustration was evident when he spoke to Congress on December 7, 1915: "The gravest threats against our national peace and safety have been uttered within our own borders. There are citizens of the United States, I blush to admit, born under other flags but welcomed by our generous naturalization laws to the full freedom and opportunity of America, who have poured the poison of disloyalty into the very arteries of our national life."

Despite that statement, Wilson for the most part tried to keep hostility to Germans from getting out of hand, even up to the last minute before the United States entered the war. In his speech to Congress on April 2, 1917, in which he asked Congress to declare war on Germany, Wilson reminded Americans that he was acting only in armed opposition to their irresponsible government and wished to demonstrate sincere friendship to the German people:

> We shall, happily, still have an opportunity to prove that friendship in our daily attitude and actions towards the millions of men and women of German birth and native sympathy, who live amongst us and share our life, and we shall be proud to prove it towards all who are in fact loyal to their neighbors and to the Government in the hour of test. They are, most of them, as true and loyal Americans as if they had never known any other fealty or allegiance. They will be prompt to stand with us in rebuking and restraining the few who may be of a different mind and purpose. If there should be disloyalty, it will be dealt with with a firm hand of stern repression; but, if it lifts its head at all, it will lift it only here and there and without countenance except from a lawless and malignant few.

As soon as the United States entered the war, Wilson issued a set of twelve regulations restricting the rights of German-born males ages 14 and up, including bans on owning munitions and on living within a half mile of military installations as well as a provision for preventive detention. On November 16, the government would issue eight more rules applying to 250,000 male "enemy aliens." The new rules mandated that

"enemy aliens" must register with authorities, carry their registration cards at all times, and report any change of address or job. They also broadened the exclusion zones, from which German men and boys were prohibited; now Washington, D.C., itself was an exclusion zone. The following April, the prohibition extended to an estimated 220,000 German women.

In May 1917, President Wilson created three internment camps for German civilians as well as for merchant marines and soldiers on German ships that were in American ports when the United States entered the war. Camps in Forts Oglethorpe and McPherson in Georgia and Fort Douglas in Utah housed conscientious objectors, civilian internees, and German prisoners of war. Eventually, Fort Oglethorpe was reserved for enemy aliens and Fort McPherson for prisoners of war to keep the two groups, who did not get along, separate. In July 1918, a fourth camp, at Hot Springs, North Carolina, in the Blue Ridge Mountains, was turned over from Labor Department to War Department control to provide separate housing for the officers and crews of German merchant ships that were in U.S. ports when Wilson declared war on Germany. Because such measures had been under discussion since the previous December, the government was able to move quickly to set up the camps. The government had been monitoring activities of German and Austro-Hungarian groups for three years, and thus had a pool of information to help it decide whom to arrest. At first it attempted to be selective. From May through October 1917, the government had interned just over 900 German aliens; mass arrests would not come until after December 1917, when Congress declared war on Austria-Hungary. By the end of the war, the administration had arrested more than 6,000 individuals considered to be potential threats—including American citizens—for offenses that included merely speaking in public in favor of Germany, or even of neutrality.

Wilson made a point of staffing the barracks system with officials whom he believed to be moderate. Although authority rested with the Justice Department, Wilson made sure that responsibility did not fall directly under Assistant Attorney General Charles Warren, who had drafted the three recent major laws dealing with hostile foreigners and whom Wilson considered to be something of an extremist. Wilson's deputies tried to en-

sure that the treatment of prisoners was fair, notably that of German sailors who had been seized, in no small part to ensure that American POWs were treated well. The manner of arrest was another matter entirely. Arresting officers and vigilante groups like the American Protective League—a volunteer group with loose ties to the Department of Justice, boasting more than 250,000 members at its peak—often did not obtain warrants until weeks after they had detained their quarry. The cases of those arrested during the initial sweeps in May and June of 1917, for example, were not actually investigated until August.

Instead, John Lord O'Brian was placed in charge of the new War Emergency Division, which handled the arrests and preventive detentions. O'Brian appointed four deputies, including the young J. Edgar Hoover. He also shifted the power to arrest into the hands of local U.S. marshals, whom he assumed would be best able to assess the potential threats in their communities. Unfortunately, these largely illiterate political appointees could not even tell Germans from other Europeans. According to Raymond K. Cunningham, who has documented the detainment camps extensively, the overzealous marshals indiscriminately detained Greeks, Dutch, French, Belgians, Ukrainians, Poles, and others. (Being arrested must have come as a shock to the French and Belgian detainees, whose homelands were engaged in a bitter fight against Germany—especially the Belgians, whose country was depicted in propaganda posters as a maiden being "raped" by the Huns.) In a country where hardly any Americans were separated by more than a few generations from their immigrant ancestors, everyone was a suspect, and even long-established Americans had to "prove" their loyalty. This meant that the camps would also come to house native-born citizens who were tarred by the mere suspicion of disloyalty.

Retired army officers ran the camps, each of which housed several hundred inmates at a time but was designed to hold up to 1,800. Fort Douglas War Prison Barracks Three, for example, housed 784 men, mainly civilians who held German or Austro-Hungarian citizenship. Rows of barbed wire surrounded the fifteen-acre compound, which was monitored by heavily armed sentries. At first, the atmosphere inside the

camp was relatively lenient. Civilian residents received pay for work they performed in the camp, and they were allowed to form the Association of Interned Civilians, which met weekly with the camp's executive officer, Major Emory Scott West.

The Swiss Legation inspected the camps and confirmed that they met Hague Convention standards for prisoners of war, a very low bar to clear, considering that nearly all of the inmates were civilians who had never been near a theater of war. It was a good thing, then, that many of the camps exceeded those standards. Fort Oglethorpe had a camp commissary where inmates were allowed to buy supplies, which they funded with their wages of twenty-five cents a day. Prisoners' wives were allowed one two-hour weekday visit each week, and prisoners could accept food and clothing from their families. The commandant encouraged inmates to participate in sports and recreation, including occasional field meets with prizes. Some prisoners even had gardens of their own to tend, published camp gossip sheets, and taught their fellow inmates. At Hot Springs, inmates built a replica of a German village, "complete with a miniature Gothic church made of wood and flattened cans," according to military historian William B. Glidden. Fort Oglethorpe had billiards tables and a piano.

In the autumn of 1917, security was tightened dramatically after repeated efforts by members of the Industrial Workers of the World (IWW, or Wobblies) to tunnel out of the camp. At Camp Oglethorpe in September, more than 100 rebellious IWW prisoners attacked other internees who disagreed with their propaganda; in October, authorities at Fort Douglas disciplined Wobblies for repeated tunneling efforts; various escape attempts there involved at least sixteen tunnels, various bomb plots, and coded messages, according to an account by Cunningham. The longer the prisoners remained, the more restive they became—especially those who had been most stridently opposed to the Wilson administration's policies. Wintertime brought outbreaks of scarlet fever and flu, and although camp personnel tried to administer proper medical care, forty-six inmates at Fort Oglethorpe died in the 1918 flu epidemic. As the war

progressed, the atmosphere at the camps deteriorated; yet the growing unrest would merely bolster the government's rationale for continuing to detain their inmates.

On Armistice Day, November 11, 1918, inmates at Fort Douglas rioted. The atmosphere calmed dramatically within a week, however, when influenza swept through the compound, infecting about half of the camp's 676 residents; the camp doctor's pleas to the surgeon general for additional medical staff went unheeded. When Senator Reed Smoot inspected Fort Douglas in March 1919 from the vantage point of the inside of a car that drove in and out, he reached the conclusion—and wasn't shy about stating it publicly—that the internees were a "bunch of criminals." (Smoot would later cosponsor the infamous Smoot-Hawley Act.)

Although other war powers released prisoners within a few months of the war's end, arrests in the United States continued until February 1919. Before Attorney General Thomas W. Gregory left office in the spring of 1919, he released one-third of the internees and repatriated another third of them (who had voluntarily accepted this option) to Europe. When he left, however, his successor, A. Mitchell Palmer, kept the camps open to house dissidents detained during the Red Scare that followed the Bolsheviks' victory in Russia. The camps did not close until June 30, 1920, more than eighteen months after the armistice. It wasn't an effort to restore justice that closed them, but an effort to reduce government spending. When the camps closed, their demise received little, if any, public attention.

In the time since, America has all but forgotten about the internment camps. Unlike the shameful camps in which Japanese Americans were interned during World War II, the three Great War detention centers have not been cited, even by the few historians who have paid them attention, as a national embarrassment. There were no legal battles over *habeas corpus* requests, which dissidents had used during the Civil War and which would prompt notable Supreme Court debates in World War II and during today's "war on terror." Indeed, there was so little public comment about the camps that Richard O'Connor's otherwise exhaustive history of

German Americans during the Great War explicitly states that they were not interned.

Reinforcing the idea that the camps had done the job that they were supposed to do in keeping certain individuals out of general society, accounts of trouble within the camps tend to portray those responsible as agitators who tried to push their pro-German or anarchist propaganda on the other inmates.

Historian Mitchell Yockelson, who has researched the camps extensively, calls them "one of the true success stories for the War Department during World War I." Yockelson cites one prisoner who, after his release, wrote the commandant thanking him for "Excellent, fair, and just treatment" at the camp: "I shall never look back upon those days with regret, they have been a wonderful lesson for me, and have in many ways developed that democratic idea, that is so truly American." Historian William Glidden notes that 173 of the German naval prisoners applied to stay in the United States and become citizens, suggesting that the internment could not have been so bad.

The camps had flourished under the cover of false patriotism, like that which had inspired the Robert Prager lynching and turned his murder into a reason to silence immigrants and citizens alike. A *Washington Post* columnist expressed the prevailing sentiment in the days after Prager's death: "Prager apparently was an ignorant foreigner, who should have been promptly arrested and sent to an internment camp." The indignant columnist continued, criticizing the widely repeated ideal of America that Israel Zangwill had immortalized in his 1908 play *The Melting Pot*: "If this war has demonstrated anything, it is that we are a melting pot that does not melt. There is widespread sentiment in this country now that the man who lives in America henceforth must be an American."

But what did that mean, to "be an American"? The columnist was wrong about the war's having demonstrated a new requirement of loyalty and patriotism. What the war had done was to redefine what it meant to become American, in ways that were not for the better.

3

Becoming American

In Brighton Beach, a heavily Russian neighborhood in Brooklyn, New York, a group of Russian senior citizens are sitting in a community center civics class preparing to take the examination to become naturalized U.S. citizens. The teacher, a no-nonsense New Yorker dressed in serious brown, begins quizzing her students on their homework assignment on the U.S. Constitution: to imagine what a Twenty-eighth Amendment might be. A man in the front row reads carefully but emphatically from the statement he'd written out: "To allow citizens over 65 years old to pass the citizenship exam in our native language." He speaks the last bit of the sentence in triumph, and looks up to applause from his classmates.

"Tamara?" the teacher asks a woman with blue-tinted glasses, pale-blue hair, a leopard-spot vest, and a very Russian sense of fashion. "What would you propose?" Tamara nods her color-coordinated head. "No rent increases!" she answers emphatically. "You still think we should live under communism!" the teacher replies. Everyone laughs.

The teacher surveys the room. "How about someone else?" Lydia, a tiny red-haired woman, speaks up from the back row. "The Twenty-eighth Amendment would be for universal health care. Forty percent of Americans don't have health insurance. But they have it in lots of countries: in France, China, Canada." Another student chimes in: "People should be allowed to be president once they have lived here for twenty

years, even if they are not natural-born Americans. I think about my grandchildren. They were seven years old when they came here, but they will be Americans."

The teacher smiles. "Very good. Now I have another question for you. It's been over 200 years since the Constitution was written, and there have been only twenty-seven amendments so far. Why so few amendments?" she asks. Tamara sniffs authoritatively. "Very good Constitution," she says, nodding vigorously and prompting nods all around her.

"What about an amendment to fine people if they fail to vote?" the teacher asks. Heads shake all around the room in a unanimous negative. A woman wearing a headband and a dark shawl raises her hand. "It's a free country!" she says indignantly, prompting cheers.

Welcome to America, a country whose dearest principles ring true to the people coming to our shores. Here is a classic example of the role that immigrant organizations play today, and have played throughout history, in bringing together the newest Americans to help them become part of society in their adopted country.

⌣•⌣

How do you make an American? It depends on whom you ask, but there seem to be three major approaches. One, the melting-pot theory, holds that newcomers assimilate almost automatically, by absorbing American values. Another assumes that some people will become American because the culture of their homeland is similar enough, but that people who come from cultures that are too different will never become American, so there is no use trying. Under the third view, which Americans today often associate with the early twentieth-century United States, new immigrants need instruction in how to become American.

The Americanization movement of the early twentieth century was born as a way to show that the eugenics movement was wrong to contend that the new southern and eastern European immigrants would never assimilate. White "established" American educators and social workers put their efforts toward providing language and cultural education to adults

and schoolchildren. At Chicago's Hull House, the most famous institution of the nationwide Settlement House movement created to give
people the tools to escape inner-city poverty, social worker Jane Addams
helped immigrants assimilate while letting them celebrate their homelands; urging students to tell stories of their own customs was part of the
process of learning English. Giving immigrants familiar subject matter on
which to practice their English, this method was intended to help them
value their roots and respect those of others. At the same time, classes on
subjects such as food preparation, home sanitation, civics, hygiene, and
child rearing were designed to replace the rough peasant habits that so
many of the new immigrants brought from the Old World.

This version of Americanization sought to instill patriotism through
example so that immigrants would want to take the oath of citizenship
and assimilate of their own free will—not because they were coerced. It
worked because Americans who were born here joined efforts with those
of the ethnic associations that had long dedicated themselves to helping
recent immigrants integrate into American society. Since the early days
of the Republic—the Charitable Irish Society was founded in 1737 in
Boston, the Hibernian Society for the Relief of Emigrants from Ireland
in 1790 in Philadelphia, and the Sons of Herman for German-speaking
immigrants in the 1840s—such groups organized community activities
such as sports and theater, served as business and employment networks,
sold life insurance, and acted as burial societies. Some placed agents directly at Ellis Island to help the newly arrived find lodging, work, and
community. Their work, though it was done under ethnic umbrellas, was
quintessentially American, both for its roots in civic voluntarism and for
its underlying "can-do" ethos. Indeed, American voluntarism flowered in
the late nineteenth and early twentieth centuries as never before or
since, as sociologist Theda Skocpol has shown; it was a time of astound-
ing growth for large civic associations.

In encouraging immigrants to embrace common civic aspirations, the
ethnic associations and settlement houses became a major force in ex-
changing and transforming the cultures that immigrants brought with
them, stripping away the bad and leaving the good to mingle with those

who likewise had come to America for a better life. This was the model that Israel Zangwill presented in his 1908 play *The Melting Pot*, whose title would become an enduring metaphor for what it meant to become American. A Broadway hit, the play was a latter-day Romeo and Juliet story of two immigrants, the Jewish violinist David Quixano, whose family had escaped the pogroms, and the social settlement worker Vera Revendal, whose Cossack forebears had caused them. At the end they stand on the roof of the settlement house. "There she lies, the great Melting Pot—listen! Can't you hear the roaring and the bubbling?" David says. "There gapes her mouth—the harbour where a thousand mammoth feeders come from the ends of the world to pour in their human freight. Ah, what a stirring and a seething! Celt and Latin, Slav and Teuton, Greek and Syrian, black and yellow . . ." Vera adds, "Jew and Gentile." David continues: "Yes, East and West, and North and South, the palm and the pine, the pole and the equator, the crescent and the cross—how the great Alchemist melts and fuses them with his purging flame!"

Although the essential message of the melting pot was that it allowed people to cast off prejudices and racial hatreds, even Vera and David probably would have been shocked at the idea that to become American, immigrants had to give up the part of their identity that rested fondly in their homeland. On the contrary, it was through homeland connections that people plugged in to the networks they needed to succeed in America. In Jewish communities, *Landsmanshaftn*—hometown associations—helped bring immigrants together around memories of the homes to which many of them could not return because of the pogroms that had annihilated many of their relatives and sent the survivors fleeing to America.

In many cases, America allowed immigrants to put into action ideas that had been suppressed at home. The Turnverein gymnastics associations, originally created in Germany to help prepare youths to resist Napoleon, were involved in the failed 1848 German revolution, which sent hundreds of thousands into exile, many in the United States. With the motto "Sound Mind in a Sound Body," the Turners took on an Ameri-

canized name and became involved in social justice causes as well as in integrating immigrant youths into their new American communities.

At the same time, the pull of the homeland remained strong. From 1901 to 1920, 36 of every 100 immigrants to America went back to their home countries for good. From 1971 to 1990, by contrast, only 23 of every 100 immigrants went home: Contemporary immigrants are more likely to stay than the Great Wave immigrants were. A hundred years ago, steamships took at least sixteen days to cross the Atlantic ocean. Thus, a visit home was a major undertaking, so migrants—even the many who went back and forth as seasonal laborers—had to be far more committed to making the trip than today. There were many reasons to do so, some involving the homeland itself and some involving the ideals and dreams that America had nurtured.

In the late nineteenth and early twentieth centuries, governments were well aware of the importance of encouraging their people to return once they had made their fortunes on America's gold-paved streets and to send money while they were still earning it. For its part, China required women and children to stay behind when Chinese men left to work in America so that the men would feel obliged to send money home and one day return to reunite with their families. From 1900 to 1906, immigrants sent home 12.3 million postal money orders from New York to their home countries. Then, as today, home-country governments used carrots and sticks to make sure that emigrants would send money back. In Italy, a 1913 law allowed emigrants to regain Italian citizenship by returning for two years, and their children born abroad were still deemed to be Italians. Another proposal, which never came to fruition, would have given political representation in Italy to Italians living abroad.

The money that went back to Europe was substantial, as detailed by Mark Wyman: an average of $850 from each immigrant to Galicia each year before the war; between $250 and $1,000 from returning Italians; $400 to $600 from Transylvanians. (To get a better idea of the size of these funds, consider that today's equivalent of $100 in 1913 dollars would be nearly $2,000, a twentyfold increase.) In many places, returning

migrants bought up significant amounts of local land. Immigrants brought back not only money but skills, making a tremendous impact on the European economy: "To many, the impact of the returned emigrants was less in carrying back scissors and pulp-making machines than in knowing how to tackle projects, big projects." Charles Hallgarten returned to Germany to become a banker and to promote adult education and civic projects; Thomas Edison's former assistant, Siegmund Bergmann, opened an electric works in Berlin. Scandinavian re-migrants brought back farming techniques to improve drainage, breeding, and cultivation and initiated the first large-scale poultry operations. Across Europe, the Americanized returnees pushed for improvements to schools and public services and led workers rights movements.

Immigrants to America came to play an important role in spreading American political ideals around the world. Two of Poland's greatest heroes, Casimir Pulaski and Tadeusz Kosciuszko, fought both in defense of their Polish homeland and in the American Revolutionary War; Pulaski was mortally wounded in the battle of Savannah. The United States harbored many of the rebels who led the 1798 Irish uprising and many of those who fought throughout the nineteenth century for Irish independence. Eamon de Valera, Ireland's great freedom fighter and later its prime minister and president, was born in the United States and returned here many times to raise funds for the Irish cause; he raked in $10 million during one trip to the United States in 1920. Many other heroes of the struggle for Irish independence had spent time in America, bringing organizing skills and funds back to Ireland. José Martí worked from exile in Spain and Venezuela to free Cuba from Spanish domination and planned the ultimately successful Cuban revolution during the years (1881–1895) he lived in New York. Even before Marcus Garvey's Universal Negro Improvement Association launched a pan-African improvement movement from New York in 1914, the Jamaican-born leader had (unsuccessfully) urged the Jamaican government to stick up for the rights of its migrant workers in Central America.

Even immigrants who had their sights on their homelands—indeed, especially those who dreamed of changing life back home for the better or

of one day returning permanently—understood that it was in their best interests to master American culture. It is a truism that immigrants return home either because they fail—like the family that Frank McCourt immortalized in his memoir, *Angela's Ashes*—or because they succeed. Defining success was something else—whether it meant learning new skills, earning enough to keep the family from starving, or moving up the socioeconomic ladder. For the worker who sought to improve his station in life, the more familiar he became with American customs and the English language, the more successful he could count on being. Nevertheless, the longer an immigrant intended to stay, the more likely he was to dedicate himself to adopting "American" ways of life, and in turn to improve his fortunes.

There were, however, many workers who were focused only on the short term and who had neither the time nor the inclination to dedicate themselves to "Americanizing." For the many temporary workers, to whom even the relatively low wages they earned in America were vastly beyond what they could have dreamed of in Europe, often there was no time to learn English beyond the little required on the factory floor. As the urban population of unskilled immigrants grew in the late nineteenth and early twentieth centuries, they became more visible—and so did the foreign traits that made them stand out, inciting the growing movement to restrict immigration. It was becoming clearer than ever that it was crucially important to integrate newcomers into American society, even temporary ones not necessarily inclined to changing their habits. And it also was clear that Americanizing was not necessarily so much about culture but more about class and socioeconomic status.

~·~

Frances Kellor, a sociologist who lived at Hull House, made Americanizing immigrant workers her personal mission. She took elements of the Settlement House movement's lessons and incorporated them into a broad civic movement backed by the business community and a nod from government. After serving on the New York State Commission on

Immigration in 1908, she later would become head of the state's Bureau of Industries and Immigration as the first woman to lead a state agency. "From the moment [the immigrant] arrives in America he needs the creative aggressive attention of American institutions," Kellor wrote. In 1909, she helped organize a New York chapter of the North American Civic League for Immigrants, a group whose original configuration in Boston was concerned with counteracting negative foreign influences. She rechanneled its efforts into promoting assimilation through English classes and distribution of pamphlets containing useful information. (Recently the U.S. Citizenship and Immigration Services, a branch of the Department of Homeland Security, issued a new book of such information for immigrants, the first in many years.) As the parent organization's politics became more reactionary, she distanced the New York chapter from it and in 1914 reconstituted her group as the Committee for Immigrants in America, a federal agency funded by wealthy private bankers.

Among the businessmen who embraced Kellor's work, Henry Ford became a legend for his relentless and often farcical drive to forge a new middle-class industrial ethos. Three-quarters of Ford Motor Company's nearly 13,000 workers were born in other countries, and the largest groups of foreign workers came from the very places that the eugenics movement had deemed to be the darkest, most ignorant corners of Europe: Poland, Russia, Romania, Italy, Sicily, and Austro-Hungary. To mold these workers' behavior to the exigencies of the mass production line, Ford created the Ford Educational Department, which took Americanization to extremes. Instructors and inspectors cared not only about ensuring that employees' habits at work conformed to the company's expectations but also insisted that employees' home lives met its exacting standards. Workers who ended up in less-than-ideal living circumstances were entirely at fault, one of Ford's manuals implied: "The company will not approve, as profit sharers, men who herd themselves into overcrowded boarding houses which are menaces to their health." Company manuals prescribed "clean, well conducted homes, in rooms that are well lighted and ventilated." Inspectors visited workers' homes to

ensure that they met standards of cleanliness and morality, to the extent that if a woman was present in the home, the worker was required to produce a marriage certificate. Inspectors also interviewed family and neighbors. If an inspector found a worker's home and lifestyle to be substandard, the company would move to turn things right, providing loans, grants, and paycheck advances.

In the Ford company classroom, students had to walk up to the blackboard to explain to the class how a "good American" behaved. They were encouraged to declare their good Americanness out loud. The Americanization graduation ceremonies were the height of absurdity, with adult graduates compelled to put on a pageant as if they were schoolchildren, descending a mock gangplank into a giant pot, which teachers stirred with ten-foot ladles until the students emerged outside the pot as full-fledged, flag-waving Americans. Looking back at the Americanization period, it is hard not to see the roots of today's gaudy patriotism and of the American obsession with the Stars and Stripes. The Frenchman Bernard-Henri Lévy, in a trip across America in 2004 and 2005 for the *Atlantic Monthly*, commented on how shocked he was at the fetish Americans have made of our flag.

When hostilities broke out in Europe in 1914, the drive to Americanize the immigrant intensified. The civic and business groups Kellor had assembled worked together to promote a National Americanization Day, July 4, 1915. As many as 150 cities across the country held mass naturalization ceremonies and celebrations in which children sang patriotic songs. Recognizing that no amount of Americanization could or should diminish immigrants' love of their countries of birth, President Wilson told Philadelphia immigrants being naturalized on Americanization Day, "I certainly would not be one even to suggest that a man cease to love the home of his birth and the nation of his origin—these things are very sacred and ought not to be put out of our hearts—but it is one thing to love the place where you were born and it is another to dedicate yourself to the place to which you go." Why, after all, would we want to create a citizen out of someone who does not love the land where they were born? He continued with a warning: "You cannot dedicate yourself to America

unless you become in every respect and with every purpose of your will thorough Americans. You cannot become thorough Americans if you think of yourselves in groups."

❦

During the war, the mostly benign—if often bizarre—Americanization of the turn of the century turned into a forcible Americanization by fear. At risk of losing their jobs or worse, immigrants did their best to avoid showing "ethnic" traits in public. Casting off their foreign pasts was the key to becoming Americans—not Polish-Americans or German-Americans, just plain, unhyphenated *Americans*. "The hyphen is a minus," the Ford Motor Company continued to teach its employees throughout the war, until a financial crisis at the company in 1920 cut off funding for its paternalistic reeducation program.

As the war in Europe escalated, the whole nation was grappling with the role of the roughly one-third of the population that was foreign born. "One's affections may be divided, but his allegiance and patriotism are inseparable; and this applies with equal force to the men and women of all nationalities who have made our country their home," Columbia University Professor William R. Shepherd noted in a speech to the German University League's anniversary meeting in New York City's Waldorf-Astoria Hotel on October 30, 1915. "Affection for the land of one's ancestors, and sympathy with it in an hour of adversity, are no evidence of disloyalty to the United States, so long as we ourselves are not parties to the conflict. This we have not been, and, God willing, we never shall be!"

America's entry into the Great War hostilities brought a new urgency to the work of the Americanizers, who feared that unnaturalized and unassimilated immigrants posed a threat to national security. Americanization thus completed its journey from idealistic paternalism to farce to monster. From the tolerant message "Many Peoples, But One Nation," Kellor's campaign slogan turned into the stern "America First." The fighting in Europe added to the pressure to draw a clear line between what it was to be American and what it was to be European. In the mind

of Americans, the Old World became a cauldron of primitive politics and rivalries. Newspaper magnate William Randolph Hearst wrote in the *Chicago Evening American*: "The war is attributable to the survival in Europe of medieval institutions long outgrown by modern society to the prosecution of imperial policies in the selfish interest of greedy hereditary dynasties."

Today we hear, ad nauseam, that America's roots are essentially European. Indeed, Europe sells: just listen to the accents of the models in advertisements used to sell cosmetics, cars, jewelry, lotions, and anything intended to convey a sense of luxury. This could not be more different than a century ago. Though we celebrate America's European heritage today, the highest imperative a century ago was to make it clear that America was *not* Europe. "Why is all of Europe waging this Awful War?" asked an editorial in a Wisconsin paper, the *Two Rivers Report*, on September 5, 1914. "Whose is the fault for the breakdown of civilization in Europe? For broken down it is, signally and completely. In the United States, the paper implied, even groups that fought bitterly elsewhere could live "in peace and harmony." But in Europe, they were tearing each other apart. Kingcraft has failed; statesmanship has failed; privileged-class society has failed; they have been weighed in the balance and found wanting."

Criticism of Europe implicitly elevated American democracy and mores as a superior system that had created a superior society. Unfortunately, beneath these confident proclamations lurked the fear that perhaps America had not shaken off the habits of Old Europe and that recent arrivals might still carry remnants of European character that could infect this country. As fear trumped hope, the new American patriots invoked national unity as an excuse to destroy the atmosphere of tolerance that had helped us become a nation in the first place.

Americans of English descent pitted themselves against those of German descent. As the United States moved closer to supporting England instead of remaining neutral, the idea of America as a nation influenced by the cultures of many peoples was replaced by the idea of Anglo America, which conveniently preserved the illusion that Continental rivalries had not crossed the Atlantic. Thus, anyone who was pro-English was seen as

being fully American, while anyone who preferred neutrality—Germans and many Irish who had their own bone to pick with England—now was defined as being un-American. All reflected the interests of their home-lands, but the English received two winks and a nod. Many German Americans opposed the Kaiser even more than Anglo-Americans did; af-ter all, part of the reason they had come to America was to escape his regime. A pamphlet from the Society of the Friends of the German Repub-lic reflected this view: "Are you a friend of the German Republic? Do you wish to see the old country freed from its blood-stained militaristic oppres-sors and the execration of the world which those criminals have brought upon it?"

The National German-American Alliance, founded in 1901, urged "all Germans to gain their citizenship as soon as they were legally entitled to it; to take an active interest in public affairs, and to practice their civic duty with regard to the ballot box, fearlessly and according to their own consciousness." The group promoted German language and literature and fought against Prohibition, which by targeting mainly German breweries was clearly an ethnic attack cloaked in temperance talk. By 1915, it had close to 3 million members. For the National German-American Al-liance, which had hoped for neutrality in the war, the U.S. decision to side with England was heartbreaking. Its member groups honored their heritage by organizing relief drives for German, Austrian, and Hungarian victims of the war, thus managing to support the German people while re-maining loyal to the United States. Despite the group's role in promoting American citizenship and assimilation, its ongoing advocacy of neutrality attracted negative attention from the press and Congress, and its charter was withdrawn in 1918.

Woe to anyone who did not fall in with the prevailing wartime version of what it meant to be American, especially those who exercised some of the fundamental rights based in the very democracy that had made us strong. Victor Berger, a Milwaukee politician whom servicemen would burn in effigy because of his opposition to the war, had gotten his start in American civic life through the Turners. Born in Nieder-Rehbach, part

of the Austro-Hungarian Empire, Berger emigrated at age 18 to the United States in 1878. He earned his living in Milwaukee as a metal-worker and then journalist and publisher. He established three news-papers and in 1901 became a cofounder, with Eugene Debs, of the American Socialist Party. In 1910, Berger was elected to the U.S. House of Representatives as the first Socialist Party member of Congress, though he was no radical. *Collier's Weekly* took note of his aversion to taking the extreme ground, and he would openly scoff at Upton Sinclair and IWW as "well-meaning but impossible crazy chickens." He hated the German Kaiser and disapproved of the tolerance Milwaukee Germans showed to-ward the *Vaterland*—a stance that ended up costing him any chance in 1914 of regaining the congressional seat he had lost in 1912.

Berger had become a vocal opponent of America's involvement in the war because of his aversion to imperialism in any form, because he be-lieved the war was merely a way for capitalist businesses to add to their profits, and because he believed it was not in America's vital interests to fight in Europe. Just as he denounced the Kaiser's autocratic behavior, he also criticized the U.S. government's abuse of citizens' rights during the war. For exercising his right to free speech in defense of American princi-ples and the Constitution, Berger would be branded as anti-American. For writing a series of editorials criticizing the draft, even though he took pains to encourage his readers to obey the law, he was accused of violating the Espionage Act, and his newspaper, the *Milwaukee Leader*, had its second-class mailing privileges suspended, making it virtually impossible for him to continue publishing. He was indicted under the Espionage Act in 1918—while a candidate for a Wisconsin seat in the U.S. Senate—and tried before a judge who had made disparaging comments about both Ger-man Americans and pacifists. Weeks before the trial began, he was elected to Congress by an 18 percent margin over his nearest opponent. In February 1919, a jury convicted him of sedition, and he was sentenced to twenty years' hard labor at the federal penitentiary at Leavenworth, though he was allowed to remain free on bail during appeal. Congress voted to vacate his seat, but he ran again in 1919 and won 55 percent of

the vote. Again, Congress refused to let him take office, so the seat remained vacant. The U.S. Supreme Court reversed his sentence in 1921, vindicating Berger and those who had supported him, and suggesting that their idealistic faith in the power of American values was not, after all, in vain. They had believed in America despite the persecution that had been carried out in its name. After the war, Jane Addams recalled:

> All of us, through long experience among the immigrants from many nations, were convinced that a friendly and cooperative relationship was constantly becoming more possible between all peoples. We believed that war, seeking its end through coercion, not only interrupted but fatally reversed this process of cooperating good will which, if it had a chance, would eventually include the human family itself. The European War was already dividing our immigrant neighbors from each other. We could not imagine asking ourselves whether the parents of a child who needed help were Italians, and therefore on the side of the Allies, or Dalmatians, and therefore on the side of the Central Powers. Such a question was as remote as if during the Balkan war we had anxiously inquired whether the parents were Macedonians or Montenegrins although at one time that distinction had been of paramount importance to many of our neighbors.

The nation had abandoned the idea that encouraging immigrants to participate in society would quickly put them on a clear path toward engaged citizenship. Although noncitizens, especially those who had applied for naturalization, had long been allowed to vote in state and local elections and to hold public office in more than forty states and territories, states now moved to bar immigrants from voter rolls and municipal electoral slates and ended noncitizens' right to vote in 1926. "With the quickening tempo of war, the enlightened tactic of education for immigrants steadily gave way to the harsh technique of repression," legal scholar Jamin Raskin has written. Thus, instead of engaging newcomers in their communities right away, America added to the forces that would

break down the sense of neighborliness and kinship. Instead of becoming citizens completely out of their own volition and love for America, immigrants became naturalized partly out of fear of being different and of being marked as traitors and losing their jobs or worse as a result.

"Any man who carries a hyphen around with him carries a dagger that he is ready to plunge into the vitals of the republic," Woodrow Wilson said on September 25, 1919, contradicting previous statements, in his final speech to rally support for the stillborn League of Nations. Americans had lost confidence in the founding values that made ours the greatest country in the world, and so they betrayed those values.

America's ethnic fraternal organizations already had disproved the idea that the hyphen was a minus: despite their "foreignness," these groups had been the backbone of efforts to create new Americans in a way that respected American ideals. "The efforts of immigrants to resist forced Americanization broadened the definition of liberty for all Americans," historian Eric Foner has written. Immigrants and their sympathizers wondered what happened to the values of tolerance, civic duty, education, and respect for difference tempered by a striving toward unity. Immigrants may have conformed outwardly, but they defended the ideals that had brought them here in the first place. As one Polish newspaper put it, the forced Americanization movement had "not the smallest particle of the true American spirit: the spirit of freedom."

In the aftermath of the war, with only a few exceptions, the once-thriving ethnic associations disintegrated. The Irish-dominated Knights of Columbus, thanks to having established an official partnership with the War Department, saw its membership rise after the war, but it was an exception. The Ancient Order of Hibernians, which like most Irish groups had been deeply ambivalent about being on the same side as England in the war, began hemorrhaging members and never recovered. The Sons of Herman, once one of the largest German fraternal associations, disbanded nationally in 1921, leaving only a few state chapters behind. "Suddenly, German churches and societies changed their names. Fraternal groups rescinded their longstanding policies allowing foreign-language lodges.

Group badges that used to sport the black, red, and gold of the German empire suddenly turned red-white-and-blue," wrote Theda Skocpol and her colleagues of the demise of ethnic voluntary groups. The vibrant world of ethnic societies, with their emphasis on public service and education and their international outlook, withered. Becoming American came to mean simply hiding anything foreign, not celebrating the democratic ideals that had helped this country make one people out of all the nations of the world.

~•~

Between the danger of sea travel and the hostile atmosphere in America, the war had dramatically reduced immigration. The number of new arrivals declined to 300,000 in 1916 from 1.4 million in 1914. For the nativist movement, the war's end was an opportunity to make this lull permanent. Existing nativist groups rallied together, and new groups mushroomed. The American Legion mushroomed on a nationwide level, explicitly linking its recommendations to the threat from Red Russia. "[In] Legion thinking it was invariably the alien—never the 'hundred percent American'—who carried the pest of bolshevism to our shores," wrote historian Jacobus ten Broek about the group's aims.

The American Legion's message found its way into popular culture, especially the new motion picture industry. Following the model of the successful wartime propaganda films, many the movies of the late teens and early twenties warned of the threat posed by unbridled immigration. In the 1920 movie *Shadows of the West*, American Legionnaires expose a (fictional) Japanese plot to control California agriculture. The Native Sons of Golden West, repeating the mantra that America was at risk of a "peaceful invasion" of Asian hordes and other immigrants, created in their 1919 convention a Committee on Asiatic Matters and threatened to impeach the governor if he did not call a special session of the legislature to create new anti-Japanese legislation. The California Grange (founded in 1867 and thus one of the oldest restrictionist organizations, although immigration was only one issue among many for its farmer

members) carried out a similar campaign to limit immigration. In 1920, former *Sacramento Bee* publisher V.S. McClatchy and state senator J.M. Inman organized the Japanese Exclusion League of California, an organization that would tirelessly lobby until succeeding in 1924 to persuade Congress to pass the Japanese Exclusion Act. This law prevented Japanese from naturalizing and laid the foundation for the terrible wrongs that the government would carry out against America's ethnic Japanese in World War II.

While wartime xenophobia was still high, a new menace appeared: the success of the Bolshevik revolution, which conjured the double specter of nationalism and communism. Several bombings in the summer of 1919—including one on June 2 that partially destroyed Attorney General A. Mitchell Palmer's home—made very real the fear that America faced an insidious threat on the home front. Against this backdrop, Palmer convinced President Wilson that America was at risk of nothing less than a Russian communist takeover, led by the more than 60,000 agitators supposedly identified by the U.S. government.

"Sharp tongues of revolutionary heat were licking the altars of the churches, leaping into the belfry of the school bell, crawling into the sacred corners of American homes, seeking to replace marriage vows with libertine laws, burning up the foundations of society," Palmer warned in an essay "The Case Against the Reds." In this scenario, civil liberties—especially for immigrants of German or Russian descent—took a back seat to national security. "Upon these two certainties, first that the 'Reds' were criminal aliens and secondly that the American Government must prevent crime, it was decided that there could be no nice distinctions drawn between the theoretical ideals of the radicals and their actual violations of our national laws," Palmer declared.

The Great Red Scare had begun. Persecution of one immigrant group had made it easy to extend to other foreign groups—even if "foreign" included Americans who merely sympathized with foreign ideas and causes. The Alien and Sedition Acts of 1798 (all repealed or expired by 1802) had given the United States powers to apprehend foreigners suspected of plotting against the nation, but laws passed during the Great

War went much farther, conferring on the government vast powers to arrest foreigners for a wide range of crimes. The Espionage Act, signed into law on June 15, 1917, made it illegal to utter a disloyal word or oppose the draft. Within a few months of the law's enactment, the government had used it to arrest 900 people. On May 16, 1918, President Wilson signed into law an amended version of the 1917 Espionage Act, now known as the Sedition Act because of the provision that gave the government unlimited powers to censor and punish dissidents. Under the most famous application of the law, the Socialist presidential candidate, Eugene V. Debs, was sentenced to ten years in prison for his public opposition to the war.

The government prosecuted more than 2,000 people under the Espionage Act from 1917 through 1920, winning convictions on just over half. The effects of these laws would last long beyond the end of the Great War, setting precedents for the apprehension of alleged enemies of the state during World War II and again during the Cold War. In effect, immigrants served as test subjects for laws that later would be applied against citizens.

Between November 1919 and January 1920, the government arrested and held without charges 6,000 American citizens, mostly naturalized Eastern European Jews. Attorney General Palmer's men did not bother to get warrants before bashing their way into the offices of unions as well as of communist and socialist groups. They were especially zealous in their arrests of immigrants, and in December 1919 deported 249 of them, including the feminist writer Emma Goldman, on the ship *Buford*, bound for the Soviet Union. To be sure, Goldman had a long, checkered history of run-ins with the law, including ties to the attempted assassination of a union-buster. Her reputation had also been tarnished when President William McKinley's assassin claimed that her speeches had inspired his crime. She was finally imprisoned not because of firm evidence of guilt in any substantive crime but for opposing the draft, and she was denaturalized. Recalling her departure as the ship pulled out of New York Harbor, Goldman wrote bitterly of the irony of having been stripped of her citi-

zenship for the newly created crime of exercising her First Amendment right: "Through the port-hole I could see the great city receding into the distance, its sky-line of buildings traceable by their rearing heads. It was my beloved city, metropolis of the New World. It was America, indeed America repeating the terrible scenes of tsarist Russia! I glanced up—the Statue of Liberty!"

Joseph Yenowsky, a Connecticut clothing salesman who had immigrated from Russia, was convicted in 1920 and sentenced to six months in jail for supposedly telling a bond salesman that he considered Lenin to be "the greatest, the most brainiest man on earth today"—comments that Yenowsky denied having made. Ironically, according to an account in the *Nation*, Yenowsky was an American Legionnaire who had taken an immediate dislike to the bond salesman because the salesman had never fought in the army.

This general effort to root out radicals also netted two Italian immigrants, Nicola Sacco and Bartolomeo Vanzetti, for a bank robbery and murder that many people believed was an excuse to arrest them for their long histories of political agitation and anarchist militancy. Their six-week trial became one of the most controversial political events of the century, ending with their conviction on July 14, 1921. When they were executed on August 23, 1927, many Americans continued to believe that they were innocent.

The main question was not whether the government was right to apprehend the anarchists and radicals who allegedly embraced the idea of violent overthrow of the U.S. government; it was how many of its targets were actually guilty of such agitation, and whether Palmer and his young assistant J. Edgar Hoover could not have contained them through means that respected American ideals and values. As Jane Addams wrote in indignation to the *Chicago Tribune*, "While many of these arrested aliens might be legitimately liable to deportation, the methods employed were not those to give them an impression of even-handed justice and of lawful procedure; that the entire situation was a dangerous departure from the Anglo-Saxon tradition of arresting a man for his overt act and not for his opinions."

Immigrants were on alert: looking, acting, and sounding different put them at risk. In his inaugural address in 1921, President Warren G. Harding did nothing to allay their fears: "I wish for an America no less alert in guarding against dangers from within than it is watchful against enemies from without," he declared. "Due concern for making all citizens fit for participation will give added strength of citizenship and magnify our achievement," he added, challenging immigrants to prove their commitment to American society.

After the war, the commonly accepted definition of becoming American was no longer primarily a positive one—gaining skills, learning English, participating in one's community, improving one's standard of living. It now took on a distinctly negative sheen: to hide evidence of one's past, to ostracize those who looked different, to distance America from Europe. It became easier to say what America was not than what Americans believed their country to be. "A nation conceived in antonyms," as historian Daniel T. Rodgers has called it, America had lost touch with the unifying vision that had enabled the country to bring together so many different people.

Writer Willa Cather, whose novellas and short stories had vividly depicted the lives of German and Scandinavian immigrants on America's Great Plains, understood the danger of shutting out the rest of the world, stamping out any indications that Americans all had come from different origins, and enforcing a false uniformity. Shortly after the National Origins Quota Act was passed in 1924, she lamented: "This passion for Americanizing everything and everybody is a deadly disease with us." She understood all too well that Americanizing had very little to do with being American.

~·~

Ironically, some of the most eloquent analyses of what makes America great have been written by thinkers who were not born here. J. Hector St. John de Crèvecoeur, born in Normandy, came to the United States in 1759, at 27 years old and settled in Orange County, New York. "What

then is the American, this new man?" Crèvecoeur asked in letters published in 1782 reflecting on his life as an American farmer. "He is an American, who, leaving behind him all his ancient prejudices and manners, receives new ones from the new mode of life he has embraced, the new government he obeys, and the new rank he holds. He has become an American by being received in the broad lap of our great Alma Mater. Here individuals of all races are melted into a new race of man, whose labors and posterity will one day cause great changes in the world. Americans are the western pilgrims." Though his words today still stand beside Alexis de Tocqueville's among the truest expressions of what is great about America, this American citizen never, in fact, stopped being a Frenchman. He returned to France in 1780, then came back to America a few years later as French consul; he eventually settled back in France, where he died in 1813.

Few thinkers are as closely associated with what we now call "the American Creed" than the Swedish Nobel laureate, Gunnar Myrdal. "Americans of all national origins, classes, regions, creeds and colors, have something in common: a social *ethos*, a political creed. It is difficult to avoid the judgment that this 'American Creed' is the cement in the structure of this great and disparate nation," Myrdal wrote in *An American Dilemma*, the classic 1944 study of race relations in America. "These ideals of the essential dignity of the individual human being, of the fundamental equality of all men, and of certain inalienable rights to freedom, justice, and a fair opportunity, represent to the American people the essential meaning of the nation's early struggle for independence." Myrdal's greater point was that American reality often falls far short of these ideals.

To thinkers like Crèvecoeur, Tocqueville, and Myrdal, and to the scores of millions of immigrants who have been drawn to our shores, Americans' most powerful shared cultural symbol is civic, not ethnic: the idea of liberty and the pursuit of happiness, especially when it comes to economic prosperity. Under their version of the creed, the *idea* of America—a common aspiration toward progress and individualism tempered by a commitment to one indivisible nation—is a force strong

enough to hold together people of different cultures. This idea is what America lost in the aftermath of the First World War, a loss that would be felt over the course of the twentieth century in all aspects of American life, from our relationship with the rest of the world to national unity at home.

—4—

The Eagle and the Ostrich

T he First World War thrust America onto a global stage, where it was now not only the economic leader of the world, a magnet for immigration, and a beacon of hope but also a political and diplomatic force in the world. After the trauma of the war and its divisive impact at home, however, Americans wanted very little to do with the rest of the world. Instead of capitalizing on its new global stature, America turned inward, both socially and economically, closing the doors to immigration and to trade. The eagle became an ostrich.

Before World War I, immigration was an integral part of enormous economic and social changes that had resulted from a long cycle of expanding global ties. In the late nineteenth century, many international trade treaties were signed, helping increase the exchange of capital and goods to a frenzied pace that would not be matched for a century. Just before the Great War, Great Britain was investing 7 percent of its national income abroad, a level to which no industrial economy has come close since the end of that era of globalization. In 1913, exports were around 30 percent of Great Britain's gross domestic product. By comparison, today all trade (exports and imports) makes up only about 21 percent of the GDP of the United States, the clear leader of a globalized economy. "By 1914, there was hardly a village or town anywhere on the globe whose prices were not influenced by distant foreign markets, whose infrastructure

was not financed by foreign capital, whose engineering, manufacturing, and even business skills were not imported from abroad, or whose labor markets were not influenced by the absence of those who had emigrated or by the presence of strangers who had immigrated," wrote Kevin O'Rourke and Jeffrey Williamson in *Globalization in History*.

Immigration was a pillar of this international economy. The United States, Argentina, and Brazil, the nations that took in the most immigrants, were also the fastest-growing economies in the world. Between 1870 and 1910, mass migration increased the U.S. labor force by 24 percent, dramatically boosting overall economic growth. But the price of this abundant labor supply was that it lowered the wages of the least skilled workers. The increasing numbers of unskilled migrants in the late nineteenth century "tended to flood labor markets at the bottom in destination countries, thus lowering the unskilled wage relative to the skilled wage, to white-collar incomes, to entrepreneurial returns, and to land rents," according to Williamson. The poorest of the poor included immigrants as well as people born in America who felt that the newcomers had usurped their place.

Even as the international flow of people, goods, and capital helped the trans-Atlantic economy grow as never before, it also worsened the gap between the poorest and wealthiest Americans, a difference that became impossible to ignore because of the dramatic increase in the size and visibility of the poorest part of the population. American attitudes toward the global economy were as ambivalent as they were toward immigration. This ambivalence soon would help create what historian Harold James called "a dangerous interplay" of monetary policy, trade policy, and migration law that eventually would not only lead to the Great Depression but also deepen and prolong its effects.

Economic tensions thus surely acted in tandem with emotions stirred up by the Great War, adding to the pressure that had been building since the late nineteenth century to restrict immigration. The biggest issue was the lowest-wage immigrant workers, whose presence both lowered the wages of the least skilled workers and made it clear that class divisions were still highly relevant in America—one more unpleasant reminder

that America had not freed itself completely from the Old World. "Class" was supposed to be the Achilles' heel of Europe, not America.

Although the business community had fought mightily to derail efforts to limit immigration, the Red Scare spooked many employers, who worried that immigrants might spread Bolshevik ideas among their workers. Thus, major business associations, who had long been a primary source of opposition to immigration reform, agreed to a compromise: a temporary quota. Congress responded with draconian immigration reform measures that marked the beginning of the end of an era of globalization. In 1921, it passed the Johnson Act, which instituted a quota system designed to sharply reduce immigration. The lawmaker who introduced it, Albert Johnson, was an American Legionnaire and a former member of the Asiatic Exclusion League and the Dillingham Commission member who two years later would be elected president of the Eugenics Research Association. The new law limited immigration to 3 percent of the existing number of each country's immigrants to the United States as counted in the 1910 census, with a ceiling of 355,000 per year. It was the biggest change in immigration law since 1882, but for the nativists, the fight was not over: their goal was to tighten the bolts further and lock them in place permanently.

In 1923, Calvin Coolidge became president after President Harding died, and he made it clear that he would maintain the isolationist course that Harding had set out. "New arrivals should be limited to our capacity to absorb them into the ranks of good citizenship," Coolidge declared in his first message to Congress. "Those who do not want to be partakers of the American spirit ought not to settle in America."

In May 1924—election year—Coolidge signed into law the Johnson-Reed Act, also known as the National Origins Quota Act, which dramatically tightened the 1921 quota system, ensuring that for the next four decades immigration would be limited largely to the "good" people of northern and western Europe. It also required new immigrants to obtain visas before entering, a measure that gave individual consular officers considerable latitude in deciding who would or would not be allowed to enter the country. Given that the director of consular services from 1909 to 1937, Wilber J. Carr, had firmly nativist leanings, it is not hard to guess

what their priorities were. In addition, the new law reduced the immigration quota to 2 percent of the existing number of each country's immigrants as counted in the 1890 census. Basing the quota on that year's census was significant not only because the total number of immigrants was smaller than in 1910—producing a total quota of 180,000 instead of the 270,000 that would have resulted from the 1920 census—but also because it excluded the wave of southern and eastern European immigrants who arrived after 1890. The effect was to increase the percentage of British and (ironically, considering the recent war) German immigrants, who would make up two-thirds of all immigration in the middle part of the twentieth century. It was as if a line had been drawn across the calendar to freeze in time the idea of who belonged in America.

~•~

Social, political, and economic forces collided in an upheaval that would end the Great Wave of immigration and the first age of globalization. As was typical in America, the public mood about our relationship to the rest of the world seesawed wildly, leaving in its wake shortsighted policies with unforeseen long-term consequences. As economic and political priorities competed for attention, lawmakers discussed issues endlessly but took little substantive action until problems reached a critical point. Then legislation was drafted hastily without serious consideration of its practical consequences, overcompensating in alternating opposite directions and leaving future generations to deal with the aftermath—until the newly created problems in turn became unmanageable and the cycle began all over again.

As Jeffrey Williamson has shown, globalization increases inequality *within* nations but at the same time reduces inequality *among* nations. This process of convergence is the only way to ease the pressures that force people to leave their homelands in search of work elsewhere. Ironically, it is more than likely that the way that immigration raised wages in Europe during the Great Wave era would have dramatically slowed the mass outflow of people to the United States even if the U.S. Congress had not

imposed quotas. In other words, America could have enjoyed the benefits of a more moderate level of immigration without the costs to social institutions, to our democratic ideals, to second-generation immigrants' understanding and appreciation of their parents' heritage, and to our connections to the rest of the world at a time when a breakdown of international ties would come to have catastrophic consequences.

Although immigration widened inequality in America, it helped the economy overall—and those who profited most from immigration were the ones with not only financial but also political power. This reality made it very hard for an economic argument against unfettered immigration to make headway, which is why what tipped the boat was, in the end, culture. The fear of imported radicalism combined with the undercurrents of the eugenics movement, the dislike of immigrants' peasant customs, and the doubts about immigrants' loyalty that had been inflamed during the Great War.

In time, however, the interaction between economic and cultural pressures would come full circle. Just as economic factors had provided the substantive reasons that moved America to close the gates, the consequences of the nation's turn inward would be economic—but they would worsen the original problem instead of making it better. Because the unraveling of global relationships would take place over the course of a decade, however, its impact was gradual, so that it was not obvious until too late how much damage had been done.

The full impact of the 1921 and 1924 restrictions on immigration was not felt immediately. The 1924 quota did not go into full effect, in fact, until 1929—coincidentally or not, the same year that the stock market crashed and ushered in the Great Depression. In the United States, the first impact was in construction—a sector that then, as today, both relied heavily on immigrant labor and was essential to the economy. "In the nineteenth century, construction activity had been linked to waves of immigration," Harold James explained. "For the 1920s, on the other hand, construction was the weakest point in an otherwise booming economy. From 1926 to 1929, at the height of 1920s prosperity, spending on construction fell by $2 billion, and the sector remained very weak during the

depression and the recovery of the 1930s." Elsewhere in the economy, it would have seemed that limitations on immigration were achieving what they had been intended to do: raise the standard of living and lower the unemployment rate for Americans working in manufacturing jobs. The average real income of employees rose by about 30 percent in the 1920s, compared with 20 percent between 1900 and 1920, and the average number of hours worked by each employee dropped. At the same time, the gap between skilled and unskilled workers' wages began to narrow as income and wealth distribution smoothed out.

Even as the doors were closing on immigration, the rise of American nationalist isolationism was working to protect American manufacturers from foreign products, beginning a cycle of trade protectionism that would strangle the global economy. The 1922 Fordney-McCumber Act raised tariffs and authorized further increases based on a percentage of products' "American selling prices"—which invariably were higher than their home market prices—ensured that American goods had an unfair advantage over foreign goods and encouraged the formation of U.S. monopolies. With the law coming into effect as Allied nations struggled to pay off war debts and Germany crumbled under the weight of war reparations, the drag it exerted on commerce certainly contributed to the conditions that led to the 1929 Black Monday stock market crash and the Great Depression.

The importance of stimulating trade was lost on Congress, however, which in June 1930 responded to worsening economic conditions by passing the Smoot-Hawley Act, a now-notorious piece of legislation that had, in fact, been under discussion for some time. The effects of Smoot-Hawley would be so debilitating that Vice President Al Gore's mere mention of the act during a memorable 1993 debate with Texas billionaire and sometime presidential candidate H. Ross Perot, was a decisive moment in defeating the opponents of the then-pending North American Free Trade Agreement (NAFTA). Raising tariffs to their highest levels ever, Smoot-Hawley all but closed America off from world trade. Other countries imposed retaliatory tariffs in a beggar-thy-neighbor race to the bottom that ensured the continuation and deepening of the Great

Depression. U.S. imports from Europe fell from $1.3 billion in 1929 to $390 million in 1932. U.S. businesses were hurt even worse, as exports to Europe fell from $2.3 billion to $784 million during the same period. Total world trade fell by 66 percent from 1929 to 1934, when lawmakers came to their senses and began easing tariffs. Although it had taken Congress only a few years to see the folly of economic isolationism, it would take many more years to undo the consequences, which reached far beyond the realm of economics and were more severe than anyone could have foreseen.

The unraveling of world trade networks, as nations raced to erect protectionist barriers against each others' goods, could not have sowed discord at a worse time. As Europe's economies suffered, economic nationalism turned into ethnic and racial nationalism, creating a threat that perhaps could have been confronted earlier had the world's great powers not been working at cross-purposes.

~·~

By the early 1930s, a more extreme version of the eugenics movement was taking hold in Europe. After Madison Grant's 1916 *Passing of the Great Race* was translated into German in 1925, the author reportedly received a fan letter from Adolf Hitler himself, who pronounced the book to be "my bible." By the time Grant's second solo work, *Conquest of a Continent*, was published, Americans had begun to see through the eugenicists' flawed message. As the *New York Times* noted in 1933: "Substitute Aryan for Nordic and a good deal of Mr. Grant's argument would lend itself without much difficulty to the support of some recent pronouncements in Germany." It had taken an example of others' folly for us to recognize our own.

The dramatic curtailment of immigration had certainly reduced the public squabbling over the issue, as had the general prosperity and calm of the 1920s. But if the closing of the gates had truly helped Americans unite, then the approach of World War II demonstrated a very strange definition indeed of national unity—both in terms of how well Americans

judged the now-settled immigrants to have become Americans, and in terms of the number of foreign-born individuals and groups that openly flaunted their loyalty to enemy powers. Nevertheless, clear efforts were made by the Franklin D. Roosevelt administration and by Americans in general to engage foreign-born Americans by promoting patriotic assimilation, which historian Eric Foner has described as "pluralistic acceptance of cultural diversity as the only real source of harmony in a heterogeneous society," instead of by the bullying that had characterized the First World War. The new rhetoric was intended to unite former immigrant groups in case America once again had to fight.

By various estimates, only a few million German Americans were still fluent in German and identified with the country of their ancestry. Because of the lull in immigration, America's German-born population was one-tenth of what it had been during the Great War. The vast majority were loyal Americans. Nevertheless, by 1933, the growth of German fascist groups in the United States worried the government enough that it complained to Germany. In response, the German ambassador to the United States, conveying a message from Hitler's deputy, Rudolf Hess, assured President Roosevelt that the groups had been disbanded. In reality, the number of pro-Nazi groups had risen to 800 by the end of 1938.

"The queerest birds of the most diverse kinds twittered in that wilderness, but it was a harmony of hate that rose up out of their throats," wrote Dutch author Louis De Jong in *The German Fifth Column in the Second World War*. One of these was Dr. Ignaz T. Griebl, whose successful stealing of U.S. Navy secrets was finally uncovered in 1938. Another was Nikolaus Ritter, an engineer who had worked in the United States for many years before returning to Hamburg as part of Hitler's war machine. In 1937 he gathered a network of agents, including a factory worker who obtained drawings of a secret bomb-sight mechanism. He also recruited William G. Sebold, a technician at a California aircraft manufacturer, when Sebold was vacationing in Germany. On Ritter's orders, Sebold returned to the United States and installed a "secret" radio transmitter—but in fact the secret was being kept from Germany, not from the United States. Sebold had reported Ritter's overtures to

the U.S. consul in Cologne and was cooperating with U.S. authorities. It was not Sebold but the FBI who controlled the only radio contact back to Germany from a "German agent" in America and was the central contact for Germany's entire spy network in America.

In this case, America rightly moved to repress specific members of one particular ethnic group who openly embraced disorder and aggression. On February 26, 1938, Indiana's highest court banned meetings of the German American Bund in the state. In Philadelphia the following month, riots broke out when an anti-Nazi mob crashed a local Bund party celebrating Hitler's seizure of Austria. On February 20, 1939, for Washington's birthday, some 20,000 members of the Bund rallied and Sieg-Heiled at a Nuremberg-style Madison Square Garden, even as 10,000 anti-Bund protesters gathered outside (with 1,700 police officers to head off trouble).

The Bund, however, represented a vocal but very small portion of German American fraternal life, which was otherwise overwhelmingly loyal to America. German Ambassador Hans Dieckhoff estimated in 1938 that out of the 700,000 Chicago-area Germans, only 450 were Bund members, while 40,000 belonged to other German ethnic associations. Indeed, in many cases American immigrant ethnic societies were on the front lines of the battle against the ideas that America would eventually take up arms to fight in Europe—as well as against the Bund. In 1930, a group of German Americans founded the Carl Schurz Memorial Foundation "to work toward a better integration of the German element in America with the rest of the American people." Naming itself after the German-born U.S. senator, secretary of the interior, lawyer, journalist, and general who had come to America after the failed 1848 revolution, the group would embody the sentiment Schurz had expressed at the opening of the Chicago World's Fair in 1893: "I have always been in favor of a healthy Americanization, but that does not mean a complete disavowal of our German heritage. It means that our character should take on the best of that which is American, and combine it with the best of that which is German. By doing this, we can best serve the American people and their civilization."

Most Italian Americans, including the Italo-American press, were pro-Mussolini until the Japanese attack on Pearl Harbor. Within the

Italian American community, a small but astute group was alert to Benito Mussolini's true character long before the U.S. government would be. Italian Americans, joining with the U.S. labor movement, had formed anti-Fascist societies as early as 1923, with the creation of the Anti-Fascist Alliance of North America. Because the anti-Fascist movement was heavy with unionists and radicals, however, the U.S. government saw it as a greater danger than the one it sought to avert. At the urging of the Italian embassy—which was on excellent terms with the United States at the time—Carlo Tresca, an Italian anarchist and editorialist of *Il Martello*, was arrested, charged with using the mails to send an offensive advertisement, and sentenced to a year in prison in 1925. By the early 1930s, however, a growing number of American intellectuals were beginning to join in opposition to Mussolini as well.

These undercurrents of foreign politics were of clear concern to America, and so, just as it had during the Great War, the government embarked on a propaganda campaign to promote loyalty and Americanism. In a softened version of the 1915 Americanization Day, a new holiday was held in May 1939 for naturalized citizens: "I Am an American" Day. As Secretary of State Cordell Hull declared, "We have always believed—and we believe today—that all peoples, without distinction of race, color, or religion, who are prepared and willing to accept the responsibilities of liberty are entitled to its enjoyment." In the months leading up to World War II, the Roosevelt administration, via the Office of Strategic Services, launched a full-blown propaganda campaign aimed at combating racism. The Office of War Information promoted the message that ethnic and racial prejudice undermined American values, and embraced the contributions of Italian and German immigrants to America. "We say glibly that in the United States of America all men are free and equal, but do we treat them as if they were?" asked Arthur Upham Pope, chairman of the Committee for National Morale. "There is religious and racial prejudice everywhere in the land, and if there is a greater obstacle anywhere to the attainment of the teamwork we must have, no one knows what it is."

Roosevelt himself weighed in heavily to emphasize the need for liberty and unity. "Democracy, the practice of self-government, is a covenant

among free men to respect the rights and liberties of their fellows," the president told Americans in his 1939 State of the Union Address. "In meeting the troubles of the world we must meet them as one people— with a unity born of the fact that for generations those who have come to our shores, representing many kindreds and tongues, have been welded by common opportunity into a united patriotism." It would not be long before Roosevelt would take steps that would cast serious doubt on his sincerity and illustrate the American ability, still evident today, of finding ways to hold idealistic beliefs while undermining them through action.

The year 1939 had already seen the passage of antisubversion laws and, in December, the creation of the Custodial Detention Index—a list of German, Italian, and communist suspects who were candidates for arrest, maintained by the Office of Strategic Services without legal authorization. The FBI claimed to be keeping tabs on more than 10 million people, including, naturally, a very large number of foreign-born individuals. Since the total foreign-born population was estimated at just under 5 million, it is clear that measures being sold as targeting foreigners were affecting native-born citizens as well. In May of that year, presaging the post-9/11 argument over the government's right to detain alien suspects, Congress debated whether to allow the secretary of labor to detain aliens who had been ordered deported. "I can imagine with what satisfaction Hitler will learn that his emissaries in this country have so influenced Congress that it is following his example in setting up concentration camps during peacetime," said U.S. Representative Caroline O'Day of New York.

On September 1, 1939, Germany invaded Poland. Two days later, Britain declared war on Germany. President Roosevelt declared the United States neutral. On September 9, he instated the Emergency Detention Program, which implemented by executive order the detention plan that the House had approved but the Senate turned down just weeks earlier. J. Edgar Hoover, by now FBI director, began compiling lists, and soon arrests and predawn raids began, targeting merchant marines in particular.

Reminiscent of Attorney General A. Mitchell Palmer, with whom he had collaborated as head of the General Intelligence Division antiradical

arm from 1919 to 1924, Hoover told the FBI National Academy in mid-1940: "That there is a Fifth Column which has already started to march is an acknowledged reality. That it menaces America is an established fact. That it must be met is the common resolve of every red-blooded citizen. A Fifth Column of destruction, following in the wake of confusion, weakening the sinews and paralyzing it with fear can only be met by the nationwide offensive of all law enforcement!"

Rosy government rhetoric promoting patriotic assimilation had turned to warnings that enemy spies had infiltrated America, and the national atmosphere changed accordingly. On a single day in May 1940, nearly 2,900 people submitted complaints of espionage—nearly twice the 1,600 reported in the entire previous year. *Life* magazine reported a joke circulating on Wall Street: Hitler had ordered 10,000 tanks from General Motors. Asked where they should be delivered, he replied, "Never mind that. We'll pick them up on our way through Detroit." Privately, Hoover recommended preparing legislation to allow for mass internments of foreigners going far beyond the limited detentions already authorized.

The public responded to the alarm with overwhelming support for alien registration. In a Gallup Poll conducted on June 10, 1940, some 95 percent of respondents said that all non-U.S. citizens should be required to register with the government. On June 28, 1940, Congress passed the Smith Act, which required all aliens over age 14 to register with the Immigration and Naturalization Service (INS) and provide a detailed statement of their occupation and personal beliefs. The act's better-known component, which made it illegal for anyone to advocate or teach the desirability of violent overthrow of the U.S. government, would become a notorious tool for stamping out Cold War dissent with only spurious evidence. Beginning August 27, 1940, the first of 4,921,452 aliens registered at U.S. post offices, which passed the results along to the Department of Justice. Aliens were also required to report a change of address within five days, and to reregister every three months. (The form they used to register, the AR-3, was the precursor of the "green card"—which today is actually pink—that gives immigrants resident status and permission to work.)

The bombing of Pearl Harbor on December 7, 1941, marked the end of the Roosevelt administration's lip service to patriotic assimilation. When Germany declared war on the United States and the United States declared war on Italy four days later, America's 600,000 Italian-born immigrants and their families became "enemy aliens." America's largest immigrant group had to carry ID cards and honor curfews, and 10,000 Italian-born immigrants living near America's coasts had to leave their homes. Because the registration of enemy aliens and the internment of foreigners during the First World War had generated so little controversy, there was little resistance to repeating those practices, which this time took place on a much larger scale. Not even the American Civil Liberties Union spoke out against the internment of foreigners, and when Congress voted to impose penalties for failing to obey Roosevelt's executive order authorizing internment camps, not a single lawmaker cast a dissenting vote.

The story of the internment, beginning in 1942, of more than 100,000 Japanese Americans from the West Coast Exclusion Zones—some 70,000 of them American-born citizens—is well known. So is the heroism of the battalions made up of Japanese Americans, many of whom had been told that their only way out of the internment camps was to enlist, who fought for America. Not nearly so well known is that during the course of the war, the U.S. government also interned 10,905 enemy aliens from Germany—along with 3,278 Italians, 53 Hungarians, 25 Romanians, 5 Bulgarians, and 161 others in fifty work camps across United States. (The government also apprehended 16,849 Japanese Americans outside of the West Coast Exclusion Zones.) Seizures were arbitrary, based on the slimmest of evidence: Filippo Molinari sold subscriptions to the Italian American newspaper *L'Italia* in San Jose, California, for which he was arrested and detained on the night of the Pearl Harbor attack. In New York City, authorities seized the international opera star Ezio Pinza, even though he had already applied for U.S. citizenship, and held him at Ellis Island until Mayor Fiorello LaGuardia convinced the government to allow him a second hearing.

The Germans and Italians were afforded a luxury the Japanese were not: the government considered individual evidence in tribunals under the authority of the Justice Department's Alien Enemy Control Unit. Although the Department of Justice (as has happened during the Bush administration) removed judges thought to be too lenient, non-Japanese detainees had some recourse. In 1943, courts struck down East Coast exclusion orders against two Germans, Maximilian Ebel (who had been a German soldier in the Great War) and Olga Schueller, both naturalized Americans. Even eight German saboteurs apprehended in June 1942 with explosives intended to destroy U.S. war industries received a military trial and consideration in a special session of the Supreme Court.

Anti-Japanese violence broke out across the country, again repeating the small-minded behavior that had been so widespread during the Great War. Wild accusations were made—for example, that Japanese gardeners were hiding short-wave transmitters in their garden hoses; that Japanese were poisoning vegetables sold in the market and contaminating cans of Japanese seafood with ground glass. Attorney General Francis Biddle would later write that "in Washington an energetic idiot chopped down some Japanese cherry trees." Californians plowed over a Japanese farmer's flower fields because the flowers appeared to form an arrow pointing to the airport. Within the first three weeks after the attack on Pearl Harbor, reports came in from around the country of vandalism against and even gratuitous murders of Japanese Americans, including a Los Angeles veteran of the First World War who had been honorably discharged from the U.S. Army. Hearst newspaper columnist Henry McLemore wrote on January 29, 1942: "I know this is the melting pot of the world and all men are created equal and there must be no such thing as race or creed hatred, but do those things go when a country is fighting for its life? Not in my book. . . . I am for the immediate removal of every Japanese on the West Coast to a point deep in the interior . . . Herd 'em up, pack 'em off and give 'em the inside room in the badlands."

If many Americans, including its leaders, had failed to embrace the principles of patriotic assimilation, others understood what it meant and spoke up to defend it. Sixteen months after her husband's Four Freedoms

speech extolled Americans' supposed unity of purpose, First Lady Eleanor Roosevelt assessed the state of the nation in a sober tone: "We have here a nation built with every racial strain in the world, every creed, and there is no use denying that at the present time we are allowing our prejudices to run riot very often and to lead us to do things and say things and to follow people who do and say things which cause disunity rather than unity, and every time we do that, we lay the foundation for more war, not for peace," she said in a Foreign Language Information Service press release issued on May 15, 1942, with just over two years remaining before D-Day.

It would be many years before passions died down enough for true patriotic assimilation to take hold among Americans as well as among former immigrants. The war had hardly ended before a new Red Scare set Wisconsin Senator Joseph McCarthy loose with his accusations of foreign sympathies' corrupting America. Yet eventually Americans once again came to recognize where they had gone wrong. Most of the creators of the Japanese internment camps later expressed their deep regrets over what they had done. A commission convened in 1983 to evaluate the Japanese internments concluded that they were by no means militarily necessary. President Ronald Reagan in 1988 apologized and announced that the government would compensate the internees. Full atonement, however, has been painfully slow: Italian Americans did not receive apologies until 2000, when Congress authorized the Department of Justice to document their experience. German Americans are still waiting, although Wisconsin Senator Russ Feingold introduced a bill in 2001 to establish a similar review.

~•~

McCarthy's disgrace opened the way for America to restore some of the nation's core values and undo many of the wrongs committed toward nonwhite Americans and immigrants. It certainly helped, of course, that immigration had slowed dramatically, with the foreign-born population falling from a peak of 14.8 percent of the population in 1910 to 5.4 percent by 1960. In the immediate postwar years, Americans were

grateful for the contributions of Japanese and black American troops as well as of the many other immigrants who had fought alongside white Americans, and for the brilliance of European exiles whose ingenuity had helped give us the power of the atomic bomb. At the same time, Hitler had demonstrated the horrors that resulted from taking ethnic intolerance to extremes, and many Americans were troubled by the fate of the many Jews who were doomed by our failure to provide refuge. To avoid making the same coldhearted mistake with refugees fleeing from communist bloc nations, Congress enacted several laws during the 1950s making it clear that refugees now were welcome and no longer subject to the onerous quota system. In 1952, the United States revoked provisions barring Asians from naturalizing. Across the country, the seeds of the civil rights movement had been sown, and the national mood toward immigration was shifting.

While still a senator, John F. Kennedy became active in promoting the cause of reopening the gates. "Immigration policy should be generous; it should be fair; it should be flexible," he wrote in *A Nation of Immigrants*. "With such a policy we can turn to the world, and to our own past, with clean hands and a clear conscience. . . . Some of yesterday's immigrants . . . have supplied a continuous flow of creative abilities and ideas that have enriched our nation. The immigrants we welcome today and tomorrow will carry on this tradition and help us to retain, reinvigorate, and strengthen the American Spirit." Kennedy's thoughts on immigration were couched in the name of American founding principles and the rights of man. When President Lyndon B. Johnson took office, he brought with him a history of having worked to help Jewish refugees enter the United States in the 1930s and 1940s. For their part, Republicans wanted reform to boost economic growth, and their 1960 campaign platform had argued for *at minimum* doubling the number of immigrants admitted.

This bipartisan joining of purposes resulted in the 1965 Hart-Celler Act, which abolished race-based bars to immigration and national origins immigration quotas and replaced them with hemispheric limits: 170,000 from the Western Hemisphere and 120,000 from the Eastern

Hemisphere, for a total slightly lower than the actual number of immigrants coming at the time. Within these hemispheric quotas, it allocated 20 percent on an employment basis, 6 percent to refugees from communist countries and the Middle East, and 74 percent to adult family members—including spouses, children, and siblings—of citizens and permanent residents. Spouses, unmarried minor children, and parents of immigrants who naturalized were exempt from these categories.

The new law achieved Kennedy's stated goal of undoing past prejudices in admissions. Unfortunately, just like the 1920s closing of the doors, it went too far in the opposite direction. The family preferences part of the law had massive unintended consequences that an application of simple arithmetic could have predicted. Each immigrant who naturalized could bring over an entire family, so the annual legal numbers in reality were only a fraction of the number of immigrants who could come legally. Once naturalized, an unmarried adult whose parents had brought him to the United States could then marry someone from the homeland who, once naturalized, could then bring her entire family with her. Over the course of generations, this translated into exponential growth, creating a great new wave of immigration that would change the face of America as dramatically as had the wave a century earlier.

Over the course of the previous half century, the Great Wave immigrants had worked hard to strip away evidence of their heritage, partly out of fear and partly out of the desire to succeed. Through the message that being American had come to mean pursuing a middle-class consumer lifestyle, the rise of the mass market society had intensified this drive toward the obliteration of difference. But once again, America had gone too far and was about to swing too far in the opposite direction.

As post-1950s America rebelled against the conformity that had been imposed since the First World War, ethnicity came back into play. Swedish sociologist Marcus Hansen has argued that what the second generation seeks to forget, the third generation seeks to remember; and so the grandchildren of the Great Wave immigrants began to explore what their parents had ignored or were never given to remember. Not all Americans wanted to remember, whether because they were embarrassed

by the hardships their peasant ancestors had endured in Europe and as new arrivals at the bottom of the heap in America, or because their heritage had been obliterated so well that they could not join in this ethnic revival.

The bigger problem was that because Americans had become so good at saying who they were not, they no longer could express who they were. What were immigrants to assimilate *to* if Americans themselves could not say what it is to be American? There was still, of course, the American Creed, but immigrants had found during the two world wars that Americans valued race and ethnicity more than they did the creed. And so, amid an ethnic resurgence that made it more important than ever that Americans embrace a shared unifying belief, nobody paid attention to those core values.

The problem was that both sides of the culture wars had failed to articulate a common vision. As Arthur Mann has characterized the failure of the ethnic revival of the 1960s and 1970s, "To the degree that it helped to make the differences safe, it strengthened a major democratic tenet. Yet the revival neglected to show how the persistence of ethnic differences can lead to a sense of national wholeness. It fell down in that task because it failed to transcend the crisis from which it derived." This was the price of America's loss of faith in the American Creed; too few Americans believed that this country was strong enough to overcome the differences that our pride in freedom and individualism was now leading people of all colors to celebrate. Forced Americanization had replaced the creed, which transcended ethnicity, with a racial and ethnic definition of being American. This fundamental shift, which had led to the curtailment of immigration and the cutting of global ties in the 1920s and 1930s and the internment of "enemy aliens" in World War II, erupted in full force in the culture wars of the 1960s through the 1990s, and continues today.

As the Black Power and Chicano Power movements challenged monolithic America, white former ethnics had no corresponding way to express pride of their own. America's passive sense of self was proving to be a major obstacle even before the new wave of immigration reached

critical mass. The stripping away of foreign ties had not made America stronger at all but instead had left it unable to recognize what brought its people together. A simple "American" identity was unavailable, as Nathan Glazer and Patrick Moynihan argued in their classic work *Beyond the Melting Pot*. Ethnicity, according to Glazer and Moynihan, was and would continue to be the defining factor in American life.

By 1978, Europeans were no longer the largest group of applicants for U.S. citizenship. According to the 2000 census figures (which allowed people to mark multiple races), white Americans constituted 77 percent of the population, Hispanics 13 percent, African Americans 12.3 percent, Asians 3.6 percent, and American Indians, Eskimos, Aleuts, and Pacific Islanders 1 percent. By the end of the twentieth century, whites were well on their way to becoming a minority in California as Hispanic and Asian immigrants moved in and some whites left.

Not only were the kinds of people who came to America changing, but their prominence was rising rapidly. One in eight people living in the United States today is foreign born, the highest proportion in a century and, at 34 million, the highest absolute number ever. Some 6.6 percent of the U.S. population are not yet citizens. Immigrants, who make up the majority of the population of six U.S. cities with populations of over 100,000, are changing the faces we see on city streets, in office halls and on factory floors, in classrooms and in hospitals. Faces from Bangladesh, El Salvador, Nigeria, and Laos appear not only in the gateways of New York, Florida, and the Southwest, but in the heartland. Georgia, North Carolina, Arkansas, and Nebraska are now among the states with the fastest-growing foreign-born communities.

These demographic changes have set off alarm bells among some white Americans who warn that this country is at risk of becoming Balkanized. "America with only the Creed as a basis for unity could soon evolve into a loose confederation of ethnic, racial, cultural, and political groups, with little or nothing in common apart from their location in the territory of what had been the United States of America," Samuel Huntington has warned, strategically slipping in an apocalyptic suggestion

that America could soon be no more. Patrick Buchanan similarly downplays the strength and importance of core American values as a source for common identities and aspirations: "A common belief in democracy is too weak a reed to support the solidarity of the West. It is an intellectual concept that does not engage the heart." Yet the solution they offer—a re-racialized view of America, frozen in 1776, that is all but inaccessible to anyone but those with white Anglo-Saxon Christian roots—would be nothing but a self-fulfilling prophecy. It is hard to see it as anything but defeatism, if not a deliberate attack on the American Creed that is intended to close our doors to the rest of the world.

What America needs is not a message that excludes people who have come to this country to stay but a reaffirmation of the common dreams that existed before the Great War and the immigration reforms of the 1920s that took them away, and a commitment to making sure that immigrants and Americans alike have the power to make them come true. The power of the American Creed lies not in a mere set of words on paper, but in the way Americans turn its principles into a vibrant democracy. More than ever, we must find strength in the ways that we have succeeded better than any nation in the world in bringing together disparate cultures into one people whose combined skills, talents, and determination have made them stronger. The answer is not to retreat from the world but to embrace it.

~5~

American Jobs

Perhaps it was possible to believe a century ago that America could shut out the rest of the world. Today the rest of the world is *here*. Borders have blurred as the global economy has become increasingly interdependent. America provides a market for the world's products, invests in companies around the world, and trains the world's best and brightest, who in turn transfer the knowledge they gain here to universities and businesses around the globe. At the same time, as economies in other nations develop, they create new markets for American goods and know-how. Immigrants' fluency in the cultures of other nations have made them valuable employees to the many U.S. companies who want to expand into other countries whose economies are growing faster than our own. The flow of people across borders is the nexus of ideas, commerce, innovation, and political change.

Our economic future is linked to that of other countries in trade as well as migration, to ensure both that we have the skills to produce goods and services and that we have markets where we can sell them. Today the most successful American companies are those that identify and pursue global markets. In 2004, for example, more than three-quarters of Intel's sales were outside the United States—up from 58 percent in 1996. The trend is similar for all of the biggest U.S. multinationals. Already roughly 60 percent of the revenues of the U.S. information technology

industry comes from other countries, and experts expect that number to grow.

Being so far ahead of most of the world has given America the kind of problem most countries would like to have; that is, we are what business analysts call a "mature market"—one that has reached a state of equilibrium and is no longer growing at the astronomical rates that many start-ups (or emerging economies) exhibit. Like a company that has led the market for a long time with a reliable product, America has grown so much in so many ways that it's hard to keep growing unless we adopt new strategies. The silver lining for countries that are far behind us is that the process of catching up means they have the potential to grow much faster than we can. The personal computer market in India is expected to grow by 37 percent annually until 2010, which will amount to 80 million computers. In China, 178 million computers will be purchased during the same period.

To grow, we need the rest of the world as much as the world needs us. Studies have shown that companies that have a global outlook and operations pay their workers higher wages; they also carry out the majority of investment in facilities, equipment, and research and development in the United States. These factors benefit American workers as well as businesses. "As foreign economies become more stable, productive and prosperous, they purchase more U.S. products and services—boosting sales and profitability for U.S. companies. America's economic strength lies in win-win results like these," according to a recent report of the Computer Systems Policy Project, a collaboration of the CEOs of the country's largest information technology companies. "International business is not an either-or proposition or a zero-sum game. U.S. companies need facilities here *and* abroad, workers here *and* in distant places to survive, innovate, and grow in a fiercely competitive market place," the report concluded.

Some U.S. companies find themselves becoming global exporters almost by accident. That was the case of Trek Bicycle Corp., which made its first bike in 1976 in a tiny workshop in a rented barn outside Waterloo, Wisconsin. In 1985, a handful of letters from companies wanting to

import Trek bikes to Canada landed on the desk of Trek's telemarketing director, Joyce Keehn, who had grown up on a farm—not exactly a conventional background for an international businesswoman. When she took the letters to the company's sales director and proposed trying to export to Canada, he gave her a green light and free rein. Within a year, orders started pouring in from Switzerland, and the numbers quickly made it clear just how big an opportunity there was in Europe; at the time, Europeans bought 15 million bicycles a year, compared with 10 million for Americans and Canadians combined. Trek bicycles today are sold in more than sixty-five countries, including seven wholly owned subsidiaries in Europe and Japan. Bikes are built here and exported to China—the reverse of the process Americans are more likely to imagine.

Paul Grieco, Gary Hufbauer, and Scott Bradford, economists affiliated with the Washington, D.C.–based Institute for International Economics, argue that global integration generates an extra $1 trillion to America *each year*, or $10,000 for each household. "Unfortunately for the cause of continued [trade] liberalization, Americans do not receive this money as a check marked 'payoff from globalization'," the study's authors warn. "Instead, the payoff is hidden within familiar channels: fatter paychecks, lower prices and better product choices (compare the telephones available now with the standard black model of 1980)." As these benefits slide by under the radar, headlines focus on the fate of those who are hurt by globalization—the approximately 225,000 workers who lose their jobs each year for trade-related reasons and must look for new work, often at lower wages. According to the study, the total economic impact of these lost jobs—about $54 billion in lost wages, according to U.S. government data—is a small fraction of what America as a whole gains. Yet workers' individual stories are easier to relate to and tap into all Americans' fears of economic hardship—and thus these stories will be the driving factor behind whether we keep the doors open to trade or not. Hufbauer, Grieco, and Bradford argue that if America were to return to Smoot-Hawley-style protectionism, our economy would shrink by 2.4 percent; the damage would be even worse when other countries retaliated with trade barriers against U.S. goods, which

would slice another 2.1 percent from our GDP and cause the global economy to contract even more sharply, by 7.35 percent. Consumers would suffer as well from a combination of higher prices and a smaller variety of goods available; this additional economic impact would bring the total cost within the United States to 7.3 percent of GDP—all told, $800 billion, or $7,100 for each household in America.

The problems we face as the twenty-first century opens are all too similar to those Americans faced at the dawn of the twentieth century. But this time, the stakes are much, much higher.

The globalization trend not only has resumed after its pause following World War I, but it has accelerated in many ways. Air travel, cheap telecommunications, and the Internet have made the world seem much smaller. These technologies allow today's immigrants to move easily between their new and old home countries and keep in real-time contact. To many Americans, the phone lines and air routes that connect immigrants to their homelands are a source of concern about whether today's newcomers will see any need to adopt American customs and culture. Yet these same technologies mean that immigrants come to America far better prepared today than those who came a century ago. CNN and Hollywood have already exposed the world to American culture and the English language. U.S. Census Bureau director Kenneth Prewitt noted that the immigrants counted in 2000 spoke English sooner and became educated more quickly than earlier generations. Immigrants are working hard to "Americanize" their manners. Indian computer programmers, for example, sit and watch reruns of the sitcom *Friends* to prepare for coming to the United States. Indeed, the flip side of the fear that immigrants will not Americanize may be the worry that they will master our ways too quickly and outdo us—not only when competing in our own economy but by taking the skills they learn here back to their home countries to give America a run for its money.

Today, nearly every sector of the U.S. economy has been touched by the flow of goods, people, and capital across borders. And, just as it was a century ago, migration today is a central pillar of the new global econ-

omy, both for providing workers and for circulating ideas and preferences and creating and building demand for products. The United Nations estimates that in 2000, more than 175 million people—some 3 percent of the world's population—were living outside the country where they were born. Employers around the world, especially in the wealthier nations whose populations are aging, rely heavily on these migrant workers, both skilled and unskilled. In the United States, the proportion of foreign-born people in the civilian labor force grew from 9.4 percent in 1990 to 14.1 percent in 2002.

In Henry Ford's day, the task at hand was to mold cookie-cutter workers into efficient assembly-line men and eventually into mass markets of consumers who wanted the same products—lots of them. Today, Ford's heavy-handed approach to "Americanizing" workers seems quaint, and we have moved far beyond the mass-market vision that his efforts helped to create. Today's markets are so massive that companies now think in terms of market segments, many of which are big enough to merit attention on their own. In a U.S. economy that has moved on from manufacturing and now depends on skills and innovation, cookie-cutter workers no longer fit the bill. As the rest of the global economy follows this shift toward knowledge and services, the workers who are most in demand are those who can carry out specialized scientific, financial, entrepreneurial, and innovative tasks. In the coming years, the world will be divided into those nations and enterprises that can negotiate other cultures and assess what they want and how to sell to them and those who cannot or will not do so.

Today's economy is different from that of a century ago in other ways as well, for better and for worse. Although the living standards and life expectancies of the poorest Americans have improved considerably, the concentration of wealth that accumulated over the past hundred years has created disparities far wider than in the past. The spoils tend to go to those who are fluent in other languages and cultures, creating a new divide between the cosmopolitan professionals, who cross time zones effortlessly and whose fortunes span international borders, and the majority of the

population, which sees the dissipation of borders mainly as a threat to their livelihoods and ways of life.

The social safety network introduced during the New Deal now cushions the most vulnerable members of the population in a way that was not possible during the 1880–1920 Great Wave of immigration. In theory, it should provide a fallback for the Americans whose jobs are the most likely to be affected by competition from low-skilled, low-wage migrants. In reality, no safety net is enough for those who feel that they have lost their jobs or must accept lower wages. At the same time, resentment has risen over immigrants' receiving benefits from state and federal aid programs. "As for the clipped-haired, mean-faced Demoncats who tell me I'm hateful and intolerant because I oppose the tidal wave of Turd World immigration, I say, Go find another country," wrote AM radio talk show host Michael Savage in *The Savage Nation: Saving America from the Liberal Assault on Our Borders, Language, and Culture*. "Who are you to judge me? You may think unlawful immigrants sucking the nipple of taxpayer subsidized healthcare is a good thing, but you're wrong, and I'll prove it."

Today, America is at a new tipping point for our immigration policy and our economy. Socially, America today can look back on a success story, on the ways that the supposedly unassimilable immigrants of the beginning of the century worked hard to make sure that their children grew up as Americans who would take advantage of the opportunities this country had to offer, both as workers and as consumers. We more or less weathered the culture wars of the late twentieth century and emerged as a nation that has made great strides in learning to get along but one that nevertheless still has work to do. Yet, the more things change, the more they stay the same. The tensions over immigration that have been rising over the past quarter century dovetail with growing anxiety over globalization as some skilled jobs now are following the manufacturing jobs that have moved to other countries. Resentment over immigrants' presence in this country is becoming harder and harder to ignore, and it often takes the form of economic complaints. Even as many Americans are convinced that globalization is a threat, they also believe that immigrants are taking away American jobs and costing taxpayer money.

Fears associated with globalization and with immigration have reinforced each other through the powerful (if not always accurate) image of the poorly paid foreign worker; whether he stays in his own country or comes here, he supposedly will steal an American job. This character is much more useful to the populist politician than are the hundreds of millions of foreign workers who are entering the global economy for the first time as consumers. The more the economies of other countries develop, the easier it will be for their citizens to find jobs at home without needing to disrupt their lives and leave their families in order to work at the bottom of the heap in a foreign land. Americans who fear immigration ought to want other countries' economies to grow and create jobs for their citizens. Instead, rising competition from India, China, and other emerging markets has intensified the cry to limit immigration— just as, a century ago, the call to close the doors to immigration came hand in hand with the closing of the doors to trade and worsened the problems that they were intended to solve.

一·一

There is an emotional connection between immigration and fears about jobs, welfare, and taxes—three issues that make politicians sit up and listen. Whatever the facts of the economy are, no elected official can afford to ignore these hot buttons. Unfortunately, they face two diametrically opposed arguments. On one side is the view represented by the mantra of the *Wall Street Journal*'s editorial page: "There Shall Be Open Borders" for workers as well as for goods. This view is widely held in the business world.

The other side of the argument is illustrated by the e-mail that Paul Morris, a San Pablo, California, city councilman recently mass-mailed, a tasteless "Illegal Immigrants Poem" parodying an illegal immigrant: "I cross ocean, poor and broke/take bus, see employment folk/Nice man treat me good in there/say I need to see welfare." The poem—which he claimed he'd meant to send to one person but inadvertently distributed widely— prompted both nods of approval and expressions of disgust at his attitude toward the hardworking people who keep the economy humming.

In Alabama in October 2004, only one in ten respondents to an Auburn University survey believed that immigrants made positive contributions to their community, but 42 percent blamed immigrants for crime, litter, and other social blight. More than half believed that immigrants were taking jobs away from Americans, with 34 percent of respondents strongly agreeing with that statement and 23 percent somewhat agreeing. Like many areas of the United States, Alabama has seen dramatic growth in its Hispanic population. Similarly, a 2004 Minnesota Community Project study found deep antipathy toward new immigrants, although in historical terms immigration is quite low. The state's 5 percent foreign-born population today is a sliver of the 29 percent foreign-born in Minnesota a century ago. "Concerns about immigration are intense," the report stated. "In the focus groups, participants did not hesitate to raise the issue without prompting and decry the impact on community and public schools. This hostility was largely expressed as both a perception that immigrants do not assimilate and that they take advantage of government largesse." In reality, neither position—not the one that argues that completely open borders are an unconditional good, and not the one that paints immigrants as bad for America—accurately represents the economic realities of immigration.

The 13.65 million immigrants who came to the United States during the 1990s helped create jobs and economic growth. Studies documenting the positive effects their presence has had on the U.S. economy abound. A Northeastern University study published in 2005 credits immigration—both legal and illegal—with having helped increase the total number of jobs in the country by 11.5 percent in the 1990s, when it would have grown by only 5 percent without immigration. The President's Council of Economic Advisers estimated in 2002 that immigration adds a net $14 billion in revenues to the federal budget each year.

To be sure, there are those who argue the opposite. One of the best known is a 1993 study by Donald Huddle, an economist at my alma mater, Rice University, in Houston, Texas. Sponsored by the Carrying Capacity Network, a group promoting major reductions in immigration,

Huddle calculated that immigration posed a total net cost of $42.5 billion across all levels of government. Urban Institute researchers Michael Fix and Jeffrey Passel, however, pointed out major errors in his methodology, including underestimations of immigrant income and tax revenue and generalization errors. When they recalculated tax revenue, correcting for errors, they came up with a surplus of at least $25 billion.

In 2004, the Center for Immigration Studies, another group that advocates sharp restrictions on immigration, issued a study suggesting that immigration may have contributed to job losses for U.S.-born workers. "It would be an oversimplification to assume that each job taken by an immigrant is a job lost by a native. What is clear is that the current economic downturn has been accompanied by record levels of immigration," wrote Stephen A. Camarota, the study's author. "Given the labor market difficulty of many natives, the dramatic increase in the number of immigrants holding jobs certainly calls into question the wisdom of proposals by both presidential candidates [President George W. Bush and Senator John Kerry] to increase immigration levels further."

In testimony before the U.S. House of Representatives in May 2005, however, Harry Holzer, a Georgetown Public Policy Institute expert on low-wage labor, took issue with Camarota's work. "Over the long term, immigration has modest negative effects on less-educated workers in the U.S. but other positive effects on the economy—and the latter will grow much stronger after Baby Boomers retire. American workers are thus best served by policies designed to stimulate job growth in the short term, and their own skills and incomes over the long term, rather than by policies to drastically curb immigration."

Many people think about immigration and jobs as a zero-sum game: if someone comes here, someone else must lose out for the newcomer to be accommodated. That simply is not true. Newcomers affect the economy in several ways. In some cases—like the engineers, scientists, and entrepreneurs mentioned earlier—they create products and industries that simply did not exist before, and thus add jobs and tax revenue. In other cases, an existing industry may be able to grow only when it has enough

people to do the work it needs to produce its goods. Again, by filling those slots, a company generates revenue and profits that allow it to expand. Immigrants also are consumers—they need housing, food, clothes, transportation, health care, and other goods and services, and thus provide important markets. When no existing companies provide these goods and services, immigrants create businesses to meet their needs—again, creating enterprises, jobs, and tax revenue that otherwise would not have existed. At the same time, economic analysis must take into account the effect that immigrants have on the wages of the American workers with whom they may be competing—but also on the prices of goods, some of which might have been more expensive had labor cost more or had not enough workers been available for companies to save money by producing enough to generate economies of scale.

Opponents of immigration often argue that immigrant workers, who not only are willing to work for less but also increase the labor supply, compete with and drive down pay for low-wage U.S. workers. Every time the population increases by 10 percent, Harvard economist George J. Borjas calculates, wages fall by 3 percent. By his calculation, immigration transfers $160 billion from the pockets of workers to employers each year. (Borjas also calculates that in 1998 immigrants increased the income of the U.S.-born population by about $8 billion, or $30 per American, an amount he deems too small to matter.) "The debate is not over whether the country as a whole is better off—the net gain seems to be much too small to justify such a grand social experiment. The debate is really over the fact that some people gain substantially, while others lose," Borjas argued in his 1999 book, *Heaven's Gate: Immigration Policy and the American Economy.*

More recent work argues that the gains are larger than Borjas contends and that the impact on lower-income workers is smaller. Economists Gianmarco I.P. Ottaviano of the University of Bologna and Giovanni Peri of the University of California found in a 2005 study that immigration from 1990 to 2000 increased average U.S. wages for those with a high school degree or better by between 2 percent and 2.5 percent, while

it lowered the wages of high school dropouts by 2.4 percent. They made two important assumptions that bring their estimates closer to reflecting reality than do Borjas's calculations. For one thing, they assume that when more workers are available, businesses can invest appropriately, creating more business that keeps wages steady and creating related jobs—like sales and marketing to support newly developed products.

The other important assumption is based in part on evidence that foreign and U.S.-born workers are not perfect substitutes for each other: that is, that they tend to do different kinds of jobs. As labor economist David Card concluded, "Although immigration has a strong effect on relative supplies of different skill groups, local labor market outcomes of low skilled natives are not much affected by these relative supply shocks." Among low-skilled workers, Ottaviano and Peri note, 54 percent of tailors and 44 percent of plaster-stucco mason workers were foreign born in 2000. Among crane operators and sewer-pipe cleaners, by contrast, not even 1 percent were foreign born. High-skilled workers, similarly, tend to choose different jobs as well: some 45 percent of medical scientists and 33 percent of computer engineers were not born in this country, while not even 4 percent of lawyers were foreign born in 2000. This complementarity—the difference in the jobs that immigrants and U.S.-born workers choose— benefits the United States through Adam Smith's age-old principle that the division of labor—that is, specialization—allows economies to produce more than they would have otherwise. The urban areas that Ottaviano and Peri examine offer a microcosm of the argument they make for the whole nation: the cities whose economies perform the best are those with high immigrant populations. This is exactly the opposite of Borjas's argument that immigrants cause "white flight," driving native-born Americans away when immigrants move in to cities.

The evidence is far from conclusive that immigrants are a drain on tax dollars, although the question of welfare is complicated. According to the U.S. Census Bureau, in 1999, 2.5 million households, or 21.2 percent, of foreign-born households received food stamps, Medicaid, housing, or other means-tested noncash assistance, compared with 13.5 million, or

14.6 percent, of native-born households. The bulk of that assistance was from Medicaid, partly because more than one in three of the foreign-born population has no health insurance (compared with one in six native-born Americans), and partly because foreign-born families are more likely to have more children needing health care—children who, incidentally, are likely to be U.S. born and U.S. citizens. At the same time, the typical immigrant household on welfare received about 4 percent less than a comparable native-born household.

However, looking only at government revenues paid by immigrants and at the cost of government services provided to immigrants is misleading, because it estimates only the costs and revenues that result directly from immigrants. This is only part of the picture. It does not factor in the economic benefits to consumers of the lower costs of the goods and services they buy. Nor, more importantly, does it calculate what revenues might not be there without all of the business that immigrants' labor made possible.

What makes this question even trickier is that immigrants are more likely to use more benefits than they pay for in their early years here, but to pay more into the system than they use over the course of their lifetimes. In a 1997 study, the National Research Council of the National Academy of Sciences estimated that immigrants pay an estimated $80,000 per person more in federal benefits than they take in over the course of their lifetime in America. However, immigrants without a high school education will likely use more services than their taxes finance. Right now, the taxes paid by new immigrant families do not cover the publicly funded services they use—partly because immigrant families are more likely to have more school-aged children. (Nor do these calculations take into account the subsidy to U.S. taxpayers provided by skilled immigrants who enter this country after their educations and child health care have been paid for.)

Over the long run, however, new legal immigrants will provide a net benefit of $407 billion to Social Security alone over the course of fifty years, according to calculations by the Office of the Chief Actuary of the Social Security Administration cited in a study by the National Foun-

dation for American Policy. Each year, according to data reported in the *New York Times*, Social Security contributions by illegal immigrant workers added up to approximately $7 billion, or 10 percent of the 2004 surplus; Medicare taxes brought in another $1.5 billion. Because these workers are unlikely to ever be able to draw on Social Security, that money is essentially a gift.

There are few issues on which economic reality and emotion become entangled as much as they do on immigration. Economics is a foreign language to many Americans, but emotion and patriotism are not. The result is a set of laws that at best ignore economic, demographic, and social realities, and at worst serve only the needs of special interest groups to the detriment of the population as a whole. Despite growing calls for change, politicians have hesitated to reform immigration policy, ensuring that problems will only keep getting worse and that when change does come it will be extreme and shortsighted. The real trouble with American immigration policy, then, is that we don't have one; instead, our immigration laws are a patchwork of contradictory statutes that have little to do with the economic interests of America's businesses or of America's workers. Those who benefit are the employers who have no scruples about exploiting workers who accept low wages and unsafe working conditions because they have no alternatives. This hurts American workers who cannot compete against pliant, inexpensive labor. It also hurts businesses that respect labor laws because they must compete against companies that have lower labor costs. It is far too difficult for many businesses to get the workers they need legally, so they all too often must resort to hiring workers with questionable or no documents and a precarious existence—a nightmare for an employer who needs a stable workforce.

⌣•⌣

Demographics and economics collided in the early 1980s as it became clear that the 1965 immigration reform had created a rush of newcomers far larger than intended, and from countries far afield of the European countries that previously had generated the bulk of migration to the

United States. Refugees were streaming into the United States from Vietnam, Laos, Cambodia, Haiti, Eastern Europe, and Central America—as many as one million over the course of the decade, the first time America had seen such a rush. These new faces arrived as a ballooning federal budget deficit pushed interest rates to record highs, making life harder on Main Street even as ostentatious displays of wealth on Wall Street exemplified the growing divide between the rich and the poor.

In this unstable environment, it was not surprising that illegal immigration became a focal point of national debate. In 1985, Congress passed the Immigration Reform and Control Act (IRCA), which sensibly created a way to bring people previously considered to be "illegal" out of the shadows. Not so sensibly, it failed to provide a mechanism for accommodating future business needs for workers as the U.S. economy grew. It also sensibly established the principle that immigration laws would be enforced and illegal immigration prosecuted. Not so sensible, however, was the understanding that the government, to meet the business community's need for a steady supply of labor, would more often than not turn a blind eye to the employment of illegal workers. Congress inserted significant loopholes to allow businesses to avoid prosecution. The sanctions it mandated merely prohibited employers from "*knowingly* hiring, recruiting, or referring for a fee aliens not authorized to work in the United States." For once, ignorance was a defense. As Roger Daniels has remarked, "Criminal statutes—and hiring an illegal alien is a crime—do not normally absolve perpetrators who claim that they did not know what they were doing." Similarly, as Daniels points out, Section 116 of Title I of IRCA prevented the INS from carrying out raids on any "outdoor agricultural operation" without a warrant—a provision that effectively shielded the farms that employed vast numbers of undocumented workers. The law was the bastard child of those who wanted to severely limit immigration and of the companies that wanted to ensure a steady supply of workers at low wages. Although 3 million workers gained legal status because of IRCA, the main result of the reform was to create a large and growing population of permanently marginalized immigrants even as it created a backlash against them.

By the early 1990s, it had already become abundantly clear that not only had IRCA failed to stop illegal immigration, but the weak-toothed law had created conditions that encouraged more of it. At the same time, the 1980s Latin American debt crisis and recession had added to the flow of migrants desperate to come to the United States. The U.S. economy was limping along and, like the citizens of any country having difficulties, Americans were receptive to suggestions that other people were to blame. Emphasizing immigrants' differences from mainstream America made it easier to rationalize attempts to deny them health care and schooling for their children.

On television's *This Week With David Brinkley* in 1991, the populist columnist and political adviser Patrick Buchanan asked, "If we had to take a million immigrants in, say Zulus, next year, or Englishmen, and put them up in Virginia, what group would be easier to assimilate and would cause less problems for the people of Virginia?" Buchanan, of course, would become one of the most vocal proponents of slamming the doors on immigration, a theme that would play a central role in his later U.S. presidential campaigns—two unsuccessful attempts to win the Republican Party nomination and a 2000 run on the Reform Party ticket. The conservative writer Peter Brimelow, a naturalized U.S. citizen who apparently was one of the Englishmen whom Buchanan had so fancied, chimed in with his 1995 book, *Alien Nation: Common Sense About America's Immigration Disaster*. This polemic, argued with all the fervor of a convert, drew on racial stereotypes to argue that the non-European immigrants who arrived after 1965 were tearing America apart. "It is simply common sense that Americans have a legitimate interest in their country's racial balance," he wrote. "It is common sense that they have a right to insist that their government stop shifting it. Indeed, it seems to me that they have a right to insist that it be shifted back." (In 2005, Brimelow was playing the same tune through the Web site vdare.com, which provided a home for the small but shrill contingent of others who saw immigration as the undoing of America.)

New kinds of fears arose after the 1993 World Trade Center bombing by Middle Eastern terrorists and the 1995 bombing of the Murrah Federal

Building in Oklahoma City by a white supremacist terrorist—which was immediately and erroneously attributed to Muslim supremacists. Mexico, the biggest source of immigration to the United States, loomed big as a threat in the middle of the decade, beginning with the christening of NAFTA, the rise of Mexico's Zapatista guerrilla movement, and "tequila crisis" economic collapse in 1994 amid rising interest rates and a global economic slowdown.

California's 1994 midterm elections crystallized all of these issues in the creation of Proposition 187, a ballot measure that capitalized on growing resentment of immigrants. The controversial measure aimed to deny state social services to illegal immigrants and their children—who often were American citizens. It also required state and local agencies to report suspected illegal immigrants to the INS, a policy that would have been a nightmare to implement and would have interfered with the reporting of crimes to local law enforcement agencies and cooperation with police officers. The shortsightedness of such a policy would become widely apparent several years later, after the 9/11 terrorist attacks, when communities across the United States protested and refused to comply with federal attempts to make state and local agencies into immigration police.

California Governor Pete Wilson, trailing his Democratic opponent by seventeen points, championed Proposition 187 as a central theme of his reelection campaign, which he turned around and won. And, despite the mean-spiritedness and patent unconstitutionality of Proposition 187, the measure was passed. Opponents of the law sued, arguing correctly that it infringed on the federal government's authority to regulate immigration and that the ban on schooling was illegal. After a long legal battle, the measure would be abandoned quietly in 1996. As for Wilson's party, which had made immigrant-bashing a central part of its platform, the Republicans won a landslide midterm victory in Congress that same November.

In 1996, Pat Buchanan's anti-immigrant platform helped him win the New Hampshire Republican primary for the U.S. presidential nomination. The week of his victory, I was in the Dominican Republic, where I was interviewed on a morning television program. The first question was

about Buchanan; Dominicans were horrified at the thought that he might become president and were greatly relieved when I predicted that his run soon would be cut short. This was a reminder of how closely the rest of the world watches when America validates views like Buchanan's. Certainly, the Dominicans were concerned about their own visas to America, where more than one-tenth of Dominicans already lived. But an even bigger fear was that someone with Buchanan's attitudes about foreigners had a chance at the most powerful position in the world.

Buchanan was hardly alone in holding such convictions and in trying to turn them to political advantage. Anti-immigration groups like the Federation for American Immigration Reform (FAIR), founded in 1979, took heart from the warm reception Buchanan's ideas received. FAIR's message—that immigration was to blame for crime, poverty, disease, urban sprawl, and increasing racial tensions in America—spread and spawned new groups. The California Coalition for Immigration Reform (CCIR), whose founder was fond of calling Mexicans "savages," was created in 1994 as a cosponsor of Proposition 187.

Across the country, individuals and groups took it upon themselves to make immigrants feel unwelcome. In Alabama in 1995, Madison County tax assessor Wayland Cooley prohibited Dominican and Korean immigrants from bringing interpreters to a hearing that would have granted them a homestead property tax exemption, and then denied them the credits because they did not speak English. The immigrants sued and won the more than $3,500 in back taxes they had overpaid; the court instructed Cooley not to deny any more exemptions to non-English-speakers who were entitled to them.

Opponents of immigration were particularly enamored of billboards. CCIR posted billboards on the Arizona border that read, "Welcome to California, the Illegal Immigration State. Don't Let This Happen to Your State." In 1996, billboards appeared in Queens—a New York City borough in which 55 percent of the population was foreign-born at the time—with anti-immigration messages. One proclaimed, "Over 80 percent of Americans support very little or no more immigration. Is anyone listening to us?" Another showed a white boy and the words, "Immigration is doubling U.S.

population in my lifetime. (Please don't do this to us Congress)." The community found the signs to be so offensive that immigrants of many different backgrounds organized, discovered that the signs did not have proper permits, and forced their removal. The group that put up the billboards would formally become Project USA, which describes its goals in part as, "We believe a democratic immigration policy will be one that places more importance on the wishes of the American people and less importance on the self-serving demands of immigration lawyers, corporate profiteers, and ethnic-identity special interests."

The immigrant-bashing of the previous few years culminated in Congress's passing an Orwellian trio of laws in the summer of 1996, the Illegal Immigration Control and Immigrant Responsibility Act, the Anti-Terrorist and Effective Death Penalty Act, and the Personal Responsibility and Work Opportunity Act. The laws excluded immigrants—even legal tax payers—from Social Security, Medicaid, and other benefits. They trampled such American legal pedestals as due process and judicial independence, made even the most minor of legal offenses retroactively punishable by deportation, and restricted legal immigrants' access to services that they had paid taxes to help fund. Under the new laws, parts of which would become a significant and controversial part of the post-9/11 crackdown on immigrants, immigrants no longer had the right to fair and impartial hearings or to be freed on bond pending trial. They became subject to detention and deportation for minor offenses committed years earlier, even if they had served full sentences or if their sentences had been suspended. Immigration judges lost the ability to exercise sentencing discretion, a change that has left them no alternative but to break up families and turn lives upside down with sentences far out of proportion to most infractions. Also under the new laws, judges were required to deport any legal immigrants who had been convicted of crimes with a sentence of one year or more.

Part of the momentum to pass the laws came from resentment based on many Americans' beliefs that immigrants were not becoming part of American society. Yet, ironically, these laws made it harder for many immigrants to integrate; families were broken apart and communities destabi-

lized. In response to the 1996 laws, the number of immigrants applying to naturalize rose dramatically, from just under 1 million in 1995 to 1.3 million in 1996 and 1.4 million in 1997. Many of these new Americans, however, decided to take the oath not out of pure affection for their adopted country but out of fear that they would fall victim to capricious laws.

·

Although vocal minorities know all too well how to get politicians' attention in America, the great thing about this country is that common sense eventually kicks in and we recognize when we have gone too far. That is what happened after the 1996 laws. The mean-spiritedness of Proposition 187 and the 1996 laws made it much harder to deny that a significant minority was exploiting the immigration issue unfairly. And so polls showed a sharp swing in public opinion—*away* from the restrictionists' goals. In a poll taken in July 1993, amid the anti-immigrant sentiment that would lead to Proposition 187's passage, some 65 percent of Americans thought immigration should be decreased, 27 percent thought the level should stay the same, and 6 percent thought it should increase. In September 2000, however, the proportion who thought immigration should stay the same had risen to 41 percent—surpassing the 38 percent who wanted to lower immigration—and the percentage of Americans who wanted to increase immigration had more than doubled, to 13 percent.

Pulled by conflicting sentiments about immigrants and immigration, the country seesawed the other way again. Seeing the 1996 laws as a threat to basic American values and well aware that past efforts to deny rights to noncitizens could quickly extend to citizens as well, moderate Americans and immigrant activists challenged those laws and successfully rolled back some of the stricter provisions. The outcry made it clear to many politicians that immigrants were an important and growing constituency—and that laws that hurt immigrants hurt the communities and cities around them. Even more important, immigrants were naturalizing in record numbers. They may have done so out of fear, or to ensure that they would be entitled, on retirement, to the Social Security

benefits they had paid for; but whatever the reason, they now had votes. In cities that were home to major immigrant populations, politicians shifted their tone dramatically. In New York City, Mayor Rudolph Giuliani became a champion of preserving the benefits that the 1996 laws had taken away. Across the country, politicians began taking Spanish lessons in the hope of winning over Latino constituents.

The economy helped to improve sentiment toward immigrants. In the late 1990s, when Internet commerce took off and cell phones became all the rage, technology industries were ravenous for programmers and engineers—and they needed far more than the American workforce could provide. On top of that, the so-called Y2K bug created a huge demand for programmers who could sift through millions of lines of code, chasing the hard deadline of 12:00 a.m., January 1, 2000. To meet the deadline, the software industry succeeded in convincing Congress to expand the H-1B visa program, created in 1996 to bring in skilled workers on three-year visas that could be renewed once. (The trio of other immigration laws passed that year had the unspoken aim of blocking low-income illegal workers; skilled workers—for the moment—remained mostly unscathed by the hysteria.) Demand for the visas had quickly outpaced supply, so the U.S. Congress agreed to raise the annual quota from 65,000 to 195,000 temporarily.

Yet even as the immediate battle for public sentiment seemed to be won, the about-face would give ammunition to opponents of immigration in the larger war over whom to let in to this country. The fact remained that the foreign-born population was growing faster than many American communities were comfortable with and faster than our immigration laws and bureaucracy could handle. A congressional commission led by Representative Barbara Jordan, which released its findings in 1994 and 1995, addressed these issues. The commission recommended a modest decrease in legal immigration and better enforcement coupled with better treatment of those who are here. It also suggested improvements in the ways we prepare immigrants for American citizenship, including a much-needed overhaul of the naturalization test (which a decade later is finally in progress). But immigration was too controversial a topic for any

politicians to seriously take up most of the commission's sensible recommendations. The Jordan Commission report languished, all but forgotten, and unresolved immigration issues festered. We could have made a stitch in time to save nine. Instead, the demographics now are even harder to grapple with, and the economic environment makes public opinion even more hostile to immigrants.

The technology bust of 2000, which came after Congress had dramatically increased the number of foreign computer programmers allowed to work in this country, expanded resentment of foreign workers for purportedly taking American jobs into the middle class, whereas previously such anger had been directed only at the lower-income service and agricultural sectors—the same jobs that have long been held to be the ones that Americans didn't want to do. The recession was all the more destabilizing because it followed a technology boom that had raised expectations to unrealistic levels. During the tech boom, salaries rose astronomically in the tight job market, only to come crashing down as jobs disappeared after Y2K arrived without a hitch and then rising interest rates popped the speculative technology stock bubble. High-tech start-ups that had been swimming in venture capital suddenly had to tighten their belts, and others had to close shop. In the aftermath, it was easy to blame the mostly South Asian programmers who had come to the United States on high-skill H-1B visas during the boom. No one wanted to think about how much of the boom would not have been possible at all without the workers who had labored to get systems up and running and new products to market.

When the good times ended, foreign-born and U.S.-born workers alike lost jobs, and so when the 195,000 annual H-1B visa cap came up for renewal in 2000, it was not hard for the anti-H-1B lobby to block Congress from renewing the quota increase that had been approved in 1998. In 2003, then, the annual cap fell back to 65,000, far less than what the high-tech sector had sought. On October 1, 2004, the U.S. government began processing applications for skilled worker visas for the year 2005. Before the end of the day, the entire year's quota was full: 65,000 high-skilled H-1B worker visas, minus 6,800 reserved for Chile and Singapore. In a small concession to industry, the Bush administration added 20,000

H-1B visas in November 2004 for foreigners with advanced degrees from U.S. institutions. Even after the visas were approved, continued political squabbling over which workers would be eligible significantly delayed regulations allowing companies to apply for them.

Crystallizing fears about immigration and globalization at once, the H-1B system represents the worst of both worlds: it makes it hard for legitimate businesses to get the workers it needs even as it makes it easy for unscrupulous employers to take unfair advantage of vulnerable foreign workers.

Sona Shah, who was born in India, came to the United States with her parents at age 3 and is now a U.S. citizen with degrees in physics and mechanical engineering. She went to work as a programmer at the New York City branch of Wilco Systems, which she and a British coworker, Kai Barrett, later sued over "Project Delhi Belly" (named after the intestinal distress of British officers in colonial India), which involved aggressive recruitment and alleged exploitation of Indian workers and marginalization and firing of U.S. workers.

"Wilco management thought calling their Indian recruitment effort the equivalent of 'Project Diarrhea' was appropriate," she later testified before a congressional committee on H-1B workers. "The new, mostly Indian, recruits learned they were severely underpaid. They also objected to garnishing their wages to pay for overcrowded housing. Kai and I noticed that he was paid half my wage despite having a higher degree and more experience. The foreign workforce was also subjected to captive audience, loyalty meetings where Wilco managing directors lectured these visa holders on being loyal to the company because it enabled them to be in the U.S."

"This is not an issue of Indians vs. Americans or foreigners vs. Americans," Shah cautioned. "I've witnessed attempts to pit the two groups of employees against each other: it's a divide and conquer tactic. This is not about being anti-Indian or anti-immigration. This is about reforming corporate abuse of unregulated visa programs that are out of control."

Nadarajan Sivakumar, an Indian software programmer who originally came to the United States on an H-1B visa, disagrees emphatically with

the notion that most companies who hire H-1B workers exploit them. "I had an American programmer who was paid less than me when I was hired for a very similar position," he wrote in his impassioned and charming tribute to Indian high-skilled guest workers, *Debugging Indian Computer Programmers: Dude, Did I Steal Your Job?* "Competition from H-1B workers did help bring down the skyrocketing programmer salaries, but the big corporations never discriminated against immigrant workers by paying them lower salaries," he added. Sivakumar brings the "body shops" to task for abusing H-1B workers. He also disputes the idea that Indian and American programmers' skills are interchangeable. Using the slang that consulting companies teach Indian programmers to use in America, Sivakumar quipped, "Dude, the jobs would have gone abroad ten years ago if the H-1Bs hadn't been here." A survey and analysis by the research firm Foote Partners, published in *Computerworld*, used wage data from roughly 290,000 H-1B applications for positions in programming, systems analysis, networking, end-user support, and quality assurance. The survey showed that in 2001 and 2002 the salaries of the foreign-born workers and the U.S. workers fell by about the same amount. In 2003, however, the wages of U.S. workers rebounded by between 1.5 percent and more than 6 percent, while those of H-1B workers fell by between 2 percent and 5 percent. What happened in 2003 that might have accounted for the change? The fact that H-1B wages were falling even as businesses were rushing to outsource work to offshore companies supports the theory that foreign-born workers were not competing with American workers but instead with workers in other countries. Sivakumar likely was right that the H-1B program was keeping jobs in the United States.

The economic slowdown that followed the 9/11 attacks complicated American attitudes toward immigrant labor even further. From March 2000 to March 2004, overall U.S. unemployment rose by 2.3 million. At the same time, the number of working adult immigrants increased by the same number, according to the Center for Immigration Studies, a group that advocates sharp restrictions on immigration. Jobs rebounded between March 2003 and 2004 by about 900,000, but two-thirds of the new jobs went to immigrant workers, even though immigrant workers account

for only 15 percent of working-age adults. "The findings raise the very real possibility that immigration has adversely affected native employment," the Center argued.

As any economist knows, and as Mark Twain expressed better than anyone else, statistics are not always what they seem. For starters, the broad-brush numbers do not say as much as we need to know about what the new jobs were and the circumstances under which they were created. Did the immigrants' presence push Americans out of jobs, or did it enable businesses to do work that would not have been done without the labor supply to fill those jobs? Immigrants filled 86 percent of new jobs in precision production, craft, and repair occupations from 1996 through 2002. Even with the influx of immigrants, wages in those sectors still rose by an average of 3 percent annually during that time, suggesting that if immigrant labor had not been available, many of those jobs would have gone unfilled, dampening economic growth, and wages would have risen so sharply that consumers would have felt a shock.

〜・〜

U.S. labor unions historically have viewed immigrants as a threat to U.S. jobs and wages. Recently, however, they have added promoting immigrant worker rights to their priority issues. In 2000, the AFL-CIO issued a dramatic reversal of its earlier positions, now arguing that all workers, whether immigrant or native-born, documented or undocumented, deserved the full protection of workplace rights and freedoms. "Employers often knowingly hire workers who are undocumented, and then when workers seek to improve working conditions employers use the law to fire or intimidate workers," said AFL-CIO Executive Vice President Linda Chavez-Thompson in announcing the change, which effectively withdrew unions' support of IRCA. "This both subverts the intent of the law and lowers working and living standards for all workers—immigrant and non-immigrant—in many industries. The law should criminalize employer behavior, not punish workers."

The unions changed their position because they realized a simple fact: laws that confine many foreign-born workers to a legal purgatory are a large part of the reason why unscrupulous employers are able to pay so little. A worker who knows that he risks being deported at any time is less likely to demand higher wages or protest workplace abuses. Indeed, workplace abuses commonly show up in high-profile cases involving illegal aliens. "This gap between undocumented workers' rights and remedies creates a perverse incentive for unscrupulous employers to seek out these workers, undermining not just labor policy but immigration goals as well," wrote Lori Nessel, director of Seton Hall University Law School's Immigration and Human Rights Clinic. She cites an example in which the mostly immigrant workers in a New York City garment sweatshop filed five unfair labor practice charges with the National Labor Relations Board (NLRB) after their company tried to require its employees to work forty-nine hour weeks without overtime pay. When the NLRB found good cause to prosecute the company, the firm's attorney called the INS to alert it to the presence of undocumented workers. The INS then scheduled a search of the business. "Conveniently, on the prearranged date of the INS raid, pro-management undocumented workers were told not to report to work. When the undocumented union supporters showed up for work that day, INS officers intercepted, questioned, and arrested them," Nessel wrote.

This is not an isolated case; labor activists complain that companies commonly "turn themselves in" to immigration authorities in order to smother unrest and continue exploitative practices. Immigration authorities' operating instructions require them to determine whether they might be in the middle of a labor dispute and to contact the U.S. Department of Labor and the NLRB if they suspect that is the case, yet they have tried to expel undocumented workers anyway. Employers, meanwhile, typically get by with impunity. Although companies in theory are subject to fines of up to $11,000 per illegal hire, fines are rarely imposed if the company cooperates with immigration authorities.

In the late 1990s, the INS dramatically decreased its efforts to deport illegal immigrants from workplaces. INS officials were open about the fact

that the only workers at real risk of deportation were those whose employers reported them in retaliation for exercising their right to organize. As immigration authorities threw up their hands, the number of workplace arrests fell from 2,849 in 1999 to 735 in 2001, and to 445 in 2003. In 1999, according to the Government Accountability Office (GAO—the research arm of Congress), the INS issued 417 notices of intent to fine employers for immigration employment violations; by 2001, the number fell to 100. In 2004, INS's successor, Immigration and Customs Enforcement (ICE) issued just three such notices. The same GAO report said that ICE agents spent only 4 percent of their work time on work-site enforcement.

Few cases illustrate the overlap of workplace violations and businesses' impunity than the high-profile Wal-Mart case that attempted to right both wrongs. In 2003, federal agents brought the issue of workplace enforcement to the front pages when they raided sixty Wal-Mart stores, where they arrested more than 300 undocumented immigrants. Even as the government pursued Wal-Mart for employing illegal aliens, many of those workers sued Wal-Mart, alleging abusive employment practices, including long hours with no overtime pay and the locking of workers into stores overnight. The class-action suit by the workers had not yet been resolved at this writing, but the company eventually settled with the government, escaping criminal charges and paying a fine of $11 million. That's a small price to pay compared with the $3.16 billion in profits the company announced for the quarter that ended shortly before the settlement. Nevertheless, it was four times the size of the largest payment made to the government until then—reflecting the fact that the consequences of hiring illegal workers are minimal even in the rare cases when companies are caught. The greatest cost to Wal-Mart may have been in the torrent of negative publicity generated by the case. Perhaps the cruelest cut of all was being parodied on television's *The Simpsons*, when Homer takes a job as a "Sprawl-Mart" greeter and is locked inside the store overnight with no pay.

The outcome of the Wal-Mart case may change things, but generally even when illegal aliens do complain, there are almost no consequences

for companies that violate labor standards for undocumented employees. This point was driven home in 2002, when the U.S. Supreme Court ruled that illegal aliens are not entitled to back wages even if they convince a court that their employer violated labor laws. Unscrupulous employers thus have no financial incentive to respect labor or immigration laws.

These are the practices that make it harder for American workers—as well as for businesses that do respect the law—to compete. The way to ensure that all employers respect labor and immigration laws would be to impose real fines for failure to comply. That has not happened because of a relatively simple political calculus. It is far easier to get votes and campaign money by going after an impoverished, uneducated immigrant from another country than by raking business owners over the coals. Never mind that in the end, the way to protect American workers and law-abiding businesses is to go after the businesses that break the law.

~•~

Overall, immigrants today are integrating into America's economy and society relatively well. A 1999 study by the National Immigration Forum, a pro-immigration group, found that more than three-quarters of immigrants who had lived here for forty years or more had been naturalized. By 1990, six of ten immigrants owned homes—a clear commitment to life in this new land. Poll after poll shows that immigrants place a high value on learning English, including a 2004 Zogby International poll in which 97 percent of respondents strongly (86.4 percent) or somewhat (10.9 percent) agreed that "the ability to speak English is important to succeed in this country." After dipping during the culture wars of the 1960s through the 1980s, the number of naturalized immigrants has been rising again since the 1990s—to 11.3 million in 2002 from 6.5 million in 1990. The proportion of legal immigrants who naturalize has also been rising, reaching 49 percent in 2002; although this is far below the high of 80 percent in 1950, it is close to the 52 percent naturalization rate in 1920.

Yet not all immigrants are doing well in America's economy. Among the foreign born in 2002, the poverty rate was 16.6 percent, significantly

higher than the rate of 11.5 percent for native-born Americans. Naturalized citizens, however, were no more or less likely than native-born citizens to live under the poverty level. In 2003 and 2004, according to the Pew Hispanic Center, Hispanic workers were the only group for whom wages declined two years in a row, to an average of $400 a week. Wages for white and black workers hardly changed during that period. Pew attributes the 5 percent drop in Hispanic wages to an increase in the number of new immigrants competing for similar low-skill jobs. At the same time, the number of undocumented immigrants, now estimated at over 10 million, has risen so fast that more immigrants arrive illegally each year than they do legally. By some estimates, undocumented immigrants now make up as much as 45 percent of the U.S. Hispanic population.

These low-skilled, undocumented immigrants are those who cause the most economic concern, because they displace low-wage U.S. workers, because they are less likely to succeed economically, and because they are less likely to assimilate by broader measures—both because of their economic isolation and because legal avenues are closed to them. All too commonly, Americans see a cultural explanation for the troubles this group has in assimilating. Victor Davis Hanson, in his 2003 book *Mexifornia: A State of Becoming,* blames the failure of low-income Mexican immigrants to assimilate on the geographical proximity of Mexico. "The traditional homesick immigrant was now barricaded in his new homeland by thousands of miles of ocean, with little hope of returning to the Old Country every few months, and thus had to deal with Americans," he wrote. "For the Mexican immigrant, by contrast, the Rio Grande is no ocean, but a trickle easily crossed by a drive over a tiny bridge." As we know, however, even the European immigrants of a hundred years ago went home regularly, so we can discount that explanation.

Focusing on cultural differences allows us to avoid policy explanations for why some immigrants do not assimilate as well as others and to ignore awkward truths that don't fit the stereotypes that have served as fuel for the culture wars.

Whether immigrants assimilate or not has huge implications not just for the labor market but also for the markets for U.S.-made goods. After all, the U.S. economy depends on immigrants not just to fill jobs but also to create or expand markets for U.S. products. America's 39 million Hispanics alone have a combined purchasing power of nearly $600 billion. This number is growing rapidly, since U.S. Hispanic incomes are rising at 18 percent annually, or double the national rate. By 2007, Hispanic purchasing power is expected to reach $1.3 trillion annually. Between 1991 and 2000, the number of Hispanic households earning six figures or more grew by 126 percent, far outpacing the 77 percent in the general population. *Hispanic Business* magazine estimates that the wealthiest seventy-five U.S. Hispanics represent a combined net worth of $11.4 billion. Hispanics have caught the eye of brokers such as Merrill Lynch and Charles Schwab as well as traditional banks, all eager to secure these individuals as clients.

Two out of five Latinos in the United States are foreign born; an estimated 6 million to 8 million are undocumented. That is part of the reason that only 45 percent of U.S. Hispanics have checking accounts, compared with 80 percent of the general population. Only 50 percent have credit cards, compared with 70 percent of the general population. Seeing the growth potential, banks are fighting to move into this market demographic. Financial service institutions have begun offering low-fee and low-minimum-balance accounts that they hope will deliver a combination of volume and long-term-relationship business. These business strategies depend on immigrants' being here to stay and succeeding as new Americans, not merely marking time.

___6___

The Best and the Brightest

No other country can boast as impressive a record of national and international contributions by immigrants as the United States. Of the Nobel Prizes awarded to U.S.-based researchers between 1990 and 2001, nearly half were won by immigrants or children of immigrants. Without the scientists Edward Teller (Hungary), Enrico Fermi (Italy), and Albert Einstein (Germany), we would not have developed the atomic bomb during World War II. Immigrant entrepreneurs and scientists have contributed to America's global leadership in technology and pharmaceuticals: Among the most notable are Andy Grove (Hungary) co-founder of Intel; Jeong H. Kim (Korea), high-tech entrepreneur; and Bjarne Stroustrup (Denmark), inventor of the C++ computer programming language. James Gosling (Canada), inventor of the Java language, and Linus Torvalds (Finland), inventor of Linux operating system, developed these innovations while here on the H-1B high-skilled worker visas that have become so controversial. Vinod Dham, born in Pune, India, earned his master's degree in solid state sciences in Cincinnati in 1975 and went on to become known as "the father of the Pentium chip." Microsoft's Amitabh Srivastava and Anoop Gupta are both natives of India. Another Indian-born entrepreneur, Kumar Malavilli, cofounder of Brocade Communications and chairman of the American National Standards Institute, was named to the Silicon Valley Hall of Fame in 2003 as

one of the main architects of fiber channel technology, which allowed the creation of the data disaster recovery systems that proved to be vital to the survival of companies whose offices were destroyed and human capital decimated in the 2001 World Trade Center.

In 2000, Chinese or Indian immigrant CEOs headed 29 percent of high-tech Silicon Valley companies—including Hotmail, Intel, Sun Microsystems, and Yahoo—with total annual sales of $19.5 billion and 72,839 employees. Tobias Taurel, CEO of Eli Lilly & Co., was born in Morocco. And it almost goes without saying that perhaps the world's most famous financier and philanthropist, George Soros, began his life in America as a Hungarian-born immigrant.

Immigrants have held the highest posts in American government. There is, of course, Arnold Schwarzenegger, governor of California. Former Secretaries of State Madeleine Albright (Czech Republic) and Henry Kissinger (Germany) and Joint Chiefs of Staff Chairman John Shalikashvili (Poland) were all immigrants. Tens of thousands of foreign-born soldiers fought as members of the U.S. armed forces in Iraq, and many of the first U.S. casualties were not born in this country; many were not even U.S. citizens. Indeed, immigrants have long been combatants on our side, including the celebrated Japanese battalion in World War II. The flying ace Colonel James Jabara was the son of immigrants from the Lebanese village of Merjayoun. Working in his family's grocery store in Wichita, Kansas, Jabara became an Eagle Scout, began officers' flight school while he was still a teenager, flew more than 100 combat missions in Europe during World War II, and became a legend for his courageous fighting in Korea.

The music of Isaac Stern (Russia), Zubin Mehta (India), Itzhak Perlman (Israel), and Irving Berlin (Russia) has enriched our culture. Other enduring images of America come in the form of immigrants, such as the athlete and coach Knute Rockne (Norway) and the director of *It's a Wonderful Life* and other American movie classics, Frank Capra (Italy). The writers and thinkers Elisabeth Kübler-Ross (Switzerland), Kahlil Gibran (Lebanon), and Elie Wiesel (Romania) have changed the way people think in America and around the world.

Immigrants in the arts include fashion designers Liz Claiborne (Belgium) and Oscar de la Renta (Dominican Republic), who designed First Lady Laura Bush's 2004 inaugural gown. Architect I.M. Pei (China) came here from Beijing when he was 18 years old to study at Harvard and MIT; he designed the East Wing of the National Gallery in Washington, D.C., New York City's Javits Convention Center, and the National Center for Atmospheric Research in Boulder, Colorado—and in Paris, he designed a spectacular addition to the Louvre Museum. Cesar Pelli (Argentina) designed New York City's World Financial Center and Carnegie Hall Tower, London's Canary Wharf Tower, and Kuala Lumpur's Petronas Towers, which at 1,483 feet is the world's tallest building. The accomplishments of these immigrants have spread American ingenuity and innovation to the farthest corners of the globe.

This list represents only the most prominent of America's immigrants. Our economic dependence on the world's best and brightest is far broader, from education to research to health care to R&D. In 2000, 13 percent of college graduates working in U.S. nonmilitary jobs were born in other countries. A higher proportion of these college graduates hold postgraduate degrees than do the workers who were born in the United States (43.6 percent compared with 35.2 percent). According to the National Science Foundation, foreign nationals hold 38 percent of U.S. science and engineering jobs that require doctorates.

The foreign-born population contributes a vast amount of knowledge to America; some 440,000 foreign-born individuals hold PhDs—roughly one-quarter of all the country's doctorates. Nearly half of the National Institutes of Health's 5,500 staff members with advanced degrees were born in other countries and still hold citizenship in nations other than the United States.

We depend most heavily on the world's best and brightest in science and engineering—the fields that are the biggest drivers of the present and future global economy. Our dependence on the skills of the foreign-born has been rising. In 1966, only 23 percent of U.S. science and engineering doctoral degrees went to foreigners. In 2000, the proportion had risen to 39 percent. One in four students at MIT are born abroad. Among MIT

graduate students, the proportion is even higher, at 36 percent. One in five college and university science and engineering professors were born outside the United States. At the University of Maryland at College Park, the deans of the engineering, life sciences, computer, mathematical and physical sciences departments are foreign born and U.S. educated.

Part of our growing dependence on foreign-born workers is the result of the rapid expansion of the science and engineering fields, which have outpaced the supply of U.S.-born skilled workers. In fact, more and more organizations are warning that our economy faces serious shortages of skilled workers. *Time* magazine, echoing this fear, reported in 2002 that with 76 million baby boomers retiring and only 46 million "Gen-Xers" around to replace them, America may face a shortage of 4 million to 6 million skilled workers by 2010.

The other part of the equation is that many other nations have come to realize how important science education is to getting ahead and have the growing populations and economies to generate increasing numbers of mathematicians, scientists, doctors, and researchers. In 2001, U.S. universities awarded 25,509 doctoral degrees in science and engineering fields. The same year, Chinese schools awarded 7,617—considerably fewer than the United States, but consider this: in 1981, two decades earlier, China did not award a single PhD, when the United States awarded more than 18,000. Going from zero to light speed in a matter of decades, China is soon expected to produce more PhDs than the United States. Similarly, European universities awarded 40 percent more science and engineering PhDs than the United States in 2001 and are expected by 2010 to award nearly double the number of doctorates awarded annually in the United States. If you subtract the number of foreign-born students in those groups, the numbers are even more striking. Europe's advantage rises to 60 percent, and China produces not roughly one-third but nearly three-quarters the number of doctorates produced in the United States.

Just as the best sports teams come from the big schools with large numbers of athletes, America needs access to a wide talent pool. Yet America's population is only 300 million—not even 5 percent of the world's population. Even considering that America's resources for developing home-

grown skills are (or at least should be, considering our wealth) relatively greater than those of other nations, it does not take any statistical genius to recognize that we must draw on a worldwide workforce to recruit the talent we need.

As the creative and economic engine of the world, the United States ought to be positioned to reap the benefits of globalization. We should be gearing up our efforts to ride the wave of globalization and to take advantage of the human capital pushing at our doors. The reason America attracts the world's most talented people is that our system offers the freedom and opportunity to develop and market ideas. A new idea often occurs from the combustion of two existing ideas. Connecting them provides a way to accomplish something that previously seemed impossible. The best way to generate the spark for such combustion is to get the best people around into the same room. Then, once new ideas have been brought into being, they need the proper environment to flourish—the system that is unequivocally America's greatest strength. An engine needs both air and fuel, which create combustion energy when they are mixed. In America's global growth engine, the people are the fuel and the system is the air.

To run at full capacity, however, that engine needs the highest-quality input possible. If we do not welcome the best and brightest, they may never be able to gain access to the resources they need to reach their potential—both by developing it at home and by seeking it out abroad. If human assets are not matched with the resources they need, they are wasted; ideas never happen and the development of the entire world is slowed. When other countries lack the resources or political will to allow talent to meet its potential, the United States has stepped in. But there's a bit of a chicken-and-egg conundrum here: you have to have talent to attract talent. And so we need to keep the world's best and brightest coming here, whether they eventually choose to stay or to return to their home countries to circulate the skills and ideas they gain in this country.

Richard Freeman, of the National Bureau of Economic Research, recounts a conversation that illustrates the implications of America's dependence on foreign scientists. "Speaking with a Harvard physicist, whose

most readily commercializable work was done collaboratively with overseas scientists and engineers, I commented, 'Ah, so you are helping them catch up with us,' to which I received the reply, 'No, they are helping us keep ahead of them.'"

⌣•⌣

When you look at a Rubik's Cube, you probably see a maddening game and a fad of the 1980s. What Po-Ling Loh sees is a far more complex puzzle: Is there some sort of method that could always solve it? Seeking the answer, she turned to a specialized area of advanced algebra that focuses on closed embeddings of finite groups. The project that resulted, titled "Closure Properties of D2p in Finite Groups," made her a finalist in the 2005 Intel Science Talent Search. Formerly known as the Westinghouse Science Talent Search and familiarly known as the "Junior Nobel Prize," the competition was founded in 1942 as the nation came to recognize that our security and prosperity depended on more young people choosing careers in science, mathematics, and engineering. It attracts original research projects from some 1,600 high school seniors each year from all areas of math and science. The top forty students come to Washington, D.C., for a week of interviews with judges, presentations to the public, and audiences with leading scientists as well as the president and first lady. Six Science Talent Search winners have gone on to win the Nobel Prize; ten have won MacArthur Foundation "Genius" grants; and four have won the National Medal for Science or the National Medal of Technology.

On the final weekend of the competition, a bright March day, the forty Intel Science Talent Search finalists, including Po-Ling, are presenting their work to the judges and the public in the arching main hall of the National Academy of Sciences in Washington, D.C. Despite the crowd, the noise level is surprisingly muffled, with serious hushed voices floating up into the massive domed ceiling above.

Peering out through oversized glasses, Po-Ling describes her work with the earnest manner and slight nasal accent typical of an American

midwesterner, which by all rights she is. Although her parents are from Singapore, where her two brothers were born, Po-Ling was born in New York City and has grown up in Madison, Wisconsin, where her father is a statistics professor. "Groups are the building blocks of math, just as amino acids are for biology," she explains matter-of-factly. The term "closure" in the title of her project refers to how different sets of numbers relate to each other. This specialized field of mathematics can be applied to chemistry, modern theoretical physics, coding theory, cryptography, and Internet security. By helping to identify symmetries in crystalline structures, it can distinguish fool's gold from the real thing.

Po-Ling earned perfect scores on her SATs and is first in her class of 523 students at James Madison Memorial High School in Madison, Wisconsin. Winner of the gold prize in the USA Math Talent Search for three years in a row and a $50,000 scholarship for top midwestern honors, she has also won the top individual prize, a silver medal, in the Siemens-Westinghouse Competition in Math, Science, and Technology. And she is a talented musician, having won first-place honors for vocal duet in the 2001 Wisconsin School Music Association Solo/Ensemble Festival. She plans to attend the California Institute of Technology, where her brother studies, or the University of Chicago, and eventually teach math.

Of the 2005 Science Talent finalists, nineteen—nearly half—are immigrants or, like Po-Ling, children of immigrants. They come from Singapore, India, Korea, Belarus, and China. Each is impressive individually, but as a group, their achievements are overwhelming. Olga Pikovskaya, who was born in Russia, lived in Belarus, and moved to New York at age 6, spent eighteen months researching metabolite-binding mRNA riboswitches, which are responsible for activating genes to find ways to "turn off" the cancer cell gene, as part of research inspired by her grandmother, who died of cancer. Neal Wadhwa studied the relationship between topology and geometry in "Calabai-Yau supermanifolds"—concepts in theoretical physics and mathematics. June-Ho Kim studied a possible treatment for multiple sclerosis. David Qianli, born in China, researched a process for fortifying purple-skinned sweet potatoes against viral infection. Abhi Gulati, born in India, submitted a mathematics project involving algebra

and combinatorics. Many of the students also are accomplished musicians, athletes, and community volunteers. Most appreciate their heritage.

Pooja S. Jotwani, born in Poona, India, was just a year old when her father, an electrical engineer, brought his family to America, where he had taken a job. Both her parents are now American citizens, a fact that gives her as much pride as does her Indian heritage. She went to high school not far from Miami, Florida, and was the head the youth group of the Sindhi Association of South Florida. She goes back to India to visit relatives every other year. The project that made her a finalist was research on cooling neutron stars. She is now a freshman majoring in astrophysics at MIT. Her parents didn't pressure her, she says: "It was more like 'Do what you want to do and never fall short of your dreams.'"

At the gala dinner where the finalists would be announced a few evenings later, blue and fuchsia lights project up onto the soaring 125-foot-high glass ceiling of the Ronald Reagan Building and International Trade Center, making the whole place feel a bit like a vast starship—all things considered, a fitting atmosphere. Calling the research projects "all but unintelligible to a layman," Intel Chairman Craig Barrett echoes the admiration that it is impossible not to feel for these students. Yet he also delivers a far more sobering message: America is having a harder and harder time producing the scientists we need to ensure our future. He warns that American high school seniors performed in the lowest 10 to 20 percent among industrialized nations in math; that the number of U.S. nationals choosing to major in science and engineering fields and proceeding to graduate school is dwindling; and that increasingly, the foreign-born students who make up a large part of our science and engineering fields are choosing to return to their home countries. "All of these numbers add up to a serious problem in building our next generation of scientists," Barrett warns. "The U.S. educational system to a degree has become complacent and has set its expectation levels too low," he adds.

His comment bears out Pooja Jotwani's experience. Teachers and administrators at her public school of 850 students heard about her becoming a finalist from the *Miami Herald*. Pooja and many of the finalists

had pursued their projects on the strength of their own initiative, with little or no encouragement from their schools. Many of them brushed off their schools' shortcomings, though, and pointed out that the important thing was that other opportunities existed. With enough drive, students can get access to the resources they need to pursue advanced studies. The good thing about America is that there is always a way to follow your dreams even if that path is not laid out clearly in front of you. But how much more could we accomplish, I wondered, if our educational system did a better job of instilling passion for science in the majority of students, who do not have the kind of drive that had brought these finalists here?

When the time comes to announce the ten winners, the forty finalists file up onto the stage and wait patiently. They have transformed themselves from the earnest group from the Great Hall into a dazzling group of young men and women. The girls are dressed in evening gowns and the boys in tuxedos. Some—more of the girls than the boys—already exude the poise of full-fledged adults, while others still display the acne, braces, or gangly limbs of teenagers.

The winners are announced, and it turns out that Po-Ling's mathematics project has won tenth place. At the close of the ceremony, all forty finalists stream out of the glass-encased banquet hall and into a smaller room for a reception. Members of the Chinese-language press surround Po-Ling, asking what it feels like to be the only Asian-American among the winners. She handles them with the same matter-of-factness she showed during the judging and public presentations in the Great Hall. Most of the finalists are joined by their beaming parents, but Po-Ling is alone; her parents joined her for the Siemens-Westinghouse finals and judged that she was mature enough to handle this competition on her own.

It's ironic that Po-Ling's family is not here, because they are a big part of her success story. Her two older brothers, Po-Shen and Po-Ru, are both former U.S. Mathematical Olympiad Competition champions. In 2004, Po-Shen won a National Science Foundation award, a Churchill Scholarship, a Hertz fellowship, and a National Defense Science and Engineering Graduate Fellowship.

There is something in the way immigration creates a virtuous circle that continues from one generation to the next: a desire to improve oneself that is so strong that it prompts a major life change, and then in turn feeds a drive do ever better. This example inspires the second generation, which tends to go on to high-achieving traditional careers, and continues to the third generation, which still seeks to excel but is willing to do so in riskier and more creative fields. Meeting the students and their parents, so many of whom are doctors and scientists, it's easy to understand the source of the stereotype of the overachieving immigrant's offspring, who strive to make the most of the opportunities created for them by their parents' having made the giant leap to a new country and language.

Many of the finalists were aware of this stereotype, which some— particularly Asian-Americans tired of being seen as "model immigrants"— viewed with a tinge of resentment and others accepted as a core part of their identity. Sherri Geng is one who cherished the legacy her parents bequeathed to her. Sherri's slight frame and soft smile belie the passion that she brought to her project—an automated detection system to identify seizure patterns in electroencephalograph data, for which she has applied for a patent—and that enabled her to live up to the challenge that her status as an immigrant, and the daughter of immigrants, represents. When BusinessWeek asked the finalists to write essays on topics of their choosing, she chose to recount her pride in the story of how her Chinese parents made the most of the American educational system, each earning a PhD. Her father founded Genex Technologies Inc., which employs more than thirty people; her mother is a statistician at the U.S. Postal Service in Washington, D.C. They embody qualities that are typical of immigrants: "By prevailing in the rigorous competition to enter America, they have proved themselves capable of overcoming both past and future adversity. Second, they do not take America for granted. They have a strong, even desperate desire to prove that they deserve a place in the society of their chosen country. Finally, they take pride in their native culture, and thus are determined never to tarnish its image so that other immigrants who follow will find at least an equal welcome," Sherri wrote. "They took their

poor-man's wages, their broken English, and most important of all, their hunger for a better future, and they spun it into a golden tapestry. Theirs is a legacy that will continue to grow and sparkle, because they have passed their values to me, and I am just as resolute as they to weave a place for myself in America—and then to teach my children what it means to be descended from immigrants."

The outperformance of immigrant students in the 2005 crop of finalists was not a fluke but part of what has become a pattern in American science. The National Foundation for American Policy, a nonpartisan think tank, found in a 2004 study that 60 percent of America's top science students and 65 percent of the top math students are children of immigrants. One in four of the 2004 Intel Science Talent Search finalists were born in another country; seven of the top ten winners were immigrants or the children of immigrants. The study's author, Stuart Anderson, pointed out that eighteen of the forty finalists were children of high-skilled immigrant workers here on H-1B visas, which became so controversial in 2000 during the dot-com bust. Since the H-1B workers admitted each year represent less than 0.04 percent of the U.S. population, Anderson notes, the performance of their children is statistically phenomenal. Foreign-born high school students made up half of the 2004 U.S. Math Olympiad's top scorers, and thirteen of the top twenty scorers were children of immigrants—both of these higher proportions than in the Intel competition. Anderson's findings highlight a secondary benefit of immigration that compounds the positive impact of the first generation: the children of the foreign born typically strive to meet their parents' high expectations, further fueling a strong work ethic and a quest to innovate and succeed.

⌣•⌣

America is an economic superpower because the best and brightest have come here for so long to study and collaborate with the top thinkers of America and the world. Today, our economic future depends on our universities and businesses continuing to attract scientists, scholars, and

entrepreneurs, who together generate and spread the ideas and technologies that drive the global economy. This gives the United States a tremendous advantage in setting the standards for technologies that eventually are adapted across the globe, creating new markets for our goods on our terms.

Not just our own future but that of the rest of the world depends on our ability to attract the world's best and brightest to create various hubs of learning and collaboration. These centers—like Silicon Valley and the MIT Corridor—boost our own ability to innovate but also contribute to knowledge, economic growth, and innovation around the world—including scientific breakthroughs, political and intellectual trends, the spreading of entrepreneurship and skills, and the artistic and cultural contributions that America (including—for better or for worse—Hollywood and the music industry) makes.

America is the economic engine of the world, producing 27 percent of all the world's manufactured goods and services. America's private and public investment in research and development has led to some of the biggest technological breakthroughs that have changed lives and economies worldwide. In the 1950s and 1960s, we responded to the perceived threat of the Cold War by intensifying public investment in scientific research. Our public sector has done a better job than any other country's to create an environment where industry can thrive—and where the world's best and brightest can congregate. Whether in Silicon Valley or Silicon Alley for high-tech products, the MIT corridor for biotechnology, or Wall Street for financial engineering, nowhere else in the world has it been possible to find such a concentration of talent or such an engine generating the intellectual and entrepreneurial energy that drives the global economy.

No other country can begin to compare in terms of great ideas and inventions: drugs, advanced surgical equipment—like magnetic resonance imaging—and techniques to cure diseases; agricultural advances to help farmers produce enough food to feed growing nations; financial technologies like the automatic teller machine and insurance; communications technologies like fiber optics; legal concepts like land title, allowing home-

owners to generate capital to invest in home businesses. It would be a reach to say that Al Gore invented the Internet, but there's not a bit of exaggeration in saying that America did. Our ideas and technologies spread to new countries, which adopt or refine them to generate economic growth and markets for our products. National Bureau of Economic Research economists Laura Bottazzi and Giovanni Peri have estimated that as advances in U.S. research and development advance knowledge creation in other countries, the benefit to the U.S. economy is about twenty times as high.

"International science and technology cooperation is an extremely effective way to leverage one of the defining strengths of the United States," Bruce Alberts, president of the National Academy of Sciences, told a congressional committee on science. "We benefit from an extraordinary set of personal, professional, and cultural relationships due to the many people from other countries who are working in the U.S. science and technology enterprise, and due to the large number of science and technology leaders in other countries who have been trained in the United States."

People from other countries coming here and Americans going around the world spread the knowledge generated in the United States. Industries in many poorer countries were started by expatriate U.S. managers, but growth has depended on the training of local managers; in many rapidly growing emerging economies, one of the biggest problems multinational firms have faced has been to find enough skilled middle managers.

Other countries are hungry for the knowledge that the United States is generating worldwide in management, marketing, and technology—not to mention political and policy making skills. Chile's economic transformation in the 1980s, for example, was engineered by the famed "Chicago Boys"—a group of University of Chicago–trained economists who liberalized the country's economy with sensible safeguards in place to keep speculative capital from rushing in and out faster than the country could handle.

With the collapse of communism, the rest of the world has embraced the American mantra of competition—our biggest export of all. Even the

ideas that are now challenging American dominance are the product of American influence. There is no better evidence of America's economic leadership than the fact that many of the "threats" to our economy began as ideas and inventions created here. Indeed, executives and would-be executives in other countries devour popular U.S. books on business and management; governments give generous scholarships to allow their future leaders to study in the United States.

Look at some of the policies China has put in place to spur innovation: venture capital, stock options, and research and development tax credits. Where did those ideas come from? Straight from Silicon Valley, of course. China has put its own spin on venture capital—using state funds as seed capital—but the model is unmistakably American. And in establishing a research and development tax credit, it did us one better, making the credit permanent. (The U.S. version, established in 1981, was temporary and actually lapsed in the 1990s. President Bush has proposed a permanent credit, which the business community warmly supports as a way to keep America competitive.)

In the 1980s and early 1990s, Americans were gripped by hysteria that Japan would overtake us as the world's most powerful economy. Taiichi Ohno, a Toyota manager, supposedly had developed a system for industrial production that was far superior to those used in the United States. Yet his "just-in-time" system was, in essence, an American idea thought up by the quality control expert W. Edwards Deming to control waste and ensure consistently high quality. His ideas had helped America streamline manufacturing during World War II.

America even created the conditions that led to today's wave of outsourcing. The need to deal with the Y2K bug made it imperative that companies find enough programmers to sort through billions of lines of code by midnight of December 31, 1999. Although the coding work paid well because of the simple rules of supply and demand, much of it was tedious and repetitive. Here we ended up with a paradox: work that required a high level of skill but that did not appeal to enough American workers to meet the demand for it. When the task was completed, all of a sudden—and briefly—the world had an oversupply of competent

programmers. Five months later, the technology bubble popped and the air began rushing out, leaving U.S. and foreign-born workers scrambling for jobs that paid much less than the boom-time jobs had offered. Many software programmers who had come from India and China to work in the United States went back home, where they started new businesses of their own with skills that helped drive double-digit economic growth rates—some of the fastest in the world.

An Indian-born entrepreneur seasoned in Silicon Valley, Vivek Paul, president of Wipro, India's leading offshore software service provider, is one of the best examples of how American training and work experience feed innovation around the world. This process turns "brain drain"— the exodus of the developing world's most skilled people to wealthy nations—into "brain circulation," whereby the same people return with additional skills that help their home countries develop new industries of their own.

A Public Policy Institute of California study of 2,300 foreign-born— mainly Indian and Chinese—Silicon Valley engineers found that 51 percent had been involved with founding or running a startup company in their home countries. Half traveled to their native countries at least once a year on business, and four out of five shared technology information and tips about U.S. job and business opportunities with colleagues back home.

Many developing countries have benefited from American innovation by "leapfrogging"—adapting the American technologies for their own use and adding their own innovative touches. Often this happens through active collaboration with U.S. companies and scientists. Thus, a growing number of patents abroad are being filed by U.S. companies. In fact, in many developing countries the vast majority of patents awarded go to foreigners. In 1999, India granted 633 patents to residents and 1,527 to foreigners. The 15,605 patents awarded to foreigners in China in 2002 were nearly three times the number awarded to residents. By one estimate, 85 percent of Chinese technology, for example, is controlled by foreign firms.

The flow of the world's best and brightest in and out of the United States has also spread the economic and political ideas that have made possible the sweeping changes that are helping formerly backward economies attract investment, grow, and lift hundreds of millions of people out of poverty. America has exported its way of life around the globe: spreading democracy, opening markets to American goods—and at the same time selling the appeal of living here. The immigrants and foreign students who upend their lives to come here are a measure of success in selling the idea of America to the world just as much as they are a large part of the reason for that success.

Go to any country in the world, and you will find that many of its leaders and entrepreneurs have studied or worked in the United States. Presidents and ministers—current or former—of many countries learned diplomacy and public policy at top U.S. universities. Just scratching the surface among universities in the Northeast, a partial list includes Cyprus's former Minister of Foreign Affairs George Iacovou, who attended Boston University; Jamaican Prime Minister Percival James Patterson, Brown University; Kazakhstan President Nurlan Balgimbayev, University of Massachusetts; Singapore Prime Minister Goh Chok Tong, Williams College; Turkish Prime Minister Tansu Ciller, University of Connecticut and Yale University. UN Secretary-General Kofi Annan (from Ghana), Taiwan President Lee Teng-hui, Israeli Prime Minister Benjamin Netanyahu, and Colombian President Virgilio Barco all went to MIT. There is a long list from Harvard: Ecuador's President Jamil Mahuad, British Member of Parliament John Rankin Rathbone, Canadian Prime Minister Pierre Trudeau, French President Jacques Chirac, Greek President Andreas G. Papandreou, Israeli Prime Minister Shimon Peres, Mexican Presidents Miguel de la Madrid and Carlos Salinas, Nepal's King Birendra Bir Birkram Shah Dev, Pakistani President Benazir Bhutto, and Norwegian Prime Minister Gro Harlem Brundtland.

As much as America is an engine of global growth, we also are an engine of ideas. Like the shift away from communism, the changes that are happening around the world are a combination of political and economic reforms, prompted by a mix of political and economic processes.

Being the world's sole superpower and globo-cop, the United States is pushing political change in other countries. More and more often, citizens of those countries who are living in America become part of those changes, whether they result directly from U.S. intervention or indirectly, through U.S. support of the ideas behind reform and the availability of a refuge on our soil.

In the driving snow outside the New Carrollton Ramada Inn, just outside of Washington D.C., Iraqis gathered on January 30, 2005, to vote for the first time ever to elect a democratic government in Iraq. Traveling for many hours and trudging through a snowstorm, past police barricades and through separate security lines for men and women, Iraqis came with young children and elderly parents in tow to the hastily rigged voting center in the hotel's basement. Each ballot cast earned a round of applause as these Iraqis seized an opportunity to help ensure that the values of their new home travel back to their land of birth. Many of them were voting for the first time in their lives—unless you count their voting with their feet when they chose to come to the United States.

The parking lot across the street from the hotel, which itself was surrounded by police to ensure voters' safety, was festooned with placards reading "God Bless You Iraqi Citizens" and with balloons in the red, white, and black colors of the Iraqi flag.

"This is a great day," said Mohammad Fradi, an Iraqi artist in a neatly trimmed beard with dramatic streaks of white and wearing a jaunty red scarf. "I give my day in honor of all the victims in the U.S. Army. I get this day because of the deaths of Americans, and I want the American people to know that I will not forget this day." After he voted, he called home, where his daughter, who was on her way to vote in Detroit, was all but crying with joy from watching television reports from Iraq and the polling places set up in five U.S. cities. All told, Iraqis living in the United States cast 24,335 ballots to elect the 275 members of the new Transitional National Assembly.

In the Iraqi elections, immigrants exercised political power that was the direct product of U.S. military might. Much more common are cases of immigrants gaining political power in their home countries because

of the money they earn in the United States and send home. While the very top echelons of migrant workers bring home human capital in the form of skills and technologies, those further down the socioeconomic ladder provide the old-fashioned kind of capital: cash. By providing work to migrants who keep their home countries' economies afloat through the remittances they send home, the United States thus acts as the engine of the world in another way, albeit unintentionally. In 2003 alone, immigrants sent money from the United States to Latin America over 100 million times, for a total of more than $30 billion. Not only do families send money to their relatives, but whole communities of émigrés join together in hometown associations to pool their money to build sewage systems, hospitals, soccer fields, churches, and schools back home.

Much of this money returns to America when the people who receive it buy American products. And money that does not return directly here benefits people on both sides of our borders because it gives political power to the best and brightest citizens of other countries who, for one reason or another, had to leave home. Too often, they left their countries because their own governments were so incompetent. Once they have lived in a place whose government, while not perfect, works better than any other, they and their families demand more from the governments in their homelands.

More and more countries are recognizing dual citizenship and involving their diaspora populations in homeland politics, marking a sea change in the role that émigrés are expected to play. In 2004, Dominican and Filipino Americans voted for the first time in their homeland elections. Colombia reserves a Senate seat for a member of its diaspora population, and that seat currently is held by a Colombian who has lived in the United States for many years. Mexicans have just won the right to vote by absentee ballot from abroad, and Ecuadorians hope to gain that right soon. Mindful of proposals to give Mexicans out-of-country voting rights by next year, Mexican President Vicente Fox toured Mexican communities in the United States last summer to urge them to support his party and policies. In January 2005, U.S. Representative Kendrick

Meeks of Miami sent Haitian Prime Minister Gerard Latortue—who, in-cidentally, assumed office after many years as a Florida resident—a letter asking him to "take whatever actions are necessary to allow Haitian citi-zens living in the United States to vote in Haiti's national elections later this year." America has long benefited from our relationship with world leaders who studied at our universities; now, the voices of ordinary people are adding to that influence as other countries give more power to their citizens who are living in the United States.

Clearly, America and the world both will benefit most if we harness the skills that citizens of developing countries gain in this country so that they can share them when they return to their country of birth. Even if many of them do not return, the contributions that skilled workers make to economic growth in the United States and other wealthy coun-tries may lead to scientific discoveries and innovations that benefit the whole world but that might not have occurred had those individuals not been tapped. "A brain drain is only a brain drain if significant human re-sources are irretrievably lost, and if those resources could have profitably been used in the migrant source country," labor economist B. Lindsay Lowell argues.

Some of the world's skilled and ambitious people, like a Pakistani medical informatics specialist I know, came to America because they had no possibility at all of pursuing their chosen profession in their home countries—there were no schools to train in and nowhere to use the skills once they acquired them. These are the people who hopefully one day will be able to bring their skills home and create new industries and professions where none existed before.

Often it is not just skills that they bring to their land of birth but also the notion of giving back to society, in the many places in the world where a culture of philanthropy is not as well established as in the United States. For example, Madhu Yaskhi Goud, a successful New Jersey busi-nessman, became a minor celebrity when he returned to India in 2003 for

a visit after fourteen years abroad and pledged 25 percent of his annual income to provide primary health care and education for impoverished farmers in Nizamabad, his hometown. The visit so moved him that he decided to resettle in India and run for parliament. As a member of the Congress Party ticket, he won decisively in May 2004. Although he has pledged to give up his U.S. green card, he promised to be a voice not only for his Nizamabad constituents but for nonresident Indians as well.

Like Goud, many members of diaspora communities get involved in helping their homelands, whether by funding sewage systems, providing seed capital and training for businesses, or helping clean up after natural disasters. Another Indian émigré, Naresh Trehan, a Manhattan heart surgeon, returned to India to found Escorts Heart Institute and Research Center in Amritsar. Although such commitments do not always turn into political involvement, there are many cases in which people do turn the education and skills they acquired abroad toward political causes in their homelands. This is particularly true with respect to the hometown associations that émigrés have created to channel funds toward improving living conditions for family and friends who stayed behind.

Hometown associations can dramatically change the local political landscape as association members develop political capital, and this in turn can translate into personal benefits for the groups' leaders abroad. As development economist Carol Zabin has pointed out, such leaders, who may hope to assume leadership positions in their hometowns down the road—may come to wield more influence from abroad than they could have by staying at home.

Clearly, America depends on the world's best and brightest to keep our own knowledge economy competitive. Yet the benefits of high-skilled migration are magnified when these workers return home and use what they have learned here to create the skills bases and industries their home countries need to grow. The circulation of these talented people through America helps create jobs and industries in other countries even as it opens doors for American investment and products. Just as important, it helps create goodwill for America.

—7—

Homeland Insecurity

When George W. Bush became president in 2001, he hinted in his inaugural address that policies toward immigrants would reflect his promise of compassionate conservatism: "America has never been united by blood or birth or soil. We are bound by ideals that move us beyond our backgrounds, lift us above our interests, and teach us what it means to be citizens. Every child must be taught these principles. Every citizen must uphold them. And every immigrant, by embracing these ideals, makes our country more, not less, American. Today, we affirm a new commitment to live out our nation's promise through civility, courage, compassion and character." Making his first foreign trip to Mexico, where he greeted Mexican President Vicente Fox in Spanish, Bush soon raised the idea of a guest worker program for illegal immigrants, which would largely have benefited an estimated 3 million or more undocumented Mexicans in the United States illegally.

Everything changed the morning of September 11, 2001. After jet planes crashed into the World Trade Center and the Pentagon, the Statue of Liberty closed to visitors. The policy was intended to protect an enduring symbol of American ideals. Yet the closing of Lady Liberty was emblematic of the damage that had already been done to the image of America as a country that welcomed foreigners and of the shift in Americans' attitude toward strangers. Although our open society made us the

greatest nation in the world by drawing talented and driven workers and thinkers to this country, our openness was now being questioned, with many Americans wondering whether it offered too much convenience for those who wanted to harm us.

It had been shockingly easy for the 9/11 terrorists to enter the United States. Of the nineteen hijackers, all had come on temporary visas—as students, as tourists, or on business. Every year, more than 30 million individuals—a number impossibly too large not to contain possible terrorists—cross our borders using these temporary visas. Four of the nineteen 9/11 hijackers had entered on student visas. Hani Hanjour ostensibly had been planning to study English in California. He never showed up for school, and resurfaced as the pilot of the plane that crashed into the Pentagon. Six months after the attacks, paperwork was completed granting two of the deceased hijackers visas to study at U.S. flight schools, making it shockingly clear just how bad a job the United States was doing of scrutinizing who was coming here. Other would-be terrorists also used student visas as their cover. Indian-born Dhiren Barot (*aka* Issa al Britani *aka* Bilal *aka* Abu Musa al-Hindi *aka* Abu Eissa al-Hindi), a convert to Islam, had registered as a student in New Jersey, where he conducted surveillance on potential financial industry targets, including the Prudential building in Newark, the New York Stock Exchange, Manhattan's Citigroup Center, and the International Monetary Fund headquarters in Washington, D.C. (He was arrested in London in August 2004 and charged with planning to commit murder and public nuisance.)

The question became not only how to protect our borders but also how to identify the enemies who already were among us. All of a sudden, danger lurked behind the most innocent of faces. Shortly after the 9/11 attacks, the cartoonist Mark Fiore published an animated interactive short on the Web called "Hate Time," which invited his audience to find the "neighborhood terrorist" by clicking on pop-up faces. "Not a Terrorist! Ahmed fled the Taliban and hates Osama bin Laden more than you do!" read the message that appeared when I clicked on one of the faces. "Not a terrorist! Yasuf has run the corner deli for 35 years," read another. The real culprit? Clicking on the white, pimply-faced

teenager apparently nourished with lots of junk food yielded the answer: "Congratulations! Jimbo just beat up Yasuf at the deli."

Immigrants were torn between loyalty to America and justifiable fear as hate crimes rose dramatically against anyone who looked "different." In the three days following the attacks, the Council on American-Islamic Relations received more than 300 reports of hate crimes and harassment, or about half the number reported in the entire previous year. American Sikh taxi drivers taped American flags to their windows, hoping to avoid being confused with terrorists. In California, a Yemeni grocer found a leaflet fastened to his windshield carrying death threats and anti-Arab invective; the next day, assailants shot him to death in his store. In Cleveland, a man drove his car into Ohio's largest mosque, causing $100,000 worth of damage. Not long after 9/11, Pakistanis in Long Island urged their fellow immigrants to naturalize and arranged for youths to sing "God Bless America" during the seventh-inning stretch at a Mets game. There was no doubt that they felt deep gratitude and affection for America, inspired by the opportunities this country offered them. Yet behind the flag-waving it was impossible not to discern anxiety: a fear that if they did not prove their loyalty, immigrants would lose everything they had worked for.

Shortly after the terrorist attacks, President Bush made a dramatic visit to a mosque, removing his shoes as required before entering, where he urged tolerance. Just as had happened in the First and Second World Wars, however, the government's actions undermined that message. On October 24 and 25, 2001, at the urging of Attorney General John Ashcroft, Congress approved the USA Patriot Act—an acronym for Uniting and Strengthening America by Providing Appropriate Tools Required to Intercept and Obstruct Terrorism—by a vote of 357–66 in the House and 98–1 in the Senate; President Bush signed it into law on October 26. Written largely by Assistant Attorney General Viet Dinh, who was born in Saigon during the Vietnam War and came to America as a refugee in 1978, the Patriot Act opened with a passage exhorting Americans not to discriminate against Muslims or Arabs. "Arab Americans, Muslim Americans, and Americans from South Asia play a vital role in our Nation and

are entitled to nothing less than the full rights of every American," the Act declared. "The acts of violence that have been taken against Arab and Muslim Americans since the September 11, 2001, attacks against the United States should be and are condemned by all Americans who value freedom." The Patriot Act also recognized that many Arab Americans and Muslim Americans acted heroically during the attacks on the United States, including Mohammed Salman Hamdani, a 23-year-old New Yorker of Pakistani descent, who disappeared after he went to the World Trade Center to offer rescue assistance.

But the content of the Act—and of the many other legal measures put in place to complement it—reflected America's Jekyll-and-Hyde views of immigrants. These measures dramatically expanded the government's powers to arrest and detain immigrants without charges, force immigrants to register (which in many cases amounted to handing themselves over into detention), and to eavesdrop on federal detainees' conversations with their lawyers—if it decided, as often it did not, to allow inmates access to lawyers. In practice, many of the Act's consequences would involve the very discrimination it purported to condemn.

Some of the measures in the Patriot Act made sense and were long overdue. The legislation gave federal immigration and State Department officials access to FBI files on visa questions; standardized the technology used for verifying the identities of foreign nationals seeking entry; and directed immigration officials to use biometric identifiers and tamperproof documents. But other measures carried costs that were not clearly outweighed by their benefits, including some that appeared on the surface to be quite reasonable but were designed in ways that would have serious and disturbing consequences. For example, the Patriot Act broadened the government's powers to deny admission to or deport anyone "deemed to be representatives of foreign terrorist organizations or of any group that publicly endorses terrorist acts." In principle, this makes sense. However, the power to designate who belonged to these categories was given exclusively to the attorney general's office. There were no checks and balances to protect anyone who was tagged in error, whether unintentionally or deliberately. Once the attorney general made a determina-

tion that an individual "represented" a terrorist group, government detention became mandatory, and suspects could be detained indefinitely
without being able to notify anyone, even family members, of where they
had gone.

The government applied a combination of secret warrants and the
antiterrorist provisions of the 1996 laws against the mostly Muslim immigrants seized in post-9/11 roundups, often refusing to release the identities of those seized. In another move clearly aimed at intimidating
immigrants and portraying the government as putting up a strong front
against foreign terrorists, Attorney General Ashcroft gutted the immigration appeals board, removing the five members most sympathetic to
immigrants. During the two-year period after the attacks, deportation
orders would rise 30 percent compared with the two prior years.

In a "Boondocks" comic strip pointing to the hypocrisy inherent in
the act, the strip's preteen star, Huey, clutches his Afro as Ashcroft an-
nounces on television, "So I would like to reassure Congress that my
proposed Turban Surveillance Act, which would allow the FBI to co-
vertly plant listening devices in the headgear of suspected terrorists, is
in no way meant to single out Arab or Muslim Americans." Many news-
papers yanked the comic from their pages for the indecency of pointing
out the obvious contradictions between the administration's rhetoric
and its actions.

The Patriot Act translated the fear that so many Americans felt into
a nightmare for anyone born in another country. In one case, someone
responded to Attorney General Ashcroft's request for reports of suspi-
cious behavior by calling the FBI on their Muslim neighbor after they
saw him bring home a large ceramic container, then use it to dump water in his back yard shortly afterward. The container was for cooking a
traditional meal, but he'd had to use it to bail out a flooded dishwasher.
For this, armed agents burst through his front door. In Florida, Moroc-
can immigrant Ahmed Koko received seven visits from the FBI, and he
was arrested when he called police to protest during the last one, which
it turned out was the result of a mix-up: the feds were actually interested
in his Iraqi neighbor.

In March 2004—in just another of many such stories—FBI agents stormed the Connecticut home of Rezwan Masud, a Bangladeshi-born nuclear scientist who has been a U.S. citizen since 1997. They blindfolded his wife and his six-year-old daughter and confiscated his computer and records. The reason he aroused FBI suspicion was that he had donated more than $10,000 to an Islamic charity, Benevolence International Foundation. Masud later questioned why, if the charity was so clearly a terrorist group, the U.S. government had given it a nonprofit tax ID number, and why the foundation's illicit activities should have been apparent to him and not the IRS. He also was mistakenly connected to a British Muslim terrorist supporter. Yet, Masud had also donated to Christian charities—and is a member of the National Republican Congressional Committee. Masud and his Tunisian-born wife, Awatef, who is also a scientist, sell radiation detectors and water purification systems to clients in Asia and the Middle East. On a trip to Dubai in September 2004 to install radiation detectors, United Arab Emirates officials seized his passport and arrested him. He was able to contact the U.S. embassy, which helped him get out. Apparently because his name had not been purged from international terrorist suspect lists, he was detained again in Germany and again upon reentry to the United States. No apology was forthcoming.

On the first anniversary of the September 11 attacks, a new rule harked back to the alien registrations of the two world wars. Male temporary foreign visitors over 16 years of age from thirty-three countries had to register with law enforcement authorities to be fingerprinted and photographed. Of the more than 82,000 who complied, some 13,000 were told to leave the country, many of them on minor technicalities that often were not the fault of the detainee but of the slow-turning wheels of the immigration bureaucracy. Many registrants were detained because they had fallen "out of status" when the INS delayed processing their paperwork because it was so far backlogged. During the post-9/11 crisis, the long-neglected immigration system, a headache in normal times, became disastrous for the many individuals and families who were trapped in its bureaucratic cogs.

A 16-year-old boy who had come to this country legally was separated from his pregnant mother, a permanent resident, and his stepfather, a U.S. citizen. A successful Iranian Jewish businessman who had fled Iran seeking freedom and security in America was arrested and jailed. Assessing the new mood in America, many Arabs and Muslims simply left the country rather than risk being detained arbitrarily with no notice to their families. By early 2003, the Pakistani government estimated that as many as 15,000 of 120,000 Pakistanis had fled the United States and applied for asylum in Canada.

Three members of Congress sent Ashcroft a letter to protest the program. "We have grave doubts about whether [it] has struck the proper balance between securing our borders on one hand and respecting the civil liberties of foreign students, business people, and visitors who come to our nation legally on the other," wrote Senators Ted Kennedy and Russ Feingold and Representative John Conyers. Special registration was an expensive public relations move that was as naive as it was ineffectual in identifying real terrorists: only a fool would register in the program if he truly intended harm. All it did was alienate immigrant groups and waste resources that could have been used far more effectively in a targeted information gathering initiative. The government finally ended the program just over a year later, all but admitting that it was an abject failure.

Many Americans, still in shock at the horror of the 9/11 attacks, supported the crackdown on immigrants and foreigners as a needed effort to protect our country. In a nationwide poll in the fall of 2004, Cornell University researchers found that nearly half of Americans—44 percent—believed that the United States should restrict the civil liberties of Muslims, either through registration with the federal government, close surveillance by law enforcement agencies, profiling based on their religion or heritage, or through undercover law enforcement agents' infiltration of Muslim civic organizations.

Yet many other Americans felt that foreigners were being made unfairly to pay for the attacks, that limits on immigrants' civil liberties could all too easily be applied to citizens as well, and that the moral and

practical costs to the nation of the new policies did not justify the limited benefit. They understood that just because someone really is out to get us doesn't mean we're not paranoid too. Time and again, Americans stood up in defense of immigrants who had fallen into a legal black hole.

Mohammad Sarfaraz Hussain, 18 years old and a star junior point guard for the Jamaica High School basketball team, had come to New York City from Pakistan when he was 7 years old to see his mother, who was dying of cancer. A few years later, his father died of a heart attack, and his uncle's family in Queens took Mohammad in. In February 2003, when the Department of Homeland Security ordered all male noncitizens between the ages of 16 and 35 from certain Arab and Muslim countries to register with the government, Mohammad took a day off from school to comply. Yet because his citizenship application was still tied up in red tape nearly two years after it was filed, the government ordered this model American teenager deported to a country where he no longer had any family. Mohammad's coach, his teammates, his friends, and his neighbors refused to let the "war on terror" destroy basic American values of right and wrong. They rallied together and brought his case to Representative Gary Ackerman, from Queens, who pleaded with the Department of Homeland Security to dismiss the deportation case on humanitarian grounds. Days before the teenager was supposed to appear before an immigration judge as part of deportation hearings, the interim director of the Bureau of Immigration and Customs Enforcement in New York, Ed McElroy, announced that the government would let Mohammad stay.

When the Department of Homeland Security moved to deport an Armenian family that had become a beloved part of their Colorado community, the outpouring of support on the family's behalf became national news. The Sargsyans had been conned by a family member's U.S.-born husband, who took money from them and others in Armenia in exchange for arranging visas that in some cases turned out to be fraudulent and in other cases were never issued at all. When the oldest daughter, Nvart Idinyan, filed for divorce from her husband after her family arrived in the United States in 1999 and saw that he had been abusing

her physically, he turned them in to immigration authorities. When the Sargsyans' neighbors in Ridgway, Colorado, learned that the family faced deportation, the town held a silent auction to raise $15,000 to cover legal bills, visited family members in detention, and set up a Web site, savethesargsyans.com, to chronicle the case. Cases like these became common as Americans stood up to protest the uneven enforcement of immigration laws and their enforcement in ways that often hurt immigrants who were upstanding members of their community and had done their best to follow the law.

Several American cities, large and small, passed ordinances defying Homeland Security authorities' insistence that local police departments also enforce immigration. The cities opposed the mandate for practical reasons: making police into immigration enforcers would hurt efforts to protect their communities. When Bush administration loyalists tried to punish these cities, the House of Representatives roundly defeated their proposal to withhold federal money from "sanctuary cities."

Independent groups—and indeed, the government itself—kept track of antiterrorism efforts and made their analyses public. A May 2003 congressional study concluded that the Justice Department had not even interviewed half of the 7,600 foreigners it had targeted for questioning. "None of the law enforcement officials with whom we spoke could provide examples of investigative leads that resulted from the project," the report said. "More than half of the law enforcement officers we spoke with expressed concerns about the quality of the questions asked and the value of the responses obtained." According to a report released in June 2003 by Inspector General Glenn A. Fine, 762 illegal immigrants were detained for months after 9/11. None of them were charged with terrorism. Fine chastised the government for holding many immigrants for months, without access to lawyers, on dubious evidence of terrorist ties. The report recommended, among other things, that the government develop clearer criteria for identifying terrorist suspects, improve detention conditions, and give immigration officials more say in detainees' fates. The Cato Institute calculated that even if the government's Terrorist Information Awareness program were 95 percent accurate, a search focused on the

U.S. Muslim population would turn up 299,750 false positive IDs—with only a 1.5 percent probability of finding a real terrorist. In other words, the government was wasting time and money and alienating the groups whose help it needed—all for precious little benefit to American security.

⌣•⌣

Hardening attitudes after 9/11 turned into coldhearted, small-minded behavior on the part of individuals both inside and outside government. When the citizenship application of Kichul Lee, a Korean immigrant, came up for review in 2003, U.S. immigration authorities in Seattle noted an infraction and denied him naturalization, citing a lack of "good moral character." Why? Because in 1999, he had been fined $152 for having gathered fifty-one oysters—nearly three times the state limit—from a beach near Seattle. He was not the only immigrant caught by such pettiness; in 2005, hundreds more joined a class-action lawsuit because they had been denied citizenship because of traffic tickets and similar minor infractions.

Carla Freeman, a 27-year-old South African, was waiting for approval on her application to become a permanent resident when a truck jumped a median strip and killed her American husband, Robert, as he drove to work in 2002. That got her not the U.S. government's condolences but a deportation order, shackles, and detention. Because they had only been married a year, she did not meet the two-year requirement for permanent residence. When her father became gravely ill at home in South Africa, she had to give up her appeal of the case so that she could go back to South Africa, or else risk not seeing him again before he died. Losing her immigration status got her barred from returning to the United States for ten years.

In March 2005, a group called the National Alliance erected billboards in Las Vegas reading "STOP IMMIGRATION." The community complained, prompting the billboard company, Clear Channel, to take the billboards down. National Alliance sued and got them put back up. Sometimes in cases like this nothing more resulted than media cover-

age. But more and more often, the growing tensions turned into violence and intimidation on both sides, often against South Asian and
Muslim victims. In 2003, arsonists targeted Hindu homes in Houston,
and a Savannah mosque was destroyed by fire. In 2004, a 54-year-old
Sikh man was brutally attacked in Queens by men who argued with him
over his honorary turban.

In November 2004, on the opening of deer-hunting season, a group
of white hunters tried to force a Hmong hunter, Chai Vang, to give up
his deer stand in the woods to the northeast of Minneapolis, Minnesota.
Racial slurs were involved, and Vang claims that one of the hunters
fired a shot, a charge that the hunters deny. Vang, who had lived in this
country for twenty years and was a veteran of the California National
Guard, opened fire, killing six of the hunters and wounding two others.
Shortly after the incident, signs and bumper stickers appeared saying:
"Save the Deer. Kill the Hmong." Vang was convicted of murder in September 2005 after he testified that some of the hunters indeed deserved
to die.

Some Americans, angry that the government was not doing more
to protect the borders, took it upon themselves to try to keep illegal
immigrants out. On April 1, 2005, the group calling themselves the Minutemen, armed with guns and pepper spray, began patrolling the U.S.-
Mexican border in Cochise County, Arizona. The Minutemen took care
to insist that their volunteers were not supposed to apprehend anyone
themselves, but simply to alert border authorities. One migrant who complained that Minutemen volunteers had detained him illegally (although
U.S. and Mexican authorities said the allegation was unfounded) was
photographed wearing a T-shirt reading, "Bryan Barton caught me crossing illegally into the United States and all I got was this lousy T-shirt." In
addition to the T-shirt, Barton and two other volunteers gave the man
water, a box of Wheaties, and $20. The Minutemen dismissed Barton,
a 25-year-old who billed himself as the youngest candidate ever to seek a
seat in Congress, because he had disobeyed rules not to approach those at-
tempting to cross the border. It was too bad, because his sense of humor
(the T-shirt) and his apparent humanity (providing water, food, and cash)

made for great press, which the group needed to offset accusations that its volunteers were nothing more than vigilantes.

Other groups picked up the cue. Two weeks after the Minutemen began their vigils, a similar group, the Yuma Patriots, began patrols of their own in Arizona. After the Minutemen's stint ended on April 30, there was talk of a similar effort on the Canadian border. A former Minuteman founded a California chapter whose Web site read, "If you are against us you are scum or just stupid beyond comprehension. Change sides fool. Lets [sic] not let OBL [Osama bin Laden] criminals kill the goose with the golden egg so our grandchildren suffer their foolishness. United We Stand!" Its logo, tellingly, was the "Don't tread on me" snake, not the American eagle. By late summer, the Minutemen claimed to have inspired similar movements in just about every state in the union, including states like Tennessee that did not even have international borders.

Others who resent the presence of so many immigrants are using every legal means at their disposal. In the first half of 2005, legislators introduced 150 different bills in thirty state legislatures to restrict immigrants' rights or to make it harder to prove eligibility for voting. In the November 2004 elections, 56 percent of Arizonans voted for Proposition 200, a measure requiring public officials to verify the legal status of anyone applying for state benefits or to vote, and to deny them if they could not produce documentation that they were legal. In another example of how restrictions aimed at immigrants often hurt native-born Americans too, the measure ended up preventing many citizens from voting in the November 2005 elections when they could not present the proper identification. Idaho's Canyon County announced that it would use the Racketeer Influenced and Corrupt Organizations Act, commonly called the RICO Act, to sue businesses who employ illegals. Earlier the county had tried to bill Mexico for the cost of providing services to illegal aliens and to have itself declared a federal disaster area because of the impact of illegal immigration. Because immigration authorities do not have the manpower to seize all illegal immigrants, the police chief of New Ipswich, New Hampshire, began arresting and charging undocumented immigrants with criminal trespassing, but was soon forced by a court order to stop.

The new national obsession with illegal immigration led politicians to pass laws that sounded patriotic but, in the end, would end up creating more problems than they solved. Capitalizing on security worries and resentment against illegal immigrants, anti-immigration forces launched campaigns to restrict illegal immigrants' access to driver's licenses. Several states and, ultimately, the U.S. Congress voted to require proof of U.S. citizenship or legal residence in order to receive a driver's license, a policy that law enforcement officers and sensible citizens opposed because it would merely increase the number of unlicensed drivers on the road and do nothing to enhance national security. The driver's license debate was just one more instance of trading diminished local security for a false sense of national security, wasting money and human resources. Governors complained that the federal government was giving states just $100 million to defray the cost of the new license cards that they would be required to issue as a result of the law, an amount that would barely cover the costs in the state of Virginia alone.

Despite the deteriorating atmosphere for immigrants, the optimists among them decided to work to prove their loyalty and make it clear that they loved America too. U.S. Marine Gunnery Sgt. Jamal Baadani, who had emigrated from Egypt when he was 10, wanted to cry shortly after 9/11 when his daughters told him they were afraid of being Arab. He sent friends and family an emotional e-mail: "I remember being jumped at the bus stop and the kids breaking my lunch box and kicking my food into the snow and stepping on it. . . . What I do remember most is the good that came out of that period of my life; I remember Richard Bailey, Donna, Debbie, and Connie Bristow. They stood up for me and kept me from harm's way. They taught me many things, they showed me how to go snow sledding, showed me how to play sports, how to roller skate, how to bowl, try new American foods, listen to music, and they helped me to learn English. Most importantly, they helped me develop into an average young American boy. . . . " That e-mail became the first activity of the

Association of Patriotic Arab-Americans in the Military, a group whose mission was to celebrate the patriotism of Arab Americans, particularly the more than 3,500 Arab Americans serving in the armed forces.

Nearly 70,000 foreign-born soldiers serve in the armed forces today, roughly 5 percent of the total. Of these, roughly half have been naturalized as Americans. More than 10,000 Muslims serve in the U.S. armed forces, but the largest group of today's "green card" soldiers are from Mexico and other Latin American countries—countries from which many immigrants came to the United States during their own civil wars in the 1980s.

Not long after the war in Iraq began in 2003, U.S. recruiters were actively soliciting prospective green card soldiers (and would-be citizens) in Mexico—so actively that Mexican nationalists protested. The Pentagon has made no secret of the fact that it is actively recruiting Latino males—recent immigrants and citizens alike—who now make up about 10 percent of the armed forces, as a key source of America's future soldiers. Because military service is voluntary, young men in low-income groups are the most likely candidates for a dangerous yet relatively stable career. Minorities make up 34 percent of the military but only 25 percent of the population, a situation attributed to the fact that better job opportunities are not as plentiful for Americans who are not white.

The first U.S. soldier killed in combat during the 2003 invasion of Iraq, Lance Cpl. José Antonio Gutierrez, had once been an illegal immigrant: a Guatemalan orphan who eventually obtained legal residency and joined the Marines. The United States quickly awarded posthumous citizenship to Gutierrez and nine other new immigrants killed in the Iraq war—many of whom had been trying to become citizens but had been frustrated by bureaucracy. Within weeks of the first deaths in Iraq, Congress was trying to make amends, considering no fewer than five separate bills to make the citizenship process easier for America's roughly 37,000 green card soldiers. Even as members of Congress and editorialists praised the foreign-born soldiers who were risking their lives on behalf of America, it was painfully obvious that some Americans remained as ambivalent about them as they did about all immigrants. In Los Angeles, an

immigrant soldier returned from the war in Iraq only to find that his father had been deported and his mother was fighting to stay in the country.

The reaction of the family of one of the green card soldiers killed in the Iraq war illustrates the uneasy feelings immigrants have about a country that welcomes their service in war but has been reluctant to recognize their contributions in life. Marine Staff Sgt. Riayan Tejeda, born in the Dominican Republic, was killed in Baghdad on April 11, 2003, after eight years of military service. His family refused to request posthumous citizenship. An American passport would not bring him back to life, and what was citizenship worth in a country that requires the ultimate sacrifice before it will embrace those upon whom it depends?

Responding to effusive press coverage of the green card soldiers fighting in Iraq, Mark Krikorian, of the Center for Immigration Studies, implied that immigrant soldiers were mercenaries who had not "earned" the right to risk their lives for America. Craig Nelsen, founder of ProjectUSA (and a slew of other groups dedicated to restricting immigration), said that immigrant soldiers should not be able to "crash the gates" to U.S. citizenship. Such comments dismissed the military's long history of being a way for immigrants to earn American citizenship. From 1907 to 2001, some 672,906 immigrant soldiers became citizens. Immigrant soldiers have consistently shown tremendous courage: of the 3,405 Medals of Honor that have been awarded, 715 have gone to them. During World War II the government hastily administered the Oath of Allegiance to immigrants willing to fight and, in fact, required many Japanese Americans to serve in the military as a condition for release from wartime detention centers.

Military service by immigrants is about more than just proving loyalty; immigrants provide skills that are essential to our national security. Yet the disastrous state of this country's immigration system has made it harder than it should be to take advantage of those skills. Rafed al Janabi, an Iraqi refugee who came to the United States in 1995, is married to a U.S. Marine. He passed his citizenship exam in March 2003 and joined the U.S. Army shortly after the overthrow of Saddam Hussein, when he got word that it was looking for Arabic interpreters. He passed an FBI

security check and went to Iraq in October 2004, where, side by side with American-born soldiers, he faced gunfire and rockets. He found, however, that he would not be allowed to translate because he needed clearance for access to classified materials, which he could not get until he was a U.S. citizen. But before he could be naturalized, he needed an additional, routine, security check—even though he had already been cleared by the FBI, and even though, under U.S. immigration laws that stipulate that applicants should get answers within 120 days of passing their test, Janabi should have already gotten word on his citizenship status by September. With an acute shortage of translators, Janabi's case, and those of other urgently needed personnel, ought to have been moved to the top of the list of applications to be investigated. But that did not happen.

Time and again, America was making the same mistake: failing to value the skills that immigrants bring to this country, and failing to fix the systems that would allow us to use those skills to our benefit.

—8—

Lockout

Before 9/11, only 843 consular officers handled more than 8 million visa applications annually, allowing only a few minutes for each. In Beijing, for example, U.S. consular personnel handled more than 1,000 visa "interviews" every day; staff was so short that these interviews typically lasted less than a minute. Under such tight constraints, U.S. visa officials were already having trouble keeping up. After 9/11, their task became seemingly impossible. First, every single visa applicant now had to undergo a personal interview. Second, the new rules dramatically increased the number of visitors who would have to undergo security clearances, from about 1.5 percent of applicants to nearly 3 percent. This change was understandable, but it raised the distinct possibility that the greater danger no longer lay in the possibility that we would let in our enemies, but that we would be denying ourselves the benefit of the human assets who no longer could—or even wanted to—come to America as easily as they needed to. As Fareed Zakaria, editor of *Newsweek International*, put it, "Every visa officer today lives in fear that he will let in the next Mohamed Atta. As a result, he is probably keeping out the next Bill Gates."

In early spring 2002, the U.S. government began to require a security clearance before issuing a visa to any adult male from one of twenty-six predominantly Muslim countries. The sheer bureaucratic weight of the new program, called Visa Condor, immediately slowed the visa approval

process by months. The number of visas denied rose sharply. Although relatively little short-term business travel between the United States and the Middle East had been going on before Visa Condor went into effect, the new rules definitely hurt travel—and the potential economic benefits—between the United States and Malaysia and Indonesia, two Asian tiger economies.

In July 2002, another new rule mandated security clearances before visas could be issued to anyone involved in industries on a Technology Alert List—a listing of fields with implications for national security. The Department of Homeland Security had expanded the list to include such broad subjects whose connection to security is a stretch: architecture, community development, housing, planning, and urban design. Landscaping would be removed from the list in November 2002 as a concession to complaints. However, the entire list has since been made classified, since smart travelers were getting around the Technology Alert List by avoiding listing any of the suspect industries on their visa applications. Visa Mantis (as this sensitive-technology program is called) increased the volume of required security checks from 1,000 per year in 2000 to more than 20,000 in 2003. Compounding the problem, Visa Mantis security clearances originally were valid for only one year rather than for the student or scholar's entire appointment, and thus had to be done repeatedly, adding to the workload. (After considerable protest and lobbying, the period was extended in February 2005.) Around the time the logjam was at its worst, in November 2003, the average processing time for a Mantis case was about seventy-two days, though it since has been reduced to about two weeks.

Alone, the new rules would have wreaked havoc on the visa approval process. But they were only part of the problem. Even as the government was changing the rules of the game, it was overhauling the country's immigration bureaucracy as part of the much larger consolidation of intelligence and border operations. On March 1, 2003, the Immigration and Naturalization Service was abolished and its responsibilities transferred to three departments within the new Department of Homeland Security: Citizenship and Immigration Services, Immigration and Customs Enforcement, and Border and Transportation Security. It was not an auspi-

cious sign that the handover date was three months before the deadline for a detailed implementation plan to be created. Even as visa officials were dealing with a much heavier workload, they had to cope with adjusting to and navigating an entirely new set of hierarchies and relationships within the immigration bureaucracy.

In a 2004 report, the Government Accountability Office warned that U.S. diplomats around the world were deeply troubled that the delays were hurting student and scholarly exchanges as well as scientific cooperation. "During our field visits, Beijing's Deputy Chief of Mission and consular officials at the embassy and consulates in China stated that visa delays could have a negative impact on student and scholar exchanges. They told us that the lengthy waits to obtain a visa might lead Chinese students and scholars to pursue studies or research in countries where it is easier to obtain a visa," the GAO reported. "A consular chief in Chennai, India, agreed, saying that lengthy waits are also causing Indian students to decide to study in countries where it is easier to get a visa and, therefore, the United States could lose out on intellectual knowledge these visa applicants bring to our country. Further, embassy officials in Beijing reported that visa delays in nonproliferation cooperation and scientific exchange could have enormous and lasting consequences."

As word spread of the tougher visa rules, facts bore out the diplomats' warnings: fewer people applied for business and student visas to the United States. Business applications, the hardest hit, fell from over 6 million in fiscal year (FY) 2000 to 2.7 million in FY2003. At the same time, more of those who applied were rejected: for business visas, the rate went from 28.1 percent in FY2000 to 31.7 percent in FY2003, and student visa rejections rose from 20.5 percent to 25.3 percent in the same period. As a result, the total number of nonimmigrant (temporary) visas issued fell from 7.6 million in FY2001 to just 4.9 million in FY2003, a 36 percent drop.

The nation's business and education leaders have been watching these numbers with alarm. Almost immediately, applications of foreign students to American universities fell dramatically because it became so difficult to get visas. Universities blame the application drop-off on tighter visa rules, on the growing success of countries working to make themselves more

attractive alternatives to the United States, and—most worrisome cause of all—on foreign students' no longer seeing the United States as a place where they are welcome to study or work.

"Far too many scarce resources are wasted on routine reviews of low-risk visa applications," Marlene M. Johnson, executive director of NAFSA: Association of International Educators, told the U.S. Senate Foreign Relations Committee in October 2004. "This particularly affects scientists, and people from Arab and Muslim countries; both of these populations are subjected indiscriminately to special reviews. Repetitive, redundant reviews, particularly of well known people, clog the system, frustrate applicants, and detract from our ability to focus attention where it is really needed."

The tighter visa rules dramatically affected foreign-born scholars, scientists, and doctors as well as the more than 600,000 foreign students and more than 100,000 exchange program participants who come to the United States. With a shrewd eye on implications for the supply of skilled graduates in science and engineering a few years down the road, business associations in industries from manufacturing to high-tech to services warned that their members were gravely worried about the impact on education. More immediately, they were up in arms over the way the new rules made it harder for their customers, partners, and global employees to come in and out of the United States. Businesses count losses in the tens of billions of dollars when they cannot get key clients, staff, and business partners into this country—even as other countries have become more competitive in luring business and talent. For their part, educators pointed out that foreign students contributed $13 billion to the education industry, the nation's fifth-largest service industry sector.

"If action is not taken soon to improve the visa system, the misperception that the United States does not welcome international students, scholars, and scientists will grow, and they may not make our nation their destination of choice now and in the future," the heads of twenty-five of America's leading educational institutions, including the National Academy of Sciences, the National Academy of Engineering, and

the Institute of Medicine, warned in a public statement in May 2004. "The damage to our nation's higher education and scientific enterprises, economy, and national security would be irreparable."

～•〜

In October 2002, Javad Mostaghimi, a leading scholar in thermal spray and plasma processing at the University of Toronto and author of more than 100 scholarly papers, accepted an invitation to chair a workshop at the U.S. National Science Foundation. Mostaghimi had been born in Iran but had been a Canadian citizen for nearly two decades. He still had fond memories of his time in the United States, where he had earned his PhD in mechanical engineering from the University of Minnesota in 1982. When he arrived at the airport on the way to the NSF conference, however, he was ushered into a private room for questioning: When had he last been in Iran? What had he done there? The official who was processing his paperwork then informed him that he had to be fingerprinted and photographed. Iran was one of twenty-five countries listed under the National Security Entry-Exit Registration System (NSEERS), which applied special security procedures to anyone born in those countries even if they had since been naturalized to another citizenship. Under NSEERS, Mostaghimi now was required to be fingerprinted, photographed, and questioned each time he tried to enter the United States. He declined, drove home, and refused to return to the United States until the country resumed treating visitors like him with respect instead of acting like they are criminals. Mostaghimi called Canada's minister of foreign affairs to ask him to issue a travel advisory. He also called University of Toronto President Robert Birgeneau, who in turn alerted the American Council on Education. In this case, there was a somewhat happy ending: the United States promised that Canadian citizens' birth countries no longer would trigger NSEERS procedures automatically.

Because four of the 9/11 terrorists had entered the United States on student visas, there was tremendous pressure to keep track of whether foreign students complied with the terms of their visas—mainly, whether

they enrolled and remained in good standing at the schools that sponsored their visas. On January 1, 2003, U.S. schools that hosted foreign students were required to participate in the Student Exchange Visitor Information System (SEVIS), a new electronic system that allowed the government to monitor foreign students, exchange visitors, and their dependents. The new system included a certification program for ascertaining whether or not a school did what it claimed to do. The system allowed consular officials to check whether a student applying for a visa had in fact been accepted to a school. Once the student arrived in the United States, SEVIS would alert the government if the student failed to show up for class. Preventing abuse of student visas was, in principle, a sensible idea. But the system that initially emerged did not do that. An arbitrary, unrealistic timetable was set for getting the system up and running before the administering agency was ready. Because of the rush, the software running SEVIS still had bugs when the program went into effect. At first, the State Department could not access the data, so consuls could not issue visas. Help Desk staff often were poorly trained and as a result gave wrong information. In one case, a Help Desk employee told the user that she did not need to sign a student's I-20 certificate of student eligibility; when the student showed up at the port of entry, the student found out the hard way that the signature *was* required. Many students had trouble paying the fee because only checks and credit cards were accepted as payment. Transcription errors could send a student into limbo, like one who was denied a visa because his birth date on a hard-copy form did not match the automated record. For tens of thousands of students, it was a nightmare. Students dreaded that they would fall out of compliance through absolutely no fault of their own and face the prospect of deportation or denial of entry.

"Backlogs and protracted delays in correcting the data mean that SEVIS maintains incorrect records for months at a time in some instances," Lawrence Bell, director of international education at the University of Colorado's Boulder campus, told Congress. "Changes in plans (for example, a student who was to return home after graduation decides

to stay and enter a PhD program instead) or minor issues (for example, an incorrect notice to an international student advisor that a student has dropped below a full course load) can precipitate a months-long process to correct a SEVIS record." Universities were not allowed to correct the errors but instead had to refer the changes to immigration authorities. Students on exchange programs faced even worse problems if their information was entered correctly. To fix it, ICE had to send their information back to the State Department for a new decision, which can take a year or more. Students whose SEVIS authorization is terminated because of bureaucratic error must reapply, paying an extra fee even though they had done nothing wrong.

SEVIS produces about 1,000 alerts each week. From the beginning of 2003 through the beginning of 2005, more than 81,000 students were tagged as potential violators. Of these, 3,700 merited further investigation, and officials arrested 641 people, some of whom had been identified as potential threats after they arrived here. A Pakistani national, arrested for failure to enroll, turned out to the subject of a terrorist database record entered after he arrived in the United States. A Saudi man failed to maintain his student status and later attempted to smuggle a 500,000-volt stun gun onto a commercial airplane; he since has been deported. The number of successes, however, was small compared with the damage done.

From 2002 to 2003, the Institute of International Education reported that new foreign student enrollments declined in 46 percent of American universities. International student enrollments in the United Kingdom, by contrast, rose 23 percent from 2002 to 2003; in Canada they rose by more than 15 percent, and in Australia by more than 10 percent.

The Council of Graduate Schools reported that international applications in the fall of 2003 for admission the following year fell 28 percent. In the fall of 2004, total foreign graduate student enrollments in the United States dropped by 18 percent, the first such decrease in a generation, as U.S. citizen enrollments fell by only 5 percent. The largest drop was in applications from China, down by 45 percent, and India, down 28 percent from 2003. Applications filed for fall 2005 slid by another 5 percent.

"The largest impact has been on master's and on smaller PhD departments," Michael Neuschatz, who has studied the issue at the American Institute of Physics, told me. "The larger departments also tend to be the most prestigious; they have many, many people applying and are able to have their pick. When they have problems getting any one individual into the country, they have no problem making a switch. They also are more likely to have lawyers, resources, and experience getting problems solved." In 2003, 20 percent of foreign graduate students accepted into physics programs were significantly delayed or could not attend at all because of visa problems. As a result, two-thirds of doctoral programs and nearly half of master's programs told the American Institute of Physics that some of the students they accepted in 2002 could not attend because they had trouble getting visas. In some cases, they had to appoint undergraduates as teaching assistants, cancel classes, and run other classes with no teaching assistance.

Senior scholars also have been delayed, jeopardizing long-term international collaborations, including in research on astronomy, treatments for AIDS and diabetes, and a vaccine against the West Nile virus. The Fermilab National Accelerator Laboratory, which employs scientists from eighteen different countries, had such trouble with visa-related project delays that it wrote desperate letters to then Secretary of State Colin Powell and Energy Secretary Spencer Abraham.

Even when students and scholars got into the United States, they faced daunting obstacles if they wanted to leave—either for scholarly conferences or to visit family members—and come back again. The University of Maryland at College Park reported the travails of a couple in the agricultural economics department, of Colombian and Danish nationalities, who got stuck in Bogotá, Colombia, when they went home for Christmas vacation with the husband's family; it was a month into the spring semester before they could return to their studies. Stories like this are legion in the long list of scholars trapped by the new visa regime. Li-jun Zhu, a physics graduate student, returned to China in 2002 to get married. It took more than two months to get return visas so he could complete his doctoral studies at Rice University. University of Utah

physicist Xiaomei Jiang returned to China for the funeral after her parents both died in a traffic accident, but when she tried to return was refused reentry to the United States for nine months, forcing her to redo experiments and delaying her completion of her dissertation. Yang Wang, a 26-year-old Stanford civil engineering doctoral student, frustrated at being stuck in China for ten months after visiting his parents in December 2002, started a chat room for students facing similar problems. Such chat rooms have mushroomed, many hosting two to three hundred thwarted visa applicants online at once.

Late in 2003, U.S. visa officials delayed processing the applications of two Chinese-born environmental toxicology graduate students, both from the University of Toronto, for so long that they were unable to attend a Society of Environmental Toxicology and Chemistry meeting where they had been invited to present papers. Not only did Hang Xiao and Yushan Su lose the professional opportunity, they lost the $750 they had spent in registration and travel costs.

In the wake of incidents like these, the hesitance of scholars and students, combined with educational and research institutions' embarrassment at the treatment of their guests, means that more and more, conferences involving foreign scholars will move outside the United States. This will detract immeasurably from America's role as a hub for learning and the free exchange of ideas.

"Is this a temporary blip, or the beginning of a longer-term trend?" asks Lawrence Bell, of the University of Colorado. "Of course, we won't know for some years. But that doesn't mean we do nothing until definitive data are in. No business that ignores signs that it's losing its market until it has definitively lost its market will be in business very long."

In fact, we already may have been ignoring for too long signs that the United States is losing its competitive edge as the world's premier destination for students and scholars. According to National Science Foundation data, the number of foreign doctoral students from China, India, and Taiwan studying in the United States began to drop after peaking in the mid-1990s and has shown no signs of recovering. By the end of the decade, doctoral students were already beginning to turn to other nations to study

science and technology. In other words, the post-9/11 visa problems only made an existing problem worse.

❧

In a small room at the Johns Hopkins School of Medicine in Baltimore, giant incubators gently shake carefully prepared yeast cultures, ensuring that the fragile protein cells do not settle to the bottom of the dishes and clump together. Professor Heng Zhu is almost paternal about these cells, which are so small that each dish holds ten to the ninth or tenth power—that is, as many as a trillion times a million cells. As tiny as they are, these cells hold the key to understanding human illnesses and, hopefully, to helping cure them.

While still a postdoctoral fellow at Yale, Professor Zhu helped develop a new procedure for mapping how well proteins respond to various stimuli. Because yeast proteins are so similar to human proteins, the technique holds promise for screening drug compounds to see how well they turn genes "on" or "off," thus determining how effective a drug is likely to be.

Researchers formerly had to painstakingly analyze fusion proteins in small experiments—a daunting task when you consider that the lowly yeast cell has more than 6,000 protein strains. But Zhu's high-throughput analysis technique, which isolates proteins from genes and mounts them on glass slides, called proteomic chips, allows researchers to simultaneously measure hundreds of protein samples at a time. "Using these chips, we can process two thousand strains per day," says Zhu, who is a rising star in the new field of proteomics—the genetic mapping of proteins. The chips were created by a robot in another room nearby, kept chilly enough that researchers must wear jackets if they spend much time working there.

The process involves pouring a silicone elastomer over micromachined molds; it then is cured, peeled away, and mounted on a glass slide. The proteins to be analyzed are attached to the wells and incubated, then are washed and then exposed to X-ray film and a phospho-

imager. Computers then analyze how reactive the protein kinases are. As this technique is honed, it will allow researchers to analyze several thousand up to millions of samples at a time.

Professor Zhu welcomed me one morning to his windowed office in the bright, spanking new Broadway Research Building with an apology: despite our appointment, he would have to excuse himself briefly at 10:30 A.M. to interview a prospective graduate student, a last-minute task that comes with being junior faculty. A tiny man in glasses and a cheerful yellow polo shirt, Heng Zhu has seemingly boundless energy. Over surprisingly good coffee in the light-filled cafeteria, he told me of the nightmare from which he had only recently emerged. This Kafka-esque visa tale sidelined important research and nearly prevented him from coming here.

After finishing his doctorate at Clemson University in 1999, Zhu went to Yale to map 6,400 genes in the yeast genome, a task intended to help researchers understand how disease-causing pathogens bind to proteins and thus how to isolate human proteins to make drug testing more efficient and effective. The study was so groundbreaking that after the results were published in November 2000, the National Institutes of Health awarded Yale a large grant to build on the research. Amid the breathtaking progress the team was making, Zhu, in a classic absent-minded professorism, realized in the spring of 2002 that he had forgotten to file paperwork related to his work visa. To clear up his status, he had to return to Beijing instead of simply applying from the United States. At first, the U.S. consulate in Beijing told him that his visa would be ready in two weeks. When he came back to pick it up, they instead requested more information about his career plans and sent the application into limbo.

During his first visit to the consulate, he had met with a vice consul. When he went back two weeks later as instructed, he only saw a secretary, who told him the visa wouldn't be ready. Maybe it would be another two weeks, she said, or maybe two months. It was about two weeks later when he really started to worry. All he could do was sit by the phone and wait, because he could not get back into the consulate without notification

that his visa was ready. A Chinese friend who had become an American citizen and could use his passport to get into the consulate went and tried to get answers for Zhu, but to no avail.

Ten months later, Zhu was still waiting in Beijing, and his paychecks from the Damon Runyon Cancer Research Foundation fellowship that supported him had stopped. He had missed several job interviews, including one at Harvard Medical School and one at the University of Rochester. Because his income had ceased, his car was repossessed, and he lost his apartment. "My friend packed everything and even had a yard sale," he recalled.

Yale officials pleaded his case to the State Department, but without luck. He waited in frustration for a year, during which time work on the $1.5 million project he was part of slowed dramatically because of his absence. A *Wall Street Journal* article drew attention to his plight, but he still had to wait two more months before he was able to return to his desk at Yale.

"When I finally got the visa, I had very mixed feelings. I was happy but sad too. I had lost everything—my apartment, my car," Zhu told me. "My research got stopped for a year. I would have accomplished so much more if this hadn't happened."

When he returned to the United States on April 23, 2003, he was being courted by universities in Canada and Germany as well as by Johns Hopkins, the most prestigious medical research center in the United States—indeed, in the world. The offers from Canada and Germany were very tempting, and all the more so because he and his fiancée would not have to worry about visa troubles. After all, meeting Annie Gao, who did public relations work for a telecommunications company in China, had been the silver lining of his unplanned stay in Beijing.

The University of Toronto's yeast research program boasted some of the leading scientists in the field. It was a very friendly and welcoming environment. When he and Annie visited the European Molecular Biology Lab at Heidelberg, the small but beautiful campus was very appealing, as was the top-notch student body and the center's generous funding and reputation for nurturing young scientists.

Johns Hopkins was offering a tenure-track faculty position that was hard to ignore. Still, he was reluctant to accept the offer before his fiancée saw Baltimore and decided that she could live there. And once again, visa trouble got in the way: the U.S. Embassy in Beijing refused to grant her a tourist visa to visit Baltimore. This only heightened her existing fears about going to the United States. "She was very worried about the problems visiting family and going home if she needed to," Zhu recalls. The co-head of the Johns Hopkins program, Min Li, flew to Shanghai—on a mission so important that even the SARS outbreak going on at the time did not deter him—to talk Annie into coming to Baltimore. She flew to Shanghai to meet him because SARS had made Beijing unsafe to visit at the time.

Although she could not come to the United States on a tourist visa, she would be able to enter on a spousal visa. Given the nightmare that visa red tape posed, however, the couple faced the risk that even once they were married, it would take a long time for her to be able to join him. "It was a bit risky," he says, with characteristic understatement. Nonetheless, in July 2003, with her assent, he decided to take the Johns Hopkins job, flew to the United States for the first semester, and then flew back to China. In December, he was married, and in March 2004, he returned to the United States with Annie, who now had an H-4 spousal visa.

Why, despite the way the United States had treated him, did he still choose to come here? His decision came down to the combination of funds, the opportunity to work with the world's very best people in a collegial environment, and the reputation of the Johns Hopkins medical research complex. "This is the best place to do science. Johns Hopkins is absolutely the number one hospital in the U.S., and probably the world," Zhu says.

Although Heng Zhu's story has a happy ending, his career—and the benefit to the United States of his work here—remains overshadowed by the frustrations of U.S. visa law. And the financial troubles caused by the visa delay continue to dog him, both personally and professionally. "My credit is very bad because of the situation," he says. "I thought about filing

for bankruptcy, but decided not to. Instead I got a settlement with my credit card company." That will be on his credit record for seven years, but a bankruptcy would have set him back ten years. "If I want to buy a house, forget it." The U.S. visa morass has also undermined his professional development by compromising his ability to share research insights and bounce ideas off of other leading scientists. Because he doesn't dare leave the country again, he's had to miss several important conferences held abroad: in Italy, Prague, London, and Japan.

We cannot just assume that America's promise will be enough to keep scholars like Heng Zhu in this country. Although many of the world's best and brightest have decided to take their chances and come here, many more have all but given up on America—and the rest of the world has by no means failed to notice. China is actively recruiting Chinese scholars in this country, and finding more and more takers. For every one of the world's best and brightest who stays in America, many others go back. Zhu himself immediately offers two examples without even having to think about it. One friend got his PhD and went into business in information technology with help from venture capital provided by the Chinese government. The friend who packed up Zhu's apartment for him when he was evicted while he was stuck in China did not stay here; she took her PhD in genetics to a job in Shanghai with Boston Consulting Group.

～•～

The impact on scholars and scientists is not just felt within the ivory tower or the corporate boardroom. There is also a very real human cost in the health fields that depend on a steady supply of new researchers and practitioners rising through the university ranks.

According to the U.S. Department of Health and Human Services, America faces a shortage of around 20,000 physicians. Although such shortages have dogged American health care for years, they have been worsened by visa policies that unnecessarily delay doctors' entry into this country and throw a monkey wrench into the professional lives of

those who are already here but need new visas. In 2003, for example, the UCLA medical center had to wait seven months for the visa of Faiz Bhora, a Pakistani doctor—one of the hospital's only three pediatric heart surgeons—who had just completed ten years of medical training in the United States. A rule change mandated by Congress in July 2004 means that far more doctors and scientists will face similar delays. No longer will foreign-born high-skilled professionals (those on H, L, or O visas) be allowed to have their visas reissued while they are in the United States. They now must undertake expensive and inconvenient travel to apply for new visas at U.S. consulates outside of the country.

The supply of nurses is particularly vulnerable to capricious visa policies. Late in 2004, the U.S. government decided to stop issuing "fast-track" work permits for workers from the Philippines, India, and China, which had become backlogged because of high demand that exceeded quotas for those countries. The result? At a time when the United States faces shortages of 275,000 to 300,000 nurses, those from the Philippines—by far the biggest supplier of nursing personnel—now will have to wait roughly three years to obtain green cards. In the past, hospitals could get work permits for foreign nurses in 18 to 24 months, and in 60 to 90 days for nurses already in the United States.

The visa restrictions have been hard on rural and small town health facilities, which are desperate for health personnel, and on low-income populations. Recognizing the need to attract physicians to these areas, the United States in the past had waived the educational exchange (J-1) visa requirement that foreign graduates return to their home country for two years before applying for a temporary work visa or a green card. Foreign-born graduates of our medical schools were permitted to remain in the United States after their residency training, on the condition that they work in communities where physician shortages are particularly severe. In September 1999, more than 2,000 of these international medical graduates provided care for more than 4 million Americans, many of whom would not otherwise have received medical services. At the time their extended stay here was approved, they had already spent three years undergoing postgraduate medical training in this country without causing

trouble; they had sworn to an ethical code in a field that made them unlikely to be terrorist threats; and there was a clear need for them in underserved American communities. But after 9/11, these physicians fell under the intensified scrutiny given to all visa holders and applicants. Then in April 2002, the U.S. Department of Agriculture, which had participated in obtaining these visas, pulled out of the program under pressure from what then was the Immigration and Nationalization Service. Four million of the Americans most in need of health care lost out.

Just one example of the result of this policy change was the plight of a small-town behavioral health center that had expected to hire a Jordanian psychiatrist who had completed his residency training in the United States. Under the revised rules, however, instead of beginning work at the center, the psychiatrist had to return to his home country for two years. His employer, desperate for psychiatrists willing to work in the small-town locale, was able to get the requirement waived after a one-year review, a period during which the psychiatrist waited in Jordan and the State Department conducted a database security check. When the waiver was finally cleared, the psychiatrist was told that he needed yet another security check—which took another year. In 2003, the Department of Health and Human Services stepped in to issue waivers again, but damage had already been done to the communities that could least afford it.

❧

The July 2002 Technology Alert List guidelines wreaked havoc not only on U.S. higher education but also on business. The new rules required security checks on anyone working in certain science and engineering industries, creating a nightmare for major projects and exports and pushing some firms into bankruptcy.

"Very quickly, the system backed up," says Ed Rice, who heads the Coalition for Employment Through Exports, a trade group that has worked to make visa policies more sane. "The first thing U.S. industry found out was that their business partners could not get into the country,

their customers could not get into the country, and even their own employees—if they were foreign nationals—could not get into the country." The backlog had risen to 100,000 applications, and the average processing time shot up to four months.

After the United States began requiring security clearances for adult males from Middle Eastern countries in the spring of 2002, a large U.S.-based engineering construction firm had to find new ways to continue a project in the Middle East, which it was doing as a joint venture—a frequent requirement of doing business abroad—with a Middle Eastern company. As you would expect in a project of considerable size and complexity, engineers from the Middle Eastern partner company had been traveling to the United States almost monthly to meet with the rest of the project team. When the new rules went into effect, the engineers arrived at the airport only to be told that they now needed a new security clearance *every single time* they wanted to travel to the United States. Needless to say, this would have ground the entire project to a halt. The monthly meetings were moved to London. The U.S. staff now had to spend time and money on travel, and U.S. hotels, restaurants, rental car companies, and stores lost a regular source of income.

The worst off were those who got caught abroad when the rules changed. An Indian national who had worked for years for a U.S.-based diversified technology company and was a permanent U.S. resident, went home to visit family. While he was abroad, the Technology Alert rule was expanded to include India. As he was on his way back to America (or so he thought), airline officials at the Hong Kong airport told him that even though his papers were valid, the United States would not let him back in. Many countries doing business in Southeast Asia and China faced similar problems; increasingly, they moved their meetings to Vancouver.

Even as they coped, however, businesses and trade groups quietly began lobbying their elected officials and documenting the massive impact the rules were having on American competitiveness. Eight major U.S. business groups reported in June 2004 that U.S. businesses had lost more than $30 billion because of visa delays. This finally got the government's attention. Not only did it validate the anecdotes that so many businesses had

been sharing among themselves, but it did so on the basis of a very conservative estimate, which probably understates the real cost considerably. For instance, if the estimate had included trade in services as well as trade in goods, it would have reached $65.15 billion. In addition, for some of the biggest companies in the survey, it was prohibitively complicated to estimate a specific cost, so they just reported zero.

Companies on the verge of signing major export contracts could not complete them because the prospective buyers could not get visas to inspect the goods. Foreign workers, particularly from India and China, were denied work visas in sensitive industries like biochemicals or robotics. "In fact, our report shows that the losses resulting from visa delays go well beyond lost revenues, with the unexplained and arbitrary denials escalating to cost U.S. companies much more," the report warned. "Key contracts and projects will go elsewhere; U.S. companies will increasingly move research and other facilities overseas; and, perhaps most troubling for the American entrepreneur, U.S. small businesses will pull back from international business development for fear that visa red tape will pose unmanageable obstacles." Eighty-four of 141 companies surveyed, or 60 percent, reported they had suffered a "material impact" from business travel visa processing delays. Seven of ten could not bring their own foreign employees to the United States; two-thirds had to postpone projects; half could not get their business partners or foreign customers into the United States for product inspections or training; and 43 percent felt that their company's reputation had been damaged with foreign customers or business partners.

The study looked only at short-term costs. Even more worrisome are the longer-term implications. "Every time you lose an export sale to a foreign competitor, the employment that would go with that export is lost with it," says Ed Rice. "Visa issues have contributed to the worsening trade deficit with China, and has also caused problems with Russia and India. They also have contributed to the negative impression that people overseas have of the United States." Because foreign customers tend to be repeat customers once they have established a business relationship, one lost sale can mean many times more in lost future business.

"Once a foreign business establishes a relationship with a U.S. company, they tend to come back," Rice says. "But if that tendency is impeded, they are likely to go to a new supplier—and that's who they're going to go back to the next time. Our companies understand this, which is why they get so upset when they lose a customer. They're looking at the longer-term relationship."

Yan Tianen, the general manager of a Chinese aerospace company, applied in Shanghai for a visa to come to the United States to purchase nearly $250 million worth of parts and equipment from U.S. suppliers. After many delays, he finally got the visa, with the help of a letter from Honeywell Aerospace vouching for the purpose of his trip. Unfortunately, U.S. law requires that a passport be valid for six months after the visa's expiration date. Because his visa had taken so long to come through, the passport no longer met this minimum when he arrived at U.S. immigration in Los Angeles. Officials separated Yan from his colleagues, detained him, and forcibly repatriated him less than 24 hours later. Not surprisingly, Yan took his business elsewhere—in this case, to France.

To be sure, the United States had clear authority to deny entry to someone whose documents did not meet requirements, and the airline should have caught the problem before he got on the plane. Yet in cases like these—a business traveler with a round-trip ticket whose documents would not have had problems had it not been for a delay that was not his fault—the system should have been flexible enough to avoid such a humiliating and ultimately costly confrontation.

A quarter billion dollars is no small change, but in the end Honeywell's loss was confined to one large order, a possible future employee, and possible future business. For smaller companies, their very existence is at risk. Without deep pockets of working capital or access to financing like Honeywell enjoyed, small and medium-sized companies often are one deal away from sinking or swimming. They do not have divisions in other countries that they can use to bring employees here on L-1 visas for transfers of foreign workers who have been with a firm for at least a year. Nor do they have armies of high-priced lawyers and lobbyists. Because contracts typically include clauses that make purchases contingent on clients'

ability to travel to the United States for design and drawing reviews or other inspections, visa bottlenecks can—and do—result in canceled contracts, which often make the difference between survival and collapse for small and medium-sized firms.

One clear example of how this plays out is the U.S. machine tool industry. As manufacturing left the United States for cheaper foreign locations in the late 1990s and U.S. factories closed, the machine tool industry shrunk by nearly two-thirds. The one bright spot was exports, which made up 30 percent of U.S. machine tool sales by 2002. This is not surprising: after all, America's long-standing expertise in engineering and machinery puts us at a competitive advantage. Exporting sophisticated machinery— "capital goods" in economist-speak—ought to be one of the biggest areas in which American businesses stand to benefit from global growth. China's demand for machine tools, for example, more than tripled between 1998 and 2004, to over $10 billion—just over twice the size of the total U.S. market. Yet U.S. machine tool manufacturers have had more trouble than they should in taking advantage of a growing world market. To be sure, Chinese trade restrictions and cheap currency hurt; but a big part of the problem was homemade: visa delays for security-related and export-control reasons. As a result, visa red tape has gotten in the way and threatens to drive into the ground an industry whose future depends on its ability to transform itself into one driven by exports.

"Long delays and increased denials for technology-control purposes caused substantial competitiveness problems for a number of U.S. industry sectors, but it was particularly acute for the machine tool industry," Dr. Paul Freedenberg, of the Association for Manufacturing Technology (AMT), told the U.S.-China Economic and Security Review Commission, a body appointed by the U.S. Senate, in June 2005. "The inability to secure U.S. visas for overseas customers on a timely basis directly contributed to loss of sales, shifts of sourcing to foreign competitors, and reduced business opportunities for AMT member companies. Indeed, in company after company that I visited during a recent trip to China, the difficulty in obtaining a business visa was cited by managers as a potential reason for not buying our members' products," he said.

Not long after 9/11, the Rockford, Illinois–based Ingersoll Milling Machine Company was struggling but still had hopes of surviving long enough to turn its business around. Ingersoll, like other machine tool makers, depended on exports for its very survival. A major Chinese company wanted its products and was prepared to enter into a multi-million-dollar contract that would have given Ingersoll a future. Because of post-9/11 visa delays, however, its potential client's representatives were having trouble getting into the United States to inspect the goods. Ingersoll's reputation was good enough that the Chinese firm was willing to be patient. But after seven months, it gave up. Ingersoll lost the contract and had to file for bankruptcy. The company is still in existence—though much downsized and now called Ingersoll Machine Tools—only because it was bought by Italy's Camozzi Group. It is no longer an "American" company, because of ill-conceived efforts to "protect" America.

Kanawha Scales and Systems, Inc., a firm with 200 employees, sells specialized weighing and control systems, including high-speed train load-out systems. Its export business, which included $22 million to China between 1991 and 2003, helped justify a 9,000-square-foot expansion that supports eight to twelve jobs. But Kanawha has had to adjust its sales projections because of difficulties getting visas for potential customers and overseas support personnel. Twice, it attempted to bring one of its foreign engineers to its home base in Poca, West Virginia, for technical training to support the equipment it sold in China. The engineer's first visa application was rejected outright as an "immigration threat." Kanawha tried again, seeking the advice of the U.S. Commercial Office in Beijing, sending a letter outlining the purpose of the trip and the length of the visit. The engineer presented documents to show his savings and checking accounts, home ownership, and family ties. The consular officer did not even look at the papers; thirty seconds, denied.

Another small West Virginia firm, Preiser Scientific, lost virtually all of its Chinese sales of lab equipment because it could not get visas for clients, including the supervisor of the coal quality lab for one of China's largest coal companies, who tried three times and was turned back at the window three times without even being granted an interview. A German

competitor had no trouble taking the business, by then ripe for the picking. Moore Nanotechnology Systems, based in Connecticut, had a $500,000 contract—worth 10 percent of its annual revenue—canceled five months after it was signed because its client, a Chinese university, could not get a U.S. visa for one of the professors who would use the machine.

One U.S. technology company had gotten so far as to sell its equipment to a Chinese company whose check had cleared; all the client needed was to send key personnel to the United States to be trained to use the equipment that their firm had already purchased. To accommodate the booming Asian market, the U.S. company set up a training facility in Japan. Many firms, like this one, found ways to do business, often in other countries. Although this typically involves a higher cost to the company and a loss of business for other U.S. firms, more and more companies are throwing up their hands and outsourcing work to other countries or simply moving entire facilities abroad. Most small and medium-sized businesses, however, can't afford to move their research labs and factories offshore, so they are the ones hurt hardest.

In fact, many of these small businesses do not have big enough budgets or staff to travel to every single potential customer. They rely on their customers to come to their booths at trade shows. But security backlogs have hit those too. Companies attending a big annual midwestern machine tools conference have reported that they have lost sales because many potential major customers could not get visas in time. Organizers of major international conference centers have had to dedicate staff to provide visa help and advice. They now typically ask potential attendees to register four months in advance to request an International Attendance Letter and to apply for visas three months in advance.

The International Consumer Electronics Show attracts over 100,000 people every year to the Las Vegas Convention Center for the introduction of thousands of new products and technologies. Show officials estimated that they lost more than 5,000 potential foreign visitors in January 2004 because they could not get visas; overall, just under six out of ten foreign registrants reported trouble getting visas. The Consumer Electronics Association responded with an international marketing campaign and

urged foreigners to apply earlier, which helped foreign attendance at its 2005 conference. So did a 27 percent overall increase in attendance, which is testament to the growing importance of the electronics sector in the U.S. and world economies. This is not a sector that we should cripple.

Trade shows are not the only events suffering from the impact of our border-control bureaucracy. Visa problems have affected the entire travel and conference industry, which brings $80 billion each year from 42 million visitors to this country—tourists, entrepreneurs, patients at our leading medical centers, and students. Just a 5 percent drop represents $4 billion, or roughly the annual economic output of a midsized state economy like North Carolina's, Maine's, or New Mexico's.

Anticipating the new biometric passport requirements scheduled to go into effect in 2005, the London-based trade publication *Conference and Incentive Travel* warned tour operators against taking groups to the United States after the rules take effect. Because there was no chance that British passports would meet the new standard—and U.S. officials knew that it was impossible but declined to set a realistic deadline—British travelers, who formerly did not need visas, would have to apply, pay a fee of about $120, and wait and hope for the best. "We have the prospect of three-hour check-ins, armed sky marshals and at least an hour waiting to get through immigration in the U.S.," the publication warned. "It is going to be a determined group that will go to the U.S. for a three-night incentive; agencies will almost certainly direct their clients away from a destination where the hurdles become disproportionate to the rewards." The biometrics requirements made sense as a way to help keep out impostors. Yet the politically motivated rush to get them into use on an unrealistically short schedule had created unnecessary friction—one more instance of emotion taking precedence over common sense.

New York City had hoped to host the 2004 World Indoor Track and Field Championships, but the visa hurdles made it impossible. The competition was held in Budapest, Hungary. New York lost 4,000 to 8,000 visitors and between $5.75 million and $11.5 million in revenue. The Amway network of independent business owners chose Japan over Los Angeles and Hawaii for its 2004 convention for 8,000 South Korean distributors.

In 2003, visa delays forced the U.S. National Academy of Sciences to postpone the biannual Chinese-American Frontiers of Science meeting it normally hosted for the most promising young scientists. The International Astronomical Union will hold its general assembly in Brazil in 2009, instead of Hawaii. Although perhaps not as lucrative in measurable terms as commercial or sporting events, the knowledge that will be exchanged at these events is, as MasterCard might put it, priceless.

Even as conferences formerly held in the United States move to Brazil, travel by Brazilians to the United States has fallen by 45 percent. This happened during a period when the Brazilian currency was strengthening, which normally would send droves of Brazilians to the United States and flood Bloomingdale's with avid shoppers.

⌣•⌣

Perhaps the greatest blow—although also the hardest to measure—is to the entrepreneurial spirit that has been the single biggest driver of America's success, and which so often is the essence of the immigrant experience. This sense of freedom and purpose draws people to the United States to achieve things they would not have been able to do in their countries of birth, and it provides a constant source of renewal of the American economy and of our work ethic.

Rajiv Khanna, a Punjabi-born lawyer whose Arlington, Virginia–based law firm employs around forty people, both American and foreign-born, points out the paradox of America. This is a country that relies on foreign-born talent and has done a tremendous job of welcoming many of them, yet having a competent immigration system is not a priority. "Nowhere have I felt a sense of integration more than here," Khanna says. Yet he is intensely frustrated with the U.S. immigration regime, which relies heavily on independent contractors who give incorrect information, relies on a patchwork of interest-driven laws instead of a clear and consistent policy, promotes illegal immigration through frequent amnesties, and is so capricious and arbitrary that companies frequently must resort to lobbying

members of Congress. For him, the post-9/11 backlogs are only part of a much bigger problem with how immigration works in America.

Khanna represents the plaintiffs in *ImmigrationPortal.com et al. v. Tom Ridge et al.*, a class-action lawsuit challenging the unreasonable delays in the processing of Employment-Based Adjustment of Status applications pending at the U.S. Citizenship and Immigration Services (USCIS) as well as the USCIS policy of requiring repeated applications for issuance of Employment Authorization and Advance Parole and for repeated fingerprinting. (In May 2005, a judge denied class action status.)

"If you are getting all of this intellectual treasure, at the expense of other countries, why wouldn't you want to use it?" Khanna asked. He takes issue with the all-too-common view that businesses' and workers' interests in immigration are at odds. It's far better for American workers if companies know they can find the talent they need to get jobs done. Companies that cannot fill positions quickly risk losing business, which affects many jobs in addition to whatever post they hope to fill with a foreign-born skilled worker. "If you want to protect your labor, you have to protect your business. They're not mutually exclusive."

I wanted to know more about the kind of companies and workers that were being affected by our immigration laws, so Khanna suggested that I post a request for stories on ImmigrationPortal.com, the Web site hosted by his firm. As soon as I posted my request, e-mails began pouring in from all over the country, from Irish, Australian, English, Pakistani, Indian, and Chinese workers in various stages of despair over the limbo into which America's broken immigration system had placed them. Like the plaintiffs in the ImmigrationPortal.com suit—a bioinformatics engineer, an operations research professional, an orthodontist, a chemist, software engineers, an accountant, a technical writer—they stated that they were hardworking professionals who were following all the proper legal avenues yet were unable to make any plans into the future because of the interminable delays in processing their paperwork. Many had invested money in businesses that employed American workers, creating good U.S. jobs out of innovation and sweat equity.

A 38-year-old Indian entrepreneur put his U.S. MBA to work in setting up an office here for his family's business. When he was just 23 years old, he turned his family's investment of $500,000 into a forty-employee company with sales of $3 million, over the course of five years. "My parents never wanted me to come to the U.S.A., even for education, and were totally against me living here after my education. They felt that due to my family's background, I had more opportunity in India in business than here. I knew they were right as well, but I wanted to stay for reasons more than making money. I believed in everything this country stands for, and also I was into music, culture, and most of all television shows, radio, and sports that we did not have in India back in 1990. Of course, now they get all the channels we do here. But most of all I wanted the freedom to be whatever I wanted to be."

Given his enthrallment with the sense of possibility that America offered, he was even planning to buy his family's U.S. business and apply to become a permanent resident here. In 1992, he filed the paperwork to change his H-1B skilled worker visa for a green card—and waited and waited for it to be processed. In January 1997, he got the call for an interview for final approval. Unfortunately, just two months earlier, his uncle and father had a falling out that forced him to resign from the family business. Changing jobs meant that he had to refile and wait all over again. He is still waiting for his green card. Without a green card, he could not pursue his entrepreneurial ambitions because his visa status depended on sponsorship by an employer. What is more, because H-1B visas allow their holders to stay in the United States for only six years (with limited extensions in some cases), the many delays would likely have forced him to give up and return to India. However, in 2002, he married an American citizen, which alleviated some of the pressure created by the ticking clock on his H-1B visa. Not only are he and his wife happily raising a toddler, but they also have started new businesses under her name. Although his story will likely have a happy ending with a green card, the bureaucratic delays that plagued him—like many others in similar positions—could very well have resulted in America losing his talent, ambition, skills, and, most importantly, the commitment he made to this country.

"I have given this country way more than I have taken. I made my family invest over $500,000, and created several jobs for U.S. citizens," he says. "In the last thirteen years, more than ten U.S. citizens that have worked under me have left to start successful small businesses of their own. I have paid a lot of personal taxes over the years, not to mention taxes paid by companies that I manage, that would not even be started but for my initiative. I have created a lot of competitiveness in the marketplace through the companies that I manage, that have benefited a lot of customers. My parents still think I am wasting my life and want me to come back. . . . After fifteen years, I am not quite sure I did the right thing by giving a lot of my energy and youth to this country that does not respect any of that. I would have done much better in India financially and for my family and country. I am still considering going back but it is harder now with my wife being from here and my daughter."

Throughout the course of talking with dozens of foreign-born students, scholars, and high-skilled professionals, it became clear to me that our problems lie as much in a broken bureaucracy as in a set of policies put in place to prevent terrorism. Many of the problems with our immigration system existed long before 9/11, and it was the dramatic increase in workload that created the huge backlogs in the bureaucracy. The United States deals with massive numbers of people seeking to come to this country to visit, work, or live permanently. Each day, the 15,000 employees of USCIS carry out 135,000 national security checks, process 30,000 applications for immigrant benefits, administer the naturalization oath to 2,100 new citizens, and issue 7,000 permanent resident cards. The volume of work is staggering.

Unfortunately, we have not invested properly in helping the people who are charged with handling immigration to do their jobs well. The problems in the system extend from an inefficient and often redundant security check system to barely comprehensible laws to a Byzantine phone system. The help line is staffed by approximately 500 contractors who must familiarize themselves with a 1,800-page manual well enough to give accurate answers to 82,000 callers a day. The help line tangles people up for half an hour as they slog through the keypad prompts and

kicks them off if the wait is expected to exceed thirty minutes. According to a report in August 2005, one in five callers to the help line failed in their attempt to reach a human being. Callers who do get through often reach poorly trained or inexperienced operators who are as likely as not to give incorrect information. My Canadian neighbor, whose husband is American, told me that at one in-person appointment, an immigration official yelled at her for following the advice she received from the telephone help line operator.

Our immigration laws are unnecessarily complex and all but unintelligible even to those who are hired to help explain them. New laws and regulations are passed each year, but it often takes months before they are put into effect, so many visa applicants and the companies who depend on them are caught in limbo. "The biggest frustration is that the process is so unpredictable," says Lynn Shotwell, of the American Council on International Personnel, a Washington, D.C.–based trade group. Sometimes, for example, several engineers from the same firm will apply for visas, but only some will receive them. This uncertainty, coupled with the delays, makes it virtually impossible for companies to do the planning they need to be profitable. "I see some really meritorious cases, no-brainers that should be approved for specialty workers, and they're either put through the wringer or even sometimes denied," says Howard Gordon, of the New York law firm Fragomen, Del Rey, Bernsen and Loewy, which specializes in business immigration. "Why does it take a senior executive four years to get permanent resident status?"

To their credit, USCIS, which handles applications for permanent resident status and naturalization, and the Department of Labor, which evaluates work-based applications, have put considerable effort into slashing the backlogs that caused such long waits for green cards. Ironically, as immigration lawyer Cyrus Mehta told me, their success in speeding the application process has hurt some skilled immigrants because there are not enough visas under existing quotas, and so they will have to wait indefinitely for green cards. Because the law limits what percentage of visas can go to applicants from each country, those born in the countries that send the most immigrants are out of luck for sev-

eral years. In October 2005, for example, the State Department announced that under the EB-3 employment-based category, it would only
process applications from Indian nationals who had applied for green
cards before January 1, 1998, and Chinese nationals who had applied
before May 1, 2000. "There is now a complete blackout in the EB-3 category in the whole world, and there are backlogs for India, China, and
the Philippines for the EB-2," Mehta told me in December 2005. Any
meaningful improvement will have to come from Congress. Unfortunately, this most likely is wishful thinking, since in December 2005 the
House passed up the chance to make available unused work visas from
other categories—and instead voted to erect a fence along the U.S.-
Mexican border.

Since the September 11, 2001, terrorist attacks, immigration has become dramatically more difficult. For now, the lure of research funding
and the opportunity to work with the world's best scientists is greater
than the frustration of dealing with shortsighted immigration policies
and a broken bureaucracy. But how long can America count on that
fragile balance? Why, indeed, has America failed to create an immigration system that allows businesses to get the workers they need? How
much higher will the costs to businesses and higher education rise before this changes?

━9━

If Not Here, Then Where?

For a long time, it has been easy to take it for granted that the United States is the place to be for a talented professional seeking to reach as high as possible. It would be a grave mistake to continue to make that assumption. The United States faces much more competition today for skilled workers than it did a hundred years ago. Today, we are the standard to beat, but we have let our guard down even as the rest of the world has sought to catch up. Indeed, other nations have already surpassed the United States on key measures of competitiveness: education, cosmopolitan culture, and openness to foreign workers. Thus, our increasing ambivalence toward immigrants could not come at a worse time.

"The obvious advantage to leading any race—be it a sprint or a marathon—is having everyone else scramble to catch up; the less obvious disadvantage is not being able to see how quickly those behind you *are* catching up," warn John Harker and William Archey, of the American Electronics Association. "The United States is the proverbial frog in the pot of water, oblivious to the slowly rising temperature."

The U.S. Council on Competitiveness, a national group of CEOs, university presidents, and labor leaders working to promote strategies to for economic growth and for raising the standard of living for all Americans, warned in 1999 that America's "innovation infrastructure" was decaying and threatening our long-term economic competitiveness. "Only a

decade ago, American confidence was shaken by strong competition from a single nation, Japan, the prototypical country that successfully moved from follower to leader," the group warned in a report on America's innovative capacity. "The United States is once again the world's undisputed economic power; but it is not clear that we are taking all of the necessary steps to compete in a world where more and more nations possess considerable innovative capabilities and where investments quickly flow to those locations offering the best environment to employ them."

This change is arguably one of the biggest preoccupations among those in the business world today, as judged at a very minimum by what they are reading. Thomas Friedman's 2005 bestseller *The World Is Flat: A Brief History of the Twenty-first Century* sounds a warning that America faces global competition as never before, although his alarm is tempered by his near-contagious optimism that America is capable of rising to the challenge of building on our strengths in face of the tremendous changes that are already under way. Other sage authors have sounded the clarion as well: Clyde Prestowitz in *Three Billion New Capitalists: The Great Shift of Wealth and Power to the East*, Ted Fishman in *China Inc.: How the Rise of the Next Superpower Challenges America and the World*, and Richard Florida in *The Flight of the Creative Class: The New Global Competition for Talent*.

Other nations are pushing forward, setting specific goals to help them compete to attract global talent. They have seen that the United States has succeeded thanks to the human capital that has come through our relatively open doors in the past. Wealthy and developing countries alike are upgrading their education programs, from early years through university, aggressively recruiting the world's brightest students and courting junior and senior scholars. They are investing in research and development and financing venture capitalists. They are liberalizing their immigration policies and even offering skilled workers tax incentives. Countries like China and Korea are aggressively recruiting their citizens who have been educated in the United States and Europe. And they are setting up international alliances to facilitate immigration, collaboration, and trade.

In a recent corporate shake-up, Toyota promoted five non-Japanese executives to managing officers, giving them a voice at the highest levels of management in Tokyo. In March 2005, Sony named Sir Howard Stringer, an American born in Wales and the man who turned around Sony's U.S. operations, to be its new chief executive. Nissan's turnaround is the handiwork of a Brazilian-born manager, Carlos Ghosn.

These high-profile appointments are part of Japan's effort to shed its rigid workplace strictures and an insular culture. In 1989, Japan eased its immigration rules to make it easier for skilled migrants to enter the country to work and lengthened the duration of work visas, especially for members of the Asia-Pacific Economic Cooperation regional bloc. As a result, immigration of high-skilled workers has increased by 40 percent over the last decade. Bucking Japan's long-standing reputation for resistance to immigration and outside influence, its companies have been aggressively positioning themselves globally and have actively recruited some of the world's top executives.

In Korea during the same period, the number of skilled immigrants has increased more than ten times over—and since 2003, many have been attracted in part by tax exemptions for workers in certain high-tech sectors and by tax-free allowances to finance housing, home leave, and education.

The European Union has set a target of 700,000 new knowledge migrants to be admitted by 2010. With that goal in mind, individual countries are changing their rules to make themselves more attractive. The Netherlands, for example, in the fall of 2004, streamlined the process for obtaining a residence permit for expatriate workers who earn more than 45,000 euros annually, or junior scholars under age 30 who earn at least 32,600 euros a year. In 2001, Switzerland increased its skilled worker quota for the first time in ten years, even though its foreign-born population was already one of the world's highest, at 23 percent.

Other wealthy countries have created tax incentives to court skilled migrants. Sweden allows such newcomers a 25 percent tax deduction; the Netherlands 30 percent, Austria 35 percent, and Korea 40 percent. Since January 1, 2004, France has made expatriate workers' bonuses for

work related to their assignments in France tax exempt and allowed tax deductions for home-country social security payments. Quebec exempts researchers from taxes on 75 percent of their personal income.

In addition to luring skilled workers from abroad, many countries are working to convince their own best and brightest that the opportunities to stay are promising. China's government has worked hard to implement the policy encapsulated in the slogan "Develop science to save the country." In the last several years, more than 200 venture-capital firms have sprung up in China—many of them seeded with government money. The government has been particularly active in creating "returnee startup parks," which have spawned roughly 4,000 new companies. These firms are attracting a growing number of foreign-educated Chinese back to their native land—today some 30,000 returnees work in China, and the government expects the number to increase threefold by 2010. Since 2003, more foreign direct investment—that is, investment that goes straight into companies instead of through stocks or bonds—went to China than to the United States, according to the consulting firm A.T. Kearney. In 2003, China attracted $53.5 billion—nearly double the $28.9 billion that went to the United States.

By focusing on skill building, many countries have developed new industries in which they are now outpacing the world. South Korea, for example, has invested in broadband connections to the extent that its residents are three times more likely than Americans to have broadband access (in fact, the United States, is ranked only thirteenth worldwide in broadband penetration). One notable result of this investment has been a national passion for online games—and a national technical expertise in developing new ones, a field in which it has the competitive advantage of being the first to market. "While we continue to believe knowhow and ingenuity are exclusive American brands, dozens of emerging nations are restructuring their economies and challenging our superiority," warned the American Electronics Association (AEA) in a February 2005 report. "Americans may be surprised if the next revolutionary technology is produced abroad, but we should not be."

Indeed, this prediction is already being borne out in statistics show-ing that America's share of production of prestigious scientific papers are falling. In a survey of authors of papers published in leading physics journals, *Physical Review* found that American authorship fell from a majority—61 percent—in 1983 to 29 percent in 2003. The European Union is now the leading source of new scientific literature, and Asian nations, particularly China, are surging ahead. Nearly half of the 169,028 U.S. patents granted in 2003 went to foreign companies and inventors, as the U.S. share of its own patents fell to 52 percent from 56 percent in 1996. Meanwhile, patent filings in other parts of the world, especially in Europe, have been increasing much faster than in the United States.

These indicators show that we no longer have a monopoly on attract-ing the world's best and brightest or on providing an atmosphere that al-lows them to flourish.

A century ago, America was beefing up public education. We created free, universal public education that no nation in the world could rival. Today, we are letting our students fall behind, especially in the science and engi-neering fields that are vital to economic growth and will only become more so. In 1975, the United States was third in the world in terms of the ratio of students who achieved their first university degree in natural sci-ences and engineering; the U.S. ranking has fallen to thirteenth—behind the top-ranked United Kingdom, third-ranked South Korea, fifth-ranked Taiwan, and even behind twelfth-ranked Spain, a country hardly known as a center of scientific achievement. In 1975, Americans held 75 percent of all global science and engineering doctoral degrees. Today, the propor-tion has fallen to 22 percent and is expected to drop to 15 percent by 2010. Europe and Asia both produce more science and engineering PhDs than we do.

South Korea has one-sixth the population that we do, and its economy is one-twentieth the size of ours. Yet this tiny country produces nearly the

same number of engineering graduates: 5 percent of the world's output, compared with America's 6 percent, the European Union's 17 percent, and China's 21 percent. Even Russia, which we took pride in trumping technologically and militarily during the Cold War, produces significantly more engineers than America does—and their science and engineering graduation rates are rising by 10 percent annually. This effort is paying off in computer programming. In 2004, top honors in the Association for Computing Machinery's International Collegiate Programming Contest went to a Russian university for the third year out of five.

Instead of responding to help Americans compete with the rapidly rising quality of students in other countries, the U.S. government is skimping. At the end of 2004, the Bush administration cut Pell Grants—funding to help low- and middle-income students pay for college—significantly for nearly half of the 5.3 million students who depend on the grants. Because the policy change increased the amount of money given to each of the smaller number of students who received Pell Grants, the Bush administration trumpeted it as having increased support for students, when in fact it left at least 80,000 students without any Pell money at all.

At the same time, the quality of higher education in other countries has risen dramatically, along with the number of students attending them. At the University of Toronto, the number of foreign-born students increased by 44 percent from 2001 to 2003, a change widely believed to be directly related to the post-9/11 visa problems in the United States. From 1997 to 2003, Australia increased its share of the world English-language education market from 6.6 percent to 10 percent, with enrollment more than doubling, from 49,000 to 115,000. From 2002 to 2003, Chinese enrollment in Australian colleges rose 25 percent, and Indian enrollment by 31 percent—and these increases were lower than those of previous years! During the same period, the number of Chinese students enrolled in institutions of higher education in England rose by 31 percent, and the number of Indian students by 16 percent. The British Council predicts that if this trend continues—as in all likelihood it will—by the year 2020, the United Kingdom will have tripled its international student enrollments. This is not a product of mere coincidence.

Prime Minister Tony Blair has launched a $7.8 million campaign to increase the number of international students in the United Kingdom by 75,000. His stated goal is "to have 25 percent of the global market share of higher education students."

France, Germany, and Australia are pursuing similar plans; as noted, the dramatic rise in international student enrollment is already evident in Australia. In 2004, Germany's Helmholtz Association of National Research Centers launched a fellowship program specifically for foreign scientists at the beginning of their careers. Responding to the aggressive recruiting efforts from Europe and from the growing interest among Taiwanese students in going there, the Taiwanese government increased the number of students eligible for subsidies specifically to study in Europe.

This trend is not confined to developed countries. The world's growing developing economies have built formidable institutions of their own, and reputations to go with them. "The medical school in New Delhi is now perhaps the best in the world," management guru Peter Drucker told *Fortune* magazine in a 2004 interview. "And the technical graduates of the Indian Institute of Information Technology in Bangalore are as good as any in the world. Also India has 150 million people for whom English is their main language. So India is indeed becoming a knowledge center." In a profile of the Indian Institute of Technology by the television newsmagazine *60 Minutes,* the founder of Infosys, Narayana Murthy, lamented the fact that his son had wanted to attend IIT but hadn't scored high enough on the entrance exam to get into the computer science program. His son ended up going to Cornell instead, choosing an Ivy League school as a backup. "I do know cases where students who couldn't get into computer science at IIT, they have gotten scholarships at MIT, at Princeton, at Caltech, yes, sure," Murthy added.

Seeking to capitalize on Malaysia's success in luring students from all around Southeast Asia, Singapore is supporting several new university campuses that are focused on international recruitment. More than 100,000 international students are enrolled in Indian schools. The number of Chinese students applying to Hong Kong University more than doubled from 2001 to 2004.

Even as the number of students studying in other countries grows, the overall number of students will grow dramatically as well, and the number of students who study outside of their home countries is expected, by various estimates to quadruple by 2015, to 8 million. Nonetheless, the competition for the cream of the crop will remain intense.

America's falling competitiveness in education hurts us in two ways: not only are the world's best and brightest more likely to choose other homes, but also our country is failing to produce enough Americans to fill skilled positions and to keep businesses from searching for sources of skilled workers elsewhere.

In a 2003 survey carried out by the Organization for Economic Cooperation and Development (OECD), American high school students were ranked in the bottom half of forty countries in mathematics and science skills—twenty-eighth and twenty-third, respectively; they did only slightly better in reading, where they ranked eighteenth. In mathematics and science, former Eastern bloc nations Poland and Hungary both outscored the American students. Some of the top-ranking countries in the survey are among those that are investing in research and technology centers to keep top students at home. South Korea, for example, was among the top three in reading, science, and mathematics. The United States was rated as obtaining the poorest results per dollar spent on education. Sadly, American students were among the nations with the highest percentage of students—more than a quarter—who had not advanced beyond the most basic skill levels. U.S.-based groups have reported similar findings. In 2003, for example, the National Science Teachers Association reported that just one in four U.S. high school graduates were prepared well enough to have a reasonable chance of completing first-year college science courses.

Although some countries are working hard to attract students and scholars at the higher-education level, some wealthy countries, like the United States, are flagging on preparing students through secondary school—or, at best, standing still as other countries catch up and dart ahead. Just as there was much to lament in America's performance in the OECD study, Great Britain's ranking fell from eighth to eighteenth

in mathematics (or, that is, it would have if the British government had allowed it to be included officially in the study once the poor results emerged). France fell from tenth to sixteenth place in mathematics, and Japan fell from second to sixth. The leaders? Hong Kong and Korean students ranked first and third, respectively, holding steady in both 2001 and 2004. (Finland, which has long been among the top ranking countries, was second.)

American education is lagging not only compared with other countries but, even more disturbingly, is falling short of our own businesses' expectations and needs. If this education deficit is not addressed soon, it will push more companies to move work abroad.

Nearly eight in ten respondents in a National Association of Manufacturers study believed that America's public schools are not preparing students well for the workplace. "[T]he question that many respondents raised is just how many new, higher-skill manufacturing jobs can be filled in the United States, given the shortage of skills in the labor force. Thus, what manufacturing faces is not a lack of employees—but a lack of well-qualified employees with specific educational backgrounds and skills," the trade group found. The consequence of this skilled labor shortage, intensified by the increasing attractiveness of low-cost labor in other countries, will be a business exodus of our own making.

The demand for high-skilled workers is outpacing supply in the United States. From 1990 to 2002, for example, employment in high-tech industries rose by 50 percent. During this time, the number of computer science and math degrees awarded rose by 41 percent, falling short of the pace of demand for their skills. U.S. production of computer science graduates nevertheless far outpaced its performance in the physical sciences, where the number of degrees awarded rose by just 3 percent, and engineering, where the number of degrees awarded actually *fell* by 6 percent. During the same period, the number of doctoral degrees in engineering grew by 5 percent, while math and computer science doctoral degrees grew by 9 percent. When you consider that the number of foreign students grew significantly during those dozen years, earning roughly half of those science and engineering degrees, it becomes even more

painfully obvious that Americans simply are not stepping up to do the jobs that industry demands.

As a result, many industries are reporting shortages in skills that are crucial to the information economy. A National Manufacturers Association survey published in 2001 reported that 63 percent of businesses surveyed felt there was a "moderate or serious" shortage of entry-level production employees, 77 percent for craft workers, 75 percent for operators and machinists; 65 percent for engineers; 49 percent for information technology technicians; and 47.6 percent for scientists and research and development workers.

~·~

Education is a leading indicator of the importance a nation places on human capital. Yet it is far from giving a complete picture of what attracts and nourishes human capital—in short, of what the factors are that have made the United States thrive by luring so many of the world's best and brightest to our shores. An assessment of these human capital factors can give a clearer picture of how good a job America or other countries will do in continuing to attract the world's best and brightest.

Richard Florida, a professor at George Mason University who writes about the importance of creative human capital to the U.S. and global economies, has made a valiant effort to measure the important factor "creativity": the knowledge-based activities that have become a vital part of the U.S. and world economies, and which he sees as based on talent, technology, and tolerance. The concentration of diverse communities is a key indicator of the ability to generate wealth, and a country's tolerance rating comes closest to approximating its lure on this count. To estimate how well countries are doing in attracting diverse populations, he has developed the Tolerance Index, which is based on large-scale surveys of popular attitudes toward minorities, traditional versus secular values, and the value of individual rights and self-expression. Among fifteen nations—fourteen from Europe plus the United States—the United States ranked second to last, just above Portugal and just below Ireland. Swe-

den ranked first. A more striking comparison for us may be Austria, which acquired a reputation for intolerance because of the rise of right-wing political movements yet scored sixth, far above the United States, despite our long-standing reputation for tolerance. A related measure, the Euro-Creativity Matrix, which shows whether nations are gaining or losing ground in terms of competitiveness in the creative economy, shows the United States at the bottom of the leadership quadrant and hovering near the edge of the line for nations judged to be losing ground.

Florida points out that other nations already have higher percentages of immigrants than does America (at 12 percent). Immigrants make up 18 percent of Canada's population and 22 percent of Australia's. Not surprisingly, these are two of the countries where higher education is enjoying heady days. As measured more broadly by Florida's "Global Creative-Class Index" (GCCI), the United States is ranked only eleventh worldwide in creative capacity, behind countries such as world-leader Ireland, Australia (third), the United Kingdom (seventh), and Canada (eighth).

Anecdotal evidence bears out his theory, at least in part. Ironically, given that America's success a century ago was the result of luring workers from Europe with the promise of the economic opportunities that came with a more open society, European nations in particular today are outdoing America when it comes to a business culture that can lure the world's best and brightest. Consider this: according to the *Economist*, seventeen of Britain's fifty biggest companies are run by foreigners, including Unilever and GlaxoSmithKline (Frenchmen), Vodafone (Indian), and Cadbury Schweppes (American). Only five of America's top fifty companies, by contrast, have foreign-born CEOs. To be fair, Germany also has only five, and France has only three. Companies see the benefit of foreigners' familiarity with other markets, and of the wider talent pool that they represent. Executives, for their part, apparently factor Britain's diversity into their decision: "French business is dominated by the graduates of the *grandes écoles*, and the Americans are very monocultural," one headhunter explained to the *Economist*.

This is not to say that Britain does not have immigration problems of its own; yet the British public appears to welcome the world's best and

brightest. A December 2004 British poll for the *Economist* reported that 74 percent of those surveyed believed that too many immigrants were coming to Britain; they believed that immigrants put too much pressure on government services and upset the racial balance in the country; to a much smaller degree, they believed that immigrants committed a high proportion of crimes and hurt the job market. Interestingly, four-fifths of those surveyed nevertheless believed that the country needed more skilled workers, and two-fifths thought it needed more unskilled workers.

*   *   *

Even as America fails to prepare current and future generations of workers, other nations are surpassing us in their efforts to build knowledge industries. Among OECD countries, the United States ranks only fifth in terms of total private and public research and development spending as a percentage of GDP. Businesses and governments in Japan, the European Union, and rising stars like China and India have been ramping up their R&D investments, and Taiwan, Singapore, Korea, Israel, and Ireland are all now on a par with second-tier OECD economies in R&D spending.

Between 1995 and 2002, China doubled its spending on R&D from 0.6 percent to 1.2 percent of its gross domestic product, an achievement that is all the more impressive because China's GDP was one of the fastest-growing in the world during that period. China introduced a permanent R&D tax credit to attract more investment. According to the R&D Credit Coalition, Australia, Canada, France, India, Japan, the Netherlands, Portugal, Singapore, Spain, and the United Kingdom all have more generous R&D tax regimes than the United States—and those regimes are permanent, unlike our temporary tax credit system.

R&D investment in the United States has not been growing nearly as fast as in other countries, and it is driven largely by a dynamic private sector. U.S. federal government spending on R&D has fallen from a peak of $75 billion in 1987 to around $71 billion in 2002 (in inflation-adjusted

terms). As a percentage of GDP, the drop has been dramatic, from 1.25 percent to 0.75 percent. For the first time in sixteen years, Congress cut the National Science Foundation's 2005 budget, by $105 million, to $5.47 billion. Although this cut is small relative to overall federal research and development spending, it had significant symbolic value, particularly since the government was supposed to be increasing the institution's budget under the National Science Foundation Authorization Act of 2002, which authorized doubling the NSF budget to $9.8 billion by fiscal year 2007.

The private sector has been taking up a growing share of total U.S. R&D spending over the course of decades. Preliminary 2002 data show private sector R&D at $163 million, below the 2000 peak, but more and more companies have moved their R&D operations overseas. In 2001, about 15 percent of total manufacturing R&D by U.S. companies was spent in foreign affiliates. Many industry observers expect that percentage to increase. From 1994 to 2000, for example, U.S. companies quadrupled their cumulative investments in China from $2.6 billion to $10.5 billion; by 2000, 454 companies had direct operations in China. During the same period, the volume of R&D activities carried out by U.S. majority-owned affiliates in China increased even more dramatically, from $7 million to $506 million. In China and elsewhere, these companies are luring U.S.-trained foreign-born graduates to return to their native countries, an option that has become increasingly attractive as U.S. visa laws have made it harder for them to stay in the United States.

～ • ～

Foreign countries' efforts to liberalize their immigration regimes and attract R&D operations are dovetailing with the trouble the United States has had both in educating and attracting home-grown talent and in getting foreign-born skilled workers through the decrepit visa system. Together, these elements make doing business abroad increasingly attractive and are contributing to the growth of skilled jobs outside of the United

States. Many of those jobs are new jobs created by rapidly growing markets around the world; but many also are the result of jobs leaving the United States.

What drives these decisions? It's too easy for Americans to complain that cheap labor alone is what makes other countries attractive. In reality, companies take into account many factors, including availability as well as costs of both skilled and unskilled labor, natural resources, and transportation time to market. Already by 2000, according to the consulting firm Deloitte & Touche, seven of ten new foreign affiliates of American firms were not in developing countries—which have been the focus of controversy over the shift of American jobs overseas—but in advanced, high-wage nations. If companies were only looking for wage savings, this would not be the case.

To be sure, developing countries are benefiting from the shift of operations abroad from the United States. The wire service Reuters, the banking and financial services firm HSBC, the telecommunications company AT&T, and the consultancy Ernst & Young all have set up operations in India recently. India is a clear example of a country's learning process: Starting out with call centers, India moved up to software programming and is now branching into research and development. It now employs 800,000 workers in software and back office services, with an annual output of $12.5 billion. Google, the Internet search engine, has set up engineering centers in Bangalore and Hyderabad, India, where work includes information retrieval, distributed systems, machine learning, data mining, theoretical computer science, statistics, and user interfaces. The Bangalore center, once staffing is completed, will employ around 100 engineers, a significant percentage of the company's global workforce of 1,000 employees. Google bills the Bangalore center as having a "Charter to invent." As the company's Web site for job seekers promises, "Google Bangalore's charter is to innovate, implement, and launch new Google technologies and products to a global audience. Anything is fair game and the team here gets to decide its agenda." The company billed its motivation for the Indian operations as a search for talent. It is an example of how foreign-born

workers who have spent time in the United States are bringing knowledge back to their home countries: Krishna Barat, an engineer born and educated in India who founded Google News, was in charge of hiring.

"Many overseas technology companies excel today in the very disciplines that North American executives say are crucial to driving competitive performance in their industry sectors," said Donovan Neale-May, executive director of the Business Performance Management Forum, which in a joint study with the consultancy A.T. Kearney concluded that American firms were not keeping pace with the demands of global competition. "Indian IT outsourcing companies like Infosys and Wipro have built exceptional customer intimacy and dependency with North American customers. Chinese companies such as Lenovo and Huawei have established strong strategic positions and brands in markets traditionally dominated by U.S. companies. Korean multinationals, such as Samsung, are now leaders in product innovation."

The list of companies setting up in countries like China, India, and the Philippines goes on and on: computer industry firms IBM, Hewlett-Packard, Earthlink, and EDS; the consulting firm Accenture; financial services firms American Express, Citibank, and Prudential; Delta Air Lines; General Electric, Lucent, Procter & Gamble Philippines; Thomson West publishing, Con-Way Transportation Services, Headstrong Corp consulting. As *New York Times* columnist Thomas Friedman has argued convincingly, the global playing field is flattening.

Predictions vary widely on how far this trend will go. In a widely quoted 2002 study, the consulting firm Forrester Research Inc. predicted that 3.3 million such jobs would be lost abroad by 2015 in fields including life sciences, legal services, art and design, management, business operations, computers, architecture, sales, and office support. By early 2004, nearly 500,000 U.S. business-processing jobs had gone overseas.

None of this is to say that it is a bad thing that other countries are striving to achieve excellence in areas that America once led; to argue such a case would be to succumb to the very mentality that has cost us our unquestioned lead. Indeed, it was the American example that has spurred

the rest of the world to strive to do better. What is bad, however, is America's reaction: the urge to insulate our workers from foreign competition instead of rising to meet it and, indeed, to benefit from it by encouraging the flow of the world's best and brightest through our schools and businesses. The growing anxiety over globalization also is hurting American attitudes toward immigration and tempting us to turn inward, a move that will only hurt our competitive advantage.

As research and development, software programming, customer support and service call centers, and manufacturing jobs leave the United States for other countries, offshoring has become entangled with the question of immigration, the implication being that people come here to take our jobs and then leave and take them back to their home countries. Americans have responded with indignation not at our country's leaders for failing to support workers who lose their jobs because of globalization, but instead by blaming other countries. Politicians have responded with populist efforts to give the illusion of keeping jobs in America. In January 2004, the U.S. Senate passed an amendment to keep private companies from using offshoring in contracts for work done for the U.S. Departments of Treasury and Transportation.

As with immigration, Americans look at outsourcing as an us-versus-them contest. Again, although some people will be affected more than others, the overall consequences benefit everyone. For one thing, it simply is not true that every job created in another country is a job taken away from America. Many of those jobs never would have been created at all—either in the United States or elsewhere. The rising living standards in other countries are increasing the demand for all kinds of goods, many of which will be sold by U.S. companies. A 2004 McKinsey Global Institute study calculated that for every dollar sent offshore, between $1.12 and $1.14 returns to the United States: 58 cents in savings from lower costs, 5 cents in additional exports, 4 cents in repatriated profits, and an additional 45 to 47 cents in value as labor is redeployed.

According to the U.S. Bureau of Labor Statistics, the manufacturing sector in this country lost 2 million jobs over the last two decades. How-

ever, 43 million jobs were added elsewhere in the economy. It's not good news for those 2 million factory workers, of course, but nobody would argue that we should forgo the 43 million new jobs for their sake. What we need are better ways to retrain those factory workers and help them find new jobs. Those jobs will be there: the Bureau of Labor Statistics predicts that 22 million new jobs will be created in the United States in the first decade of the millennium.

As Americans panic about what jobs will go to other countries, the real question we need to ask is: What businesses will stay here? A University of California–Berkeley study identified key characteristics of the kinds of jobs that are vulnerable to outsourcing: no face-to-face customer contact, high information content, telecommutable and Internet-enabled, high wage differential, low setup barriers, and low social networking requirements. Not surprisingly, the jobs that the National Association of Manufacturers predicts the United States will keep and excel in include just the opposite traits: higher-skilled "people professions" such as management, marketing, sales and services, and maintenance, with a premium on higher technology skills throughout.

When we hear how low the salaries are in other countries, the raw numbers are shocking—many are in the range of one-tenth to one-fourth the salaries paid for the same work in the United States. Yet after companies factor in distance, travel, training, and cross-cultural costs, wage savings for jobs like software programming may only be 20 percent to 40 percent. As wages rise in other countries—as they have already begun to do in India—the impetus to move jobs abroad will fall, and we will likely see far more jobs staying in the United States than the direst predictions suggest.

Some kinds of work are worth keeping in their home country no matter what wage differentials might be. Take the case of the German auto maker, BMW, which in 2005 opened a $1.6 billion luxury car factory not in a nearby low-wage Eastern European country but in Leipzig, where German auto workers enjoy the world's highest pay rates for that work. With engineers, designers, inspectors, and administration all working in

a star-shaped building right near the production line, the plant allows an efficient work flow across all stages of the production process. You just can't do that when you ship a factory off to another country.

In 2004, the credit card group Capital One abandoned a contract with the Indian call center operator Wipro Spectramind. Late in 2003, the financial services firm Lehman Brothers and the computer manufacturer Dell both repatriated a portion of their technical support call center jobs to the United States. Lehman's move involved twenty-six jobs on its internal help desk, although it left hundreds of software jobs in India. Dell's involved customer support for large business customers, who complained that the foreign call operators could not handle complex problems.

In a survey of 100 British companies conducted by Huntswood Outsourcing Solutions, four out of five said they would not consider sending call centers or customer service administration jobs abroad because foreign-based operators would not understand their customers well enough. Interestingly, 74 percent felt that skills shortages would make it impossible to bring outsourced services back in-house.

Does this mean that fears of U.S. talent and jobs going elsewhere are overblown? It means that healthy preparation for competition is in order, but not panic. The danger of manufacturing jobs going to other countries pales next to a much greater concern: that by failing to keep our doors open to foreign skilled workers, the United States may deprive the entire world of the engine of innovation created in the single place that the world's best and brightest come to exchange ideas.

─10─

The Day They Go Away

In *A Day Without a Mexican*, the 2004 hit feature film by a team of Mexican American filmmakers, a giant pink fog surrounds Southern California, blocking off the rest of the world and mysteriously whisking away the 14 million Mexicans who live and work there. The state, of course, descends into chaos without the cooks, gardeners, policemen, nannies, doctors, farm and construction workers, entertainers, and athletes on whose work it depends. With no one to pick fresh fruit and vegetables, they become black market goods, so profitable that drug dealers abandon the crack cocaine business to sell produce. A store runs a "Disappearance Day Sale" television ad, in which a loudmouth salesman against a garish purple backdrop begs people to buy the goods that the disappeared Mexicans are no longer there to buy. He makes a point that is all too often lost in discussions of the contributions immigrant consumers make to the American economy: They are the largest growing market of consumers, and they're central to many U.S. businesses' expansion plans and, indeed, their very survival. By making Mexican immigrants "disappear," the film drew attention to their purchasing power in a real-life way: Over the film's debut weekend, it took in $620,000 in theaters across Southern California, the second-highest average gross per screen in the state that weekend.

The satirical film made not only Mexicans disappear but all Latinos. After all, Americans all too commonly lump people from all Latin

American countries into the catchall category of "Mexican." What if we were to take the film's premise even farther, making all immigrants disappear, even the Japanese biochemist in the film, Dr. Takeshi, who runs experiments to try to determine what made the Mexicans disappear? What would a day look like without any Indian, Filipino, Chinese, Ghanaian, Russian, Bangladeshi, Vietnamese immigrants? What would America be if we were to decide to keep the doors partway shut, or close them completely?

～・～

There is plenty of real-life evidence to suggest what might happen if America's immigrants go away. Look at what happened in Malaysia when the government tried to scapegoat Indonesian, Bangladeshi, Burmese, and Filipino illegal immigrants. Between October 2004 and February 2005, the Malaysian government expelled 380,000 foreign laborers on the pretense that doing so would protect jobs and prevent crime. It said that only workers who left voluntarily—if you can consider fleeing under the threat of canings and forcible deportation to be "voluntary"—would later be permitted to return. They would, of course, have to register, in the process paying exorbitant fees. The 50,000 or so workers who didn't leave "voluntarily" and had to be removed forcibly were banned from ever coming back. Without the majority of the illegal workers who had made up 10 percent of the workforce, Malaysia's agricultural, construction, manufacturing, and restaurant businesses limped along. Just a few months later, in May 2005, severe labor shortages forced the government to beg workers, including those who had been expelled forcibly, to return.

In the United States, businesses in fields that depend on foreign-born workers have already been hurt because they have not been able to recruit the workers they need. Extrapolating the experiences of a few industries gives a gloomy picture of what might be in store on a much broader level.

Small U.S. businesses rely on a steady supply of foreign workers for jobs that are unpleasant or dangerous or require hard-to-find skills.

Since 1990, many have hired such workers through the H-2B visa program, which provides one-year visas for some of the most difficult jobs to fill—seasonal work like crab processing, landscaping, firefighting, oyster shucking, waiting tables, staffing resorts, and masonry. In Oregon, businesses have used H-2B visas for firefighters and helicopter pilots; in Alaska, for fishery inspectors; in Martha's Vineyard, for bus drivers.

The 1990 law that created the program set a cap of 66,000 H-2B visas per year, although because not all workers who are approved actually take jobs, authorities often awarded more visas than the cap allows. After 9/11, however, the number was watched more closely. In addition, many of the jobs that rely on H-2B workers are in rapidly growing industries that need increasing numbers of workers. As a result, in 2003, 2004, and 2005, the annual allotment of 66,000 visas ran out by March. The results have caused endless headaches for the businesses that depended on those workers. It has made planning all but impossible for some companies, and forced others out of business.

A Chesapeake Bay crab picking company shut down for an entire year, grimly facing the likelihood that even if it reopened, it would never regain the market share that it lost. In turn, its distributors and truckers lost work. The summer hospitality industry has taken a huge blow because the supply of visas runs out before companies can even apply for them; because the rules do not allow them to apply any sooner than 120 days before they need the workers, the year's quota is always full long before hotels and restaurants that are only open in summer can even get in line. Many businesses are going to extraordinary lengths to get around visa restrictions. Some have merged with businesses that operate during other seasons so that employees hired in winter can stay through the summer; others have opened their summer businesses early and limped along with skeleton staffs. For example, a Michigan hotel, which normally is closed during the brutal winters, opened two months early so that it could meet the rule that requires companies to apply for visas no sooner than 120 days before it needs the workers. Otherwise, by the time it filed, the hotel would be so far back in line that it stood no hope of getting visas before they ran out.

Businesses thus are faced with taking extraordinary measures to work around the visa restrictions, or else shutting down entirely. This is a problem for all types of specialized work. In 2005, more than 80 percent of a group of 800 manufacturers in a survey taken across many industries reported that they were having serious difficulties finding workers with the skills they needed. By 2010, predicts the National Association of Manufacturers, the country will face a gap of 4 million to 6 million workers, and by 2020, 14 million. Increasingly, the shortage will translate into more companies doing business elsewhere in the world. As the American Electronics Association has noted, "If a U.S. company needs a specialized worker that only could be filled by a foreign national, the company would have to hire the person in his or her native country, creating a foreign job instead of a U.S. job." Along with that U.S. job goes the work needed to take care of that worker's children, maintain a home, fuel a car, and pay tax dollars.

One Australian entrepreneur moved here on an H-1B visa as part of a high-tech startup that went public in 1999. Three years later, he co-founded a new company but then discovered that co-founders are not allowed to get green cards through the companies they have built. "Right now, I am looking at closing the new company, laying off our employees, and taking a nine-to-five job elsewhere just to get a green card. How that benefits the U.S. economy is anyone's guess," he says.

Clearly, the consequences of shutting the doors would go far beyond seasonal labor and the low-income workers from *A Day Without a Mexican*. In the short term, the impact across the entire economy of losing the best and brightest would leave some American workers happy because they would feel that their own jobs had been saved. They would earn more at first because of the labor shortage, but their raises would be quickly eaten up by inflation, as costs would rise for everything from strawberries to landscaping to software to health care. Then the other shoe would drop. Businesses very quickly would move more and more of their operations abroad. The rootless cosmopolitans, who were already well versed in other cultures, would get plum posts overseas, but most Americans would see their economic prospects plummet.

At the same time, the sealing of American borders would feed anti-American sentiment and thus close off markets for American goods and services. (Again, this is not mere conjecture but based in reality. As Clay Risen reported in the *New Republic*, European politicians recently called for boycotts of American goods, and some restaurants have refused to accept U.S. credit cards. In addition, 50 percent of Asian Europeans surveyed by Global Market Insite in December 2004 said they mistrusted U.S. companies, and 20 percent said they consciously avoided U.S. goods.) Sales of Coke and Pepsi around the world would nosedive; McDonald's would have to shut down one overseas restaurant after another. Such losses would in turn slow the U.S. economy, depriving developing economies of the engine of the world's biggest market. At the same time, Americans would shift their preferences to American brands, further dampening demand for the goods that developing economies have only recently begun to excel in producing. As people in developing countries gave up hope for new jobs, more pressure would be created for them to emigrate. Unemployment combined with hopelessness would increase global political instability, radicalism, and sociopolitical violence.

Other countries would be thrilled to benefit from a brain drain from America but would be sorry that their best and brightest could no longer go to America to study and collaborate with the world's top scientists. Some people would have to change their career choices because their countries do not offer adequate, if any, education in their fields. To make things worse, the United States would no longer seem to be so prolific in scientific breakthroughs and inventions, which in turn would slow the pace of research around the world as the flow of ideas was choked off.

Worst of all, the anti-immigration measures that had been implemented in the name of national security would end up hurting our ability to protect ourselves. With many fewer scientists capable of working on antidotes to biochemical agents and deadly viruses, we would fail to develop the knowledge we needed to protect ourselves. As for the measures that had been intended to curtail industrial espionage but that ended up making it all but impossible to do many kinds of dual-use research in this country—well, those laboratories would go to China, where it's a lot

harder to keep track of who has access to what kinds of information. We would end up losing far more technological secrets than we would have if we had kept the doors open.

Shirley Ann Jackson, President of Rensselaer Polytechnic Institute, draws a picture of what she calls "The Perfect Storm": an economic version of the tragedy that befell the fishing boat in Sebastian Junger's best-selling account. Junger's disaster, like the one Jackson describes, happened because those in charge ignored all the warning signs as they recklessly steered too close to the colossal storm system. "This other 'Perfect Storm'," Jackson told the American Association for the Advancement of Science, "comes not from meteorological patterns, but by the convergence of societal forces—demographic, educational, cultural, economic, and global. They, too, are unprecedented, and they, too, are potentially explosive."

The obstacles and opportunities abroad that contribute to the erosion of the American science workforce leaves a gaping hole in the next generation. These factors, Jackson warns, raise the question of who will be the scientists and engineers who help the United States maintain national competitiveness and leadership in the global economy. "How, for instance, can we even discuss preparing for human exploration of the Moon and of Mars without discussing who will do the science to get us there?" she asks. And what about the innovation needed to build hydrogen fuel cells or develop vaccines against HIV, SARS, mad cow disease, and avian flu?

Jackson's questions raise the prospect of a gloomy future. But at least these are challenges that we know we face. An even more frightening prospect is that we'll never know what we have lost. What if the United States had never thought to fund the network of computers that became the Internet because nobody ever dared to start us down that path?

⌣•⌣

The saddest thing that would happen if we close the doors would be the stagnation of the flow of ideas—not just for scientific inventions, but for the ideas that help people of different countries understand each other

and the ideas that are so powerful that they change the way people govern themselves. Harvard President Larry Summers, speaking for the many educators who feel the same way, has warned that if the next generation of world leaders decide to get their educations elsewhere, it will be an "incalculable loss to America."

Imagine the "University of Middle America," a medium-sized midwestern school whose smallish science and engineering departments for years have had trouble recruiting enough Americans to its graduate programs. Even at UMA, out here in College Town, U.S.A., in the middle of vast cornfields and communities of farmers who are descended from the German and Scandinavian immigrants who came a century ago, today the campus is filled with graduate students from Taiwan and Hong Kong, New Delhi and Lahore, and yes, even a few from Berlin and London. These students have come on stipends given in return for their work as teaching and laboratory assistants or for research on programs that bring in considerable sums of grant money. There is also a smaller contingent of undergraduate students who pay full tuition, freeing up university and federal resources for U.S. students who rely on the help to make it to college. With strict anti-immigration laws, this scenario would be a thing of the past.

Unlike the top-tier universities, like Harvard and MIT, with their significant legal budgets and their clout in the nation's capital, which would enable them to eventually get the students they wanted into the United States, UMA and scores of schools like it see student after student give up when their visas are still nowhere in sight when the semester starts. And they wouldn't lose only top-quality students but faculty as well. Consider the plight UMA would face when, say, three professors visit family in their home countries and then couldn't get back in to the United States—one gets held up by a security check when his name was confused with someone else's, another professor's application is lost, and the third is idled by a backlog of visa reentry applications. Two upper-level science courses have to be canceled as a result and another foisted off on an overworked assistant professor, even though it is not in her field of expertise. Because visas fail to materialize for several grad students

UMA was counting on to help staff courses, several sections of chemistry, engineering, and calculus 101 must be canceled. Undergraduates grumble at how crowded their classrooms are after the course sections are combined; it takes forever to get their grades back after exams; and they never seem to be able get the laboratory assistant's attention for important questions because she is dealing with so many students at once. Of course, when these students go home for Christmas break and complain to their younger siblings and friends, it doesn't exactly help interest more students in pursuing science and engineering.

The problem would only get worse as time passed. Frustrated by the red tape they had to go through in order to get visas here, many foreign students would just give up, withdraw their applications, and go to study in Canada or Australia instead. Word would go out that it wasn't worth the effort to go to America. Universities in Singapore, Germany, and Hong Kong, however, would see applications shoot through the roof. As multinational corporations continued to have trouble recruiting students in the United States, they would move more and more of their operations to other countries. Research funding would follow them, making international universities even more attractive and accelerating the flow of students to those places—and away from the United States. The U.S. science programs that did not have to close for lack of professors and students would have to make do on smaller budgets, wait an extra couple of years to replace aging equipment, and not even dare to hope to upgrade their facilities with the latest technology.

In theory, English would remain the international language of science. In practice, however, fewer students would have courses conducted mainly in English, and their English language skills, as would be expected, would deteriorate. It would take them longer to wade through scientific papers written in English, and when they attended international scientific conferences, their would find it difficult to communicate with others. Soon more papers would be published in Chinese, German, and other languages, and English-speaking scientists would have to wait for them to be translated. The flow of ideas around the world would slow down.

Not only would America lose its scientific and technological edge, the whole world's progress would slow. But the clogging of the exchange of scientific ideas is only the beginning; it would extend to philosophy, the arts, literature, politics, economics, and diplomacy. The very top students would still be able to get into Ivy League schools, but the large number of international students who go to second- and third-tier schools would be hit hard. A whole generation of diplomats and government bureaucrats, who otherwise would have been exposed to the United States, instead would stay at home. They would lose exposure to American customs and ideas, and instead view us through the lenses of the stereotypes bred by unfamiliarity.

As international students stopped coming to the United States, Americans, too, would feel the loss of the opportunity to interact with people from around the world, so our business and political insights into other countries would fall even farther short than they do now. Without exposure to so many people circulating in and out of America, fewer Americans would take an interest in foreign language and area studies, so we would find it all but impossible to find qualified foreign service officers, diplomats, and intelligence agents to help us understand and interact intelligently around the globe.

This is not merely a fanciful scenario. Lisa Anderson, dean of Columbia University's School of International Affairs, holds up Libya's experience as a cautionary tale. Until 1982, Libya sent some 5,000 students to the United States every year; apart from a handful of students who chose Eastern bloc universities, we were practically the exclusive destination for Libyans studying abroad. These students, who would go on to become the backbone of Libya's foreign service and domestic government, ate at backyard barbecues with Americans, making friends and becoming familiar with American culture. After the United States and Libya broke relations in 1982, the flow of students stopped.

Visiting Libya recently after a twenty-two-year absence, Anderson was impressed at how fondly those who had studied here still remembered their time in America, although more than two decades had passed. "After all that time, they had a finely grained, wistful sense of the United

States," she told me. And they were the ones working to help Libya's effort to repair its relationship with the world. Nearly every one had attended second-tier schools in the Midwest, West, and Southwest: Texas,
Oklahoma, California, Utah. But the students who came after them had
studied in Libya, and except for the lucky few who had gone to Europe,
an entire generation had a parochial outlook and little experience with
the rest of the world. "Now Libyans are thinking about how they're going
to manage life in the world after being excluded," Anderson said. "We
want the American image in the Middle East to be good, and one of the
best ways to make that happen is to bring in students," she added. How
are we going to do that if we close the doors?

The rough estimates of what we have lost so far from even a partial
closing of the doors are themselves sobering. It's frightening to consider
the losses we can't quantify at all: the people who decide not to come at
all, the contracts lost, the discoveries not made. "There are too many
people thinking this is too much of a hassle. The thing about that person is everyone else who follows him abroad, his family, his friends,
people who are from his country: they aren't going to come here because
of that," says Vic Johnson, of NAFSA: Association of International Educators. "It's an immeasurable but quite profound phenomenon. We
might wake up a decade from now and realize that we've suffered damage we didn't see while it was happening."

～•～

The University of Middle America is not the only place that would suffer when America's foreign-born go away. When the schools that produce the next generation of professionals suffer, the entire economy
does too. Because the foreign-born are so vital to science, engineering,
and technology in the United States, these areas would be hurt hard.
And, while many scientific discoveries may be fascinating but do not directly affect people's lives, when science involves medicine, people's
lives depend on them.

On the day we close the doors, the National Institutes of Health will have to drop half of the research it is doing because it no longer can find enough scientists. Research at universities around the nation trying to develop vaccines against deadly viruses and to seek cures for cancer and multiple sclerosis will be set back by years because the world's top experts are no longer coming here.

Let's look through our crystal ball at what would happen to "Hometown Hospital." The wait to get an appointment with a doctor—not just with the best doctors, but with any doctor—would become longer, and eventually too long. The shortage of nurses would become more acute. As the U.S. population ages, the demand for medical services will only go up. If there is no way to meet the demand for doctors, nurses, and technicians, not only will the cost of care rise, but the quality could be expected to fall, perhaps dramatically. With staff working overtime, deaths due to human error would rise. With increased stress, morale would plummet, prompting more nurses to quit and making it even harder for hospitals to find enough staff to ensure the safety of their patients.

This scenario also is rooted in current realities. Researchers in a 2001 study found that three out of four nurses regularly worked overtime. Another study found that nurses who worked rotating night shifts were twice as likely to commit errors and accidents and were more than ten times as likely to nod off at work than nurses on regular shifts. The Institute of Medicine estimates that at least 44,000 Americans die each year because of hospital medical errors, which are the eighth leading cause of death in the United States. That doesn't even count the 2 percent of all patients who experience some kind of preventable error. Medical residents cite fatigue as a cause for 40 percent of serious errors. In other words, the shortage in medical personnel has serious consequences for Americans.

Today, the United States has a shortage of 20,000 physicians, according to the Health Resources and Services Administration of the U.S. Department of Health and Human Services. If the gates close, that gap will expand dramatically. A 2003 survey of medical school deans and state

medical society executives, carried out by the Medical College of Wisconsin's Health Policy Institute and the University of Texas at San Antonio, showed that 85 percent of the nation's medical institutions already report shortages of physicians—and most of them saw no immediate way of solving the problem. The shortages affect every medical specialty: anesthesiology, radiology, cardiology, gastroenterology, geriatrics, dermatology, general surgery, surgical subspecialties, and psychiatry. Nearly one-third of medical schools and one-half of state medical societies reported shortages of primary care physicians. Richard Cooper, director of the Health Policy Institute, estimates that by 2020, the United States will face a shortage of 168,000 to 200,000 physicians.

Similarly, the nursing industry predicts that it will be 300,000 nurses short by 2010 and more than 600,000 nurses short by 2020. In 2000, according to the Health Resources and Services Administration, thirty states reported shortages of nurses. At the same time, the National Council of State Boards of Nursing reported, the number of U.S. nurses who took licensing examinations in 2003 fell 20 percent between 1995 and 2003. In California, where the ratio of nurses to population—563 per 100,000—is half the national average, Governor Arnold Schwarzenegger issued an emergency order in 2004 to change a law that required one nurse for every five patients. A Sacramento judge overturned the emergency order, which would have lowered the requirement to one nurse for every six patients.

The shortage of doctors and nurses will hurt older Americans who rely on medical care more than do younger generations. It will lower the quality of care even as it raises the costs to Medicare. At the same time, the closing of the doors on immigration will remove people and businesses from the economy, shrinking the pool of young working people paying into Social Security and Medicare.

Stuart Anderson, executive director of the National Foundation for American Policy in Arlington, Virginia, has analyzed data supplied by the chief actuary at the Social Security Administration and come up with the alarming warning that a moratorium on immigration would decimate the Social Security fund. His analysis can help us imagine what an

America would look like in 2055 after the immigrants have gone away. Even as the American population ages, the country has shut the doors to immigration, just as we did a century ago. All of a sudden, the annual arrivals of 800,000 new workers simply stops. America's retirees still need pensions and medical care even though there are not enough workers to pay into the Social Security fund. Financed by contributions from current employees to provide benefits for those whose employable days are over, the fund relies heavily on money paid in by the young, hard-working foreign-born population. Over a period of fifty years, the Social Security deficit has ballooned by nearly one-third. Desperate for money to appease the nation's most assertive voting bloc, the government has raised Social Security taxes to make up for the $407 billion shortfall (as measured in today's dollars). In the first ten years since the tax increase, Joe American, who was earning $60,000 in 2004, has paid an additional $1,860 in payroll taxes. Slowed by a shortfall of labor combined with higher taxes that have dampened consumption, the country's economy has grown by 0.25 percent less than it would have otherwise.

~•~

In the future, after we have closed the doors, we will be an aging nation paying higher taxes because there are no longer enough young people and because of the high costs of militarizing the borders. The drop in demand for U.S. products abroad—the product of a growing international backlash against America's decision to shut out the world—will have dealt a serious blow to U.S. corporate profits. Other countries will be the ones coming up with major technological advances and reaping the economic rewards. Together, these economic pressures will lead to social stresses far greater than those today prompting some Americans to call for us to stop immigration.

Closing the doors will not "automatically" make it easier for immigrants to assimilate here. Immigrants will read the message loud and clear: America does not want the likes of you here. The nativists will have made a self-fulfilling prophecy. Hate crimes will increase. Resentment will rise

among recent arrivals, who will be virtually cut off from family and friends, who will find it all but impossible to visit America even as those living here will fear leaving the United States because they will not be certain that they can get back in again, even when they are here legally.

Worse, the roughly 10 million undocumented workers in the United States today will be pushed even farther underground, becoming a permanent underclass. Delinquency and petty crime will rise. Economic and social problems will become an explosive mix. When white Americans rejected "ethnicity" as a way to define their lives between the world wars, they replaced it with consumerism and encouraged other Americans—indeed, the whole world—to do so as well. This obsession with material wealth has made economic inequality that much more noticeable—and heightens the tensions that, when they erupt, once again have taken on an ethnic tinge. Social and economic ills will play off of each other, pulling America into a vicious downward spiral.

America will lose influence around the globe as the flow across borders slows dramatically, hampering the best way of promoting America's image. We will lose out on the chance for people from other countries to come into regular contact with individual Americans, whom they have tended to view positively even when they disagree with the U.S. government. The decline of this tool for spreading American values and culture around the globe will occur while a rampant budget deficit—far worse than the one that looms today—forces our government to withdraw troops from around the world. No longer, at any rate, will there be any point in spreading American values and culture because we will have destroyed them.

___11___

Getting Immigration Right

I learned my first words of Spanish—"*Abierto! Cerrado!*"—while watching a door open and close on the children's television program, *Sesame Street*. At that time, in the 1970s, the show's characters Luis and Maria were two of a very small number of Hispanic entertainers familiar to a general American audience. Maria and Luis were all too rare examples of the message that you could share friendship and common goals with your neighbors even though you were different—a children's version of the American Creed. To me, however, they were just Big Bird's and Oscar the Grouch's human friends, not pivotal figures in a debate over what it meant to be American. Nor could I have understood that they were part of a transition from a version of America that wanted to ignore the varied origins of its citizens into a new place where ethnicity had value, both personal and economic.

Ethnicity was a central plot point in the scripts that ran through the careers of earlier Latino actors, like Brazilian singer and movie star Carmen Miranda, Cuban-born Desi Arnaz in *I Love Lucy* (1951–1957), and Puerto Rican Freddie Prinze in *Chico and the Man* (1974–1978). Carmen Miranda would always be the exotic Brazilian bombshell, and cultural differences formed the ongoing narrative of Desi's relationship with Lucy and Chico's contentious relationship with "The Man," his cranky boss. Desi and Chico both embodied the classic immigrant struggle to fit in even as they stood

out from their Anglo costars. It was not until the late 1970s that Latino actors began to get roles in which their ethnicity was not the central plot point—that is, in which they had begun to be accepted as Americans and not portrayed as exotic outsiders.

In 1977, the Puerto Rican actor Erik Estrada became the star of the television police series, *CHiPs,* playing an Italian American character, Frank "Ponch" Poncherello. Prime time clearly wasn't ready for a Latino star—although I doubt that the television executives thought about the fact that Italians had once been considered too "dark" and ethnic to fit into American society. Yet the fiction that Ponch was Italian never fully took hold. In a straw poll (admittedly unscientific) of my contemporaries who grew up watching *CHiPs,* everyone remembered his character as Mexican American, and not a single person remembered that he was supposed to be Italian. After the *CHiPs* series ended in 1983, Estrada's career fizzled. But his comeback in the 1990s illustrates how dramatically the pop culture market had changed. Estrada learned Spanish in order to star in the Mexican soap opera *Dos Mujeres, Un Camino,* which earned him a cool million dollars and liberated him from the "whatever-happened-to . . ." limbo. His character, Johnny, was a trucker whose heart was torn between his wife and his teenage girlfriend; hence the title, "Two Women, One Road." Cheesy as it was, the show was the longest-running and most profitable Latin American *telenovela* ever, and its U.S. audience was a big part of its success. I don't even like soap operas, but I was a (guilty) fan—and so were some of my white American friends who barely spoke Spanish. Erik Estrada had brought American pop culture full circle: from a groundbreaking role on American television as a Puerto Rican disguised as Chicano disguised as Italian to a groundbreaking role as an American actor who returned to his Latin American roots on international Spanish-language television.

As the 1990s advanced, it became clearer and clearer that there was a market in America for ethnicity, just as there had long been a market abroad for all things American. But it's not just any kind of ethnicity that the market craves. It's a peculiarly American blend of ethnic symbolism with American pop culture and literature. The former Puerto Rican child

star Ricky Martin made his name as an adult by working the Latino thing in his infectious hit song *Livin' la Vida Loca*. Teenage girls just *had* to have henna tattoos, inspired by (East) Indian designs. Talented immigrant fiction writers—Cuban American Oscar Hijuelos, Indian American Jhumpa Lahiri, Dominican American Junot Díaz, Haitian American Edwidge Danticat, Russian American Gary Shteyngart, Chinese Americans Amy Tan and Ha Jin, Mexican American Sandra Cisneros, Cuban American Christina García—have become the toast of the literary world. A literary agent once told me it was a shame I wasn't ethnic, because then I'd have an easier time finding a market when I wrote about immigration.

Ethnicity is no longer a sign of being low class: everybody wants some, but in a patently American version that translates it into a personal means of expression much like fashion or music. Genealogy has become an American pastime. The grandchildren and great-grandchildren of the Great Wave immigrants are searching for the roots that their peasant ancestors at best did not think were worth preserving and at worst wanted to hide. Americans today are as proud of being mongrels as the higher classes of earlier Americans with British and Germans roots were of their "purebred" family trees.

In Henry Ford's America, what sold was sameness as Americans replaced ethnic culture with consumer culture. In the process, consumerism replaced the American Creed as the force to which Americans turned to hold together. But, especially as the gap between rich and poor widened in the 1980s and 1990s and income disparities became the most important dividing factor in American society, it became harder and harder to rely on the cult of the dollar as a unifying principle. Many Americans reverted to a negative definition of being American: focusing on what we stripped away instead of what brought us together. Today, Heartland America still emphasizes the importance of losing the tics and habits that might make someone stand out. Many midwesterners still register disapproval by nodding and saying quietly in a clipped nasal accent, "Now that's *dif'rent*," a holdover from the post–Great Wave era when to become American was to forget who you were. In this worldview, it is easy to say what America is *not*, but impossible to say who we *are*.

With only a much-weakened American Creed to remind us of our common goals, the resurgence of ethnicity continues to feed tension between those who believe that you can be American only if you give up your past and those who believe that the freedom to hold on to your heritage—as long as it remains symbolic and not political—is part of what America is all about.

The future of America rests on which side prevails. If we revert to the isolationist, protectionist view that prevailed during and after World War I, we risk putting ourselves at a tremendous disadvantage in the global economy. At a time when America is the undisputed economic leader of the world, and when our troops are spread thin around the globe in an effort to spread democracy, it is more important than ever that we nurture our connections to the rest of the world and honor the values that helped Americans meld many cultures into one.

America is at a turning point not just in our relationship with the immigrants who come here but in the way we see our borders and our relationship with the world. The decisions we make in these areas will have a profound effect on both American society and our economy for years to come. We can choose to embrace the world and lead it, or we can close our gates and pretend to shut it out. Our choice depends in part on the lessons we take from our experiences of a century ago: whether we interpret the closing of the doors to the Great Wave as a needed pause in immigration that brought America together, or whether we take it as a cautionary tale of the negative consequences of withdrawing from the world, stifling individual expression, and dismantling the institutions that strengthened American values and national unity of purpose. It depends on whether we recognize that immigrants bring assets that are essential to the growth and health of the global economy or whether we see their differences as a threat. It depends on whether we embrace the ability of the American Creed to strip away the political divisions that come from differences, or whether we deliberately strip the creed of its power. It depends on whether or not we recognize that global prosperity—including our own—depends on people maintaining their homeland ties and taking home the skills they acquire in America and that this is not incompatible

with American values but actually reinforces them. And it depends on whether we blame cultural differences as a way of masking the real barriers to immigrants integrating into American society, an error that prevents us from finding solutions and that can make the argument that America is at risk of Balkanization a self-fulfilling prophecy.

America's greatest economic asset is its ability to attract the world's ablest and most talented individuals to a system that can harness their abilities better than any other in the world. It is the combination of those individuals and the system that has made this country the world's engine of innovation and economic growth. "Innovation seems to me to be not only encouraged but driven by interchange, with this exchange acting like a sourdough starter when you bring a bunch of people together and give them the right environment," Tracy Koon, Intel's director of corporate affairs, told me.

When the best and brightest come here—whether they are the most educated or simply the hardest working of their homeland—they can become a political and economic asset abroad as well. Immigrants' global connections boost Brand America, creating markets for American goods while spreading America's can-do attitude and democratic principles. One of our greatest challenges is to play these assets to their best advantage. Yet we must also address the downside of immigration in the context of global economic change. We have failed to protect the Americans who are the most vulnerable to economic disruptions and the pressures that keep their wages down. Our immigration bureaucracy is a failure: it locks out many of the people on whom our economy and prosperity depend, even as it does not efficiently keep out those who would harm us. Our immigration laws are a shifting labyrinth that has made it too hard for businesses to get the workers they need legally and created perverse incentives for unscrupulous employers to take advantage of the workers who remain in the shadows.

These are the issues that we must address in order to fix our immigration policies. Nothing less than our economic, social, and national security are at stake, including our global political and economic reach. What we need are pragmatic steps, not the emotional reactions that have sent

immigration policy seesawing wildly, to the benefit of none. Locking out the workers we need, as some propose, would hurt this country as well as the immigrants some seek to shut out.

America keeps getting immigration wrong because we only look at half of the story: we focus so hard on immigrants that we forget about our own role in shaping how people come here and how well they fit it. We get it wrong because we make policy based on emotion that blinds us to our own self-interest. We are intoxicated by lofty principles even when the policies we make in the name of patriotism and the American nation, taken to extremes, undermine the very principles they are supposed to defend. We exaggerate the differences between our immigrant ancestors and today's immigrants because it is a convenient mask for our own failings. We often wrongly blame immigration for being the cause of other problems—social tensions, economic inequality, job losses, abuse of workers—when in fact the tensions over immigration are merely the symptoms of those problems.

- At a time when the winners in the global economy will be those who can navigate cultural differences, Americans have lost sight of the tremendous asset that our mixed heritage gives us. Instead, we cling too tightly to the zero-sum view of the world that the Great War era created: that we cannot be Americans and something else too. This idea has never been more than an illusion, and the sooner we cast it away, the better. Instead of focusing on what we are not, we need to articulate what brings us together: a shared sense of faith and can-do optimism.

- We allow ourselves to believe that the solution to problems involving the rest of the world can be solved by merely changing policies inside our own borders.

- We have lost faith in the dreams that made us the greatest country in the world, a failing that has led us to blame others for our problems instead of relying on our strengths.

- We forget that integrating immigrants into American society involves not only immigrants' desire to become American but also the obstacles and incentives that we create for their doing so.

- We rely on a false mythology that makes us see new immigrants as far more different from earlier generations than they really are—and thus makes integrating immigrants into American society far harder than it needs to be.
- We fail to see immigration in its larger context of inequality between the world's wealthiest and poorest countries and between the wealthy and poor within countries. As long as the disparities between America and the developing world persist, there will be pressure for people to emigrate to America. But as much as many Americans complain about immigration, they also complain as jobs move to other countries and reduce the need for people to come here; we are unwilling to give up just a little bit of what we have so that everyone can have more. Think of the boy in Aesop's fable who reaches into a jar of filberts and grabs as many as he can; when he tries to withdraw his fist, it gets stuck because he refuses to let go of even a few of the nuts: he wants them all for himself. His greed causes him unnecessary misery, when leaving something for others would get him what he needs.

What, then, does America need to do to get immigration right? We need to wrest back the debate over immigration from the extremists: both those who would slam our doors outright and reserve America for those of Anglo-Saxon heritage, on one side, and, on the other, those who will not countenance attempts to bring immigration to moderate levels and who refuse to give any credit at all to the Anglo-Saxon cultural and political influences that enabled us to incorporate other cultures—however imperfectly—into one nation. We need to build on our strengths and come up with targeted solutions to shore up our weaknesses. In specific policy terms, this includes the following ideas.

- Accept responsibility for the wink-wink-nod-nod policies that created a large, marginalized population of more than 10 million people living in the shadows, and acknowledge that American employers and consumers have profited hugely from the illegal status that keeps

wages low and labor conditions dismal for so many workers. The population of immigrants who are in this country without legal papers did not grow to more than 10 million people without America's full participation in a legal charade. Our encouragement—through laws that were created with little intention of being enforced and through the widespread recognition that our economy would stumble badly without them—makes it morally wrong to force the undocumented immigrants here to pay the full legal price. The only fair solution is for America to provide a way for them to apply for legal status while also paying some sort of penalty, thus acknowledging a shared responsibility for illegal immigration.

- Provide legitimate pathways for future immigrants to come here and work legally, but put in place practical measures that make it difficult for those without documents to work here—most importantly, an employer verification program, which could take the form of electronic swipe cards. A system of this magnitude would have to be phased in over a realistic time frame and include a mechanism to provide for cases of data entry problems—perhaps a combination of provisional work approval and an efficient appeals process.

- Let the consequences of breaking immigration and labor laws fall squarely on the shoulders of those who profit from it—not on those who have been their victims. Not only is this approach morally just, it is also efficient in terms of enforcement, as it would involve prosecuting those who employ or traffic in illegal immigrants rather than going after the much larger number of individual immigrants.

- Design any guest worker policies carefully, keeping in mind the goals—seemingly contradictory but actually complementary—of promoting both integration in the host country and circulation of skills back to homelands.

- Enhance programs to make it easier for immigrants to acquire the skills they need to integrate into American society and economic life. For businesses, this could mean providing workplace education programs. For government, this means providing additional resources for civics and English-language education, which could be

financed through additional immigration processing fees paid by workers and employers.

- Give this country's immigration agencies more freedom from political interference by limiting congressional micromanagement. Congress should not involve itself in legislating—as it has done in the past—such trivial details as the content and format of immigration forms. Whenever possible, allow the immigration agencies to revise regulations on their own rather than legislating rule changes.

- Create a cabinet-level position dedicated to immigration. Right now, immigration policies are spread across many agencies whose work often overlaps and can be contradictory; most of the authority for implementing immigration policies lies within the Department of Homeland Security, whose primary mandate is not immigration per se. There is no senior official responsible solely for coordinating immigration work across agencies, nor for advising the administration on a broad approach to immigration.

- Streamline our immigration bureaucracies, put in place performance standards, and improve transparency. The State Department and the Department of Homeland Security have devoted considerable time and energy to speeding up the processing of visas and other applications, but both could do much more.

- Promote economic growth in countries that are heavy senders of immigrants. This could involve creating policies designed to promote the circulation of high-skilled workers and entrepreneurs back to their home countries. Understand that countries often pass through what economist Philip Martin has called the "migration hump," whereby emigration increases once per capita income rises enough (often through remittances) for people to afford to get out, and it does not slow again until per capita income reaches the other side of the hump, that is, until it increases to a level at which citizens no longer expect that moving to another country will improve their quality of life enough to be worth the trauma of dislocating.

- Accept that unlimited, unfettered immigration is no more the correct alternative than shutting the doors would be. Economic growth

in migrant-sending countries is part of the answer, but we should also consider reducing the adult sibling allotment of visas granted under family preferences. This would reduce the backlog for immediate family reunification, and adult siblings could still apply for visas under employment preferences.

～・～

The first step toward fixing America's dysfunctional immigration policies is to free ourselves from the wrong lessons we have taken from the past. America needs a new vision linking its immigrant past and future, allowing us to revisit the values that pulled us together and to create a blueprint for the future.

Conventional wisdom credits the closing of the doors with having helped immigrants assimilate and Americans unite. This explanation downplays the importance of the civic values that have united many previous generations of Americans. It also ignores the tremendous cost to the American social fabric of the dismantling of many of the ethnic associations whose primary mission was to help people assimilate. It fails to acknowledge that America's pulling back from the world contributed to the trade wars and the breakdown of international cooperation that led to the Great Depression and World War II. Our withdrawal redefined America as a nation united by the existence of a common enemy rather than by common dreams. Above all, by closing the doors, America wasted the tremendous asset that immigrants brought to us in the form of the ability to be conversant in other cultures, an important bridge linking ethnic groups in America with one another and with other nations around the world. In reality, Americans came together and eventually prospered in spite of—not because of—the closing of the gates.

Americans also must give up the wrong idea that today's immigrants are different from previous waves of immigrants because they want to hold on to their home country ties. This fallacy nurtures the self-fulfilling prophecy that people who have left their homelands to come here be-

cause they believe in America will never really belong because they do not look like us. It also, paradoxically, may slow the flow of ideas and funds back to home countries that depend on émigrés not only for the cash to survive but also to bring back the skills needed to build their home economies so that migration is no longer seen as the only way to survive.

We must replace our outdated ideas by affirming that we are a country committed to pursuing common goals; supporting institutions that help newcomers succeed in our society; recognizing that America is great because of the combined efforts of the people of many nations; and continuing to give people the freedom to honor their heritage as a private expression of who they are. It is time to restore faith and optimism in the ability of the American Creed to unite this nation by rescuing the melting pot metaphor and returning it to what Israel Zangwill meant it to be in the first place. The melting pot was never intended to mean that you can't be American and love another land too. It is about giving up the ethnic hatreds of the old homelands and starting over. It is about recognizing that the diversity of inputs creates an alloy that is stronger than any one element could be on its own.

John Fonte, of the Hudson Institute, has articulated some of the principles that can contribute to a renewal of ties to bind together new and existing Americans: "Patriotic assimilation does not mean giving up all of one's ethnic traditions, customs, cuisine, and birth language," he has written. "It has nothing to do with the food one eats, the religion one practices, the affection one feels for the land of one's birth, or the languages a person speaks. Patriotic assimilation occurs when a newcomer essentially adopts American civic values and the American heritage as his or her own."

As a country, we should encourage efforts to honor the little parts of daily life, the quirks and habits that make a people. We must reinforce the values that brought us together—freedom, respect for rights, justice, equal opportunity, and the desire to build and progress—and work together to amend the areas where we have failed to honor those values. We can achieve this by educating Americans about the rest of the world,

raising consciousness of our role to a level that does justice to this nation's power around the globe. We must work harder to educate immigrants about American civic values and help them connect their own stories to this country's future. This requires changes in education and immigration policy—and in Americans' own expectations.

Given the amount of rhetoric that has been flying around about how immigrants supposedly are not integrating into U.S. civic life, many Americans would be surprised at the creative, even inspiring efforts that many immigrants have made to contribute to their adopted communities, despite the long delays that have prevented many of them from taking the Oath of Allegiance for the first time as citizens. They have been adapting classic American models of civic participation and inventing new ways of being heard. As Robert D. Putnam lamented in his bestselling book *Bowling Alone: The Collapse and Revival of American Community*, Americans long ago abdicated their sense of civic commitment. Voter turnout for municipal elections typically is in the 30 percent range, and school board elections often are lucky to get people out in double-digit participation rates. Yet immigrants want to be involved members of their neighborhoods and cities. In some cities, including Chicago and six Maryland municipalities, immigrants have won the right to vote in certain local elections, particularly for school boards, and similar movements are under way in more than a dozen other states. Others are educating their fellow immigrants about their rights and responsibilities, and teaching them English. They've created membership organizations that provide financial help and moral support. In North Carolina, Latino and African American poultry workers are lobbying for better wages and working conditions. And the multiethnic Omaha Together One Community is supporting better working conditions for meat packers. Approximately 140 immigrant worker centers nationwide provide services and teach legal rights and leadership skills, Janice Fine, who has studied immigrant work centers for the Economic Policy Institute, told me. These centers represent a modern-day version of the mutual aid societies, fraternal aid organizations and settlement house movements of the late nineteenth and early twen-

tieth centuries, which helped immigrants get a foothold in America. In Brooklyn, African Americans and Caribbean and African immigrants manage a community credit union in an effort to build their neighborhood's economic base. Arab Americans are running voter registration and naturalization drives and hosting civic education workshops. In the 2002 elections, Arab American groups registered 250,000 new voters and ran forty candidates for offices, twenty-six of whom won, according to the Arab American Institute. Unfortunately, since 9/11, too many organizations have had to divert their energies from efforts to promote civic and social integration to instead defending immigrant detainees and otherwise fighting for civil liberties.

Above all, we desperately need more resources for civics and English-language education. A New York Immigration Coalition study showed that in New York City the available classes in English as a second language meet only 5 percent of the demand, and many providers of English classes must hold lotteries to decide which students to admit. In Portland, Oregon, according to a U.S. Citizenship and Immigration Services study, there are 9,000 people on the waiting list of one adult education provider alone. Houston has the capacity to instruct only about 35,000 people in English each year, although roughly 1 million people need classes. These backlogs, typical of what immigrant communities across the country face, should dispel the notion that immigrants do not want to learn English.

Another example of how short America falls on the attention we pay to our role in helping immigrants assimilate is the sad state of the test used to determine whether an applicant for naturalization is ready to become a citizen. For much of the twentieth century, the immigration officials who processed naturalization applications had the leeway to decide, as they pleased, which applicants to approve and which to turn away. Over the years, immigration offices across the United States each developed their own procedures for determining who deserved to become citizens, including lists of questions to be put to interviewees. According to Alfonso Aguilar, head of the Department of Homeland Security's Office

of Citizenship, the existing naturalization test has been used since 1986, when a group of officers at the Immigration and Naturalization Service cobbled together a list of potential questions from many of those already informally in use. Until recently, little serious thought was given on a national level to whether these questions reflected the values and ideals that new Americans should embrace, or simply encouraged applicants for naturalization to memorize trivia. An immigrant taking the exam to qualify for U.S. citizenship may be asked any one of 100 questions on a list that includes "What Immigration and Naturalization Service form is used to apply to become a naturalized citizen?" as an indicator of whether or not the respondent would make a good citizen. Even many of the questions that seem relevant to an immigrant's understanding of America include details that most Americans who were born here would be hard-pressed to answer. An official of the U.S. Bureau of Citizenship and Immigration Services recently openly acknowledged that even after working to improve the test, she still struggles to come up with the correct numbered Constitutional amendments that could be used to answer the question, "Name one amendment that guarantees or addresses voting rights." Some of the questions are ambiguous, like the one that asks what the first thirteen states were. I ticked them off in my head, only to discover that the answer was simply, "The colonies." Other questions are redundant, technical, or merely trivial.

More than ten years after the Jordan Commission recommended that the United States improve the test, Citizenship and Immigration Services is finally developing a new test that will purge the trivia and emphasize American concepts and values like freedom, equality, rights, and responsibilities. (It also, for the first time in recent history, began to publish materials to make sure that immigrants have the information they need most about life and civics in America.)

The political right quickly pounced on the test, branding it as a product of culture warriors intent on replacing American history with multiculturalism. The political left contends that the new questions are designed to make it harder for immigrants to pass the test. This sort of grandstand-

ing is part of the reason why America has fallen so far short in the efforts we need to make to ensure that immigrants succeed in our society.

⌣•⌣

Not only has America failed to articulate what it is that we expect of immigrants, but other policies have made it harder for many immigrants to become new Americans, for example policies that condemn many workers to illegal status and hurt legal immigrants who may be assumed to be undocumented. Ironically, some of the policies that make it harder for undocumented immigrants to gain legal status also make it less likely that they'll return home because they know that they may not be able to come back into the United States to return to their jobs and family. These migrants thus are both barred from becoming Americans and from nurturing their relationships with their Mexican or Central American families.

America's problem is not immigration itself, but how immigration occurs—that is, whether people come desperately across the border or give up in disgust at the failure of our bureaucracy and laws, or whether they can reasonably expect that the United States will make it feasible for the workers we need to comply with its immigration laws and to welcome them into our society as they work hard and participate in the civic life of their adopted communities. The current immigration system is inefficient, with little accountability, and contradicts itself at every turn. Many businesses are forced to choose between breaking the law or closing down. Congress can pass laws that take months or years for immigration authorities to put into effect. The body of law is so big that even few immigration officers fully understand it, so it is almost impossible to apply without running afoul of some technicality. As a result, too many applicants have to file repeatedly, wasting everyone's time and energy. Furthermore, decisions made by harried, overworked consular officers may be capricious yet are not subject to review.

We can put in place practical measures to create a sane, workable immigration policy and revive national competitiveness. The first step is

a major set of reforms to make immigration policy and the bureaucracy that administers it work for our country instead of acting as a drag on our economy and on our national outlook. Reforms would include establishing a clear legal framework for the low-wage migrant workers on whom parts of our economy depend, coupled with substantial and enforceable penalties for employers who willfully violate immigration and labor laws. The goals should be to streamline and clarify laws and procedures; to overhaul our immigration bureaucracy to instill accountability; make processing more efficient; and reduce backlogs for visas, green cards, and naturalization. The Department of Homeland Security has taken baby steps in this direction. For example, it appointed an ombudsman, who has already developed several pilot programs to streamline immigrant processing. He has developed an extensive plan to address processing times, lack of information, lack of standardization, processing delays resulting from benefits fraud, and inadequate technologies. This is a start, but a real overhaul of our immigration bureaucracy will require a serious commitment of funds and political will.

It also is essential to bring our immigration laws into line with reality. We must make sure that businesses can bring in the workers they need—legally. At the same time, we need to establish and enforce significant financial penalties on employers who circumvent immigration and labor laws. In immigration policy, as in drug policy, enforcement too often is directed against the victims but fails to punish those who benefit; police arrest users of drugs, focusing scarce resources on the little fish even as big fish swim away. Similarly, immigration enforcement efforts focus far too heavily on undocumented workers rather than on the businesses that profit the most from their labor. Scofflaws hurt the businesses that obey the law and respect workers' rights to fair pay and treatment, yet they largely go unpunished. By failing to provide a legal alternative for the workers on whom our agricultural and service industries depend, we have created an environment that encourages employers to ignore immigration laws; from there, it is just a short leap to abusing labor laws as part of business as usual.

Enforcement of immigration and labor laws would help the firms that adhere to them. It would also help U.S.-born workers because foreign-born workers would not be as likely to accept abusive working conditions—and thus would no longer offer employers as distinct an advantage over U.S. workers who know their rights and are not afraid to stand up for them. It is not the mere presence of foreign-born workers that lowers wages; the limitations we place on their rights as workers is a critical factor allowing employers to exploit them. By making it harder for employers to exploit migrant labor, we would level the playing field for U.S. workers instead of tilting it more steeply against them, as current policies do.

A real enforcement policy will only work if businesses can get the workers they need legally. If we are to succeed in creating a sustainable immigration policy, those on opposing sides of the debate—those who would slam the gates shut and those who would throw them wide open—must agree on a fundamental compromise that is fair to everyone. Immigration advocates must acknowledge that strategies to moderate immigration—including real enforcement measures and changes in the way we determine who may come to the United States—need to be part of any solution. This approach, based on nationalist and egalitarian principles, has had respectable advocates throughout history: abolitionist and diplomat Frederick Douglass, labor leader Samuel Gompers, and, more recently, Barbara Jordan.

Today, the idea of finding ways to reduce immigration is anathema in certain circles. Yet a modest decrease in certain kinds of immigration would allow America to put a priority on access to the skills we need, even as we could more easily implement policies aimed at ensuring that new immigrants integrate successfully and that Americans can accommodate them—because, let's be honest, successfully integrating immigrants into American society requires changes on both sides. Not all migration is good. In an ideal world, no one—neither human rights activists and immigration advocates nor enforcement officers and border communities inundated by an impoverished, desperate, transient population—wants to see people risking death in the desert or on the seas in the hopes of reaching a

life that, at best, may be merely less awful than the one they left behind. There are ways to reduce immigration moderately—particularly illegal immigration—without resorting to draconian measures that would worsen the very problems they are supposedly meant to fix.

At the same time, those who advocate restricting immigration must concede that the only way to end illegal immigration is to implement a system that allows the people our economy needs to come here legally. An increase in legal immigration—not indiscriminate, but based on a carefully thought-out approach to matching legal immigration with our country's needs—will reduce the number of people coming illegally. By taking business away from clandestine traffickers and eliminating the tremendous waste of energy that undocumented workers put into getting around obstacles, such a policy would rechannel labor and resources into productive economic activities here and in immigrants' home countries.

How, then, do we decide how many people to let in? One of the questions most frequently posed in opinion polls on immigration is whether we should let in more immigrants, fewer immigrants, or if the current immigration flow is just right. According to a 2005 Pew Hispanic Center report, immigration fell by 25 percent between 2001 and 2004, already a significant drop. However, immigration had accelerated so much in the late 1990s that even this decline in immigration left us with an annual inflow of 1.2 million immigrants—roughly the number coming around the time of the Jordan report, which advocated reducing immigration modestly in the mid-1990s.

This change in numbers undoubtedly resulted in part from the chilling of the climate for immigrants in the United States after 9/11, but it was not the result of setting a specific target. The problem with setting specific target numbers of immigrants is that it is virtually impossible to do so. And, in cutting off legal immigration, we encourage people to come in clandestinely. Indeed, data confirm that illegal immigration has increased when legal avenues have been shut off. According to the Pew Hispanic Center study, the proportion of illegal immigrants as part of total immigration inflows to the United States rose between 1992 and 2004, a period during which legal immigration became more difficult be-

cause of the combination of backlogs and new security checks. During this period, the number of new unauthorized immigrants came to exceed the number of authorized immigrants. The pressures for people to come to America are so intense that even measures intended to make life here more difficult for illegal immigrants do not effectively deter them from coming; that much is obvious from the increasing numbers of undocumented aliens crossing the borders even in face of laws intended to deny them driver's licenses and make it easier to deport them. As sociologist Ramona Hernández has shown, when home country conditions are desperate enough, workers are willing to risk leaving, even as conditions in the potential host country become more hostile.

This increase in illegal immigration happened, incidentally, during a period when the United States was dramatically increasing spending on trying—unsuccessfully—to seal its borders. Between 1985 and 2002, overall immigration enforcement spending rose fivefold, from $1 billion to $4.9 billion, including an increase from $291 million to $1.6 billion for border control.

Some restrictionist groups, like the Center for Immigration Studies, have proposed enforcement through attrition—that is, making it so difficult for undocumented aliens to live and work here that they simply give up and go home. This would be done through laws intended to prevent people from obtaining driver's licenses if they don't have a Social Security number, to prevent people from receiving government services or voting without proof of citizenship, and to prevent their children from receiving birthright citizenship, as well as through the policies of companies like Greyhound Lines, which refuses to sell bus tickets to anyone without documents. This is not the solution, not least because it would in effect force all Americans—particularly Latinos, who are more likely to be asked for identification—to carry proof of citizenship. What is more, many of these people are likely to stay here anyway, because even a marginal life in the United States is better than a life of no hope in their home countries. The result would be a growing underworld population of broken families and desperate lives—a threat to social stability and the opposite of the American Dream.

The best we can hope to do is to create very rough measures that will moderate the flow of people.

First, we need to change expectations that encourage people to come in hopes of bringing more and more family members. Second, we need to address the underlying home country conditions that drive people to emigrate in search of a living wage. Third, we need to focus enforcement efforts on those who profit most from illegal immigration: the human traffickers and the employers who abuse labor and immigration laws. Increased cooperation with other governments is crucial for apprehending and penalizing the like of the Mexican and Central American *coyotes* who smuggle people across borders. Enforcement against unscrupulous employers, however, can only be effective once we have taken steps to legalize the undocumented population that already is present.

The reason immigration has grown so quickly since 1965, when 1920s-era quotas were abolished, was the family reunification program. The program extended to adult siblings of U.S. citizens as well as citizens' sons and daughters—and their spouses. Unmarried adult children of U.S. permanent residents are also allowed in. As any high school mathematics student could appreciate, the 1965 law exponentially increased the rate of immigration by tying each immigrant to several other new immigrants, bringing the immigration rate back up to the early-twentieth-century levels that had proved to be so destabilizing and ultimately detrimental to sensible immigration policy, not the least of which was that it delayed parents from being reunited with children or spouses. For over a decade, family reunification has averaged well over 200,000 newcomers annually; it accounted for 63 percent of all immigration in 2001. By contrast, only 16 percent of legal immigration is employment based.

One simple and practical way to help ensure that immigration is orderly would be to dramatically cut back family reunification while preserving nuclear families with minors and expanding work-based visas. This would reduce expectations that one anchor family member could bring in many more. By reducing adult family preference categories, we could slash the application backlog for spouses and dependent children, who should be the priority of family reunification anyway (they make up

less than half of the annual family preference entrants). At the same time, we would open up slots for business and job-based visas and make it easier for foreign-born workers to switch jobs under those visas, or switch to entrepreneurial visas. By freeing workers of constraints tying them to the employer who initially brought them here, we give them more leverage and thus make it harder for employers to pay lower wages that in turn would hurt U.S. workers' ability to compete. A change like this also could let some steam out of the war of words over immigration.

If the state of immigration—particularly illegal immigration caused by desperation—is to shift from the chaotic logjam it is today to something more rational and productive, U.S. policy also needs to address the reasons people feel that they have no choice but to leave their homes. Immigration policies must, like drug policies, be effective in two spheres: they must influence not only demand in the destination country but also supply in the source country. The only way to slow desperation-driven migration is to reduce desperation. That means finding ways to encourage economic development in migrant-sending nations, especially by engaging migrants in helping their home countries and in encouraging the circulation of ideas and the transfer of skills and technology.

Paradoxically, in the long run, the best way to slow desperate immigration is to let people come here, build their skills, and then take those skills back to their homelands. Also paradoxically, the best way for people to help their homelands is to adapt as fully as possible to American society, for this is the key to succeeding here. By encouraging people to study here and to go back and forth freely, we can encourage brain circulation and the creation of industries that will provide jobs in migrant-sending countries and markets for U.S. goods.

We should set caps on skilled immigration at levels high enough to avoid bottlenecks during times of peak demand, and give preferences to those who have studied in our universities. It has become a mantra in the high-tech industry—I've heard this idea attributed to at least three different executives at different companies—that America ought to staple a green card to the back of every diploma our universities issue to foreign-born students. To get a visa today, students must prove something that is

extremely difficult for bright young persons who likely have no idea what they will do after completing a degree program four or more years in the future: that they reside in a foreign country that they have "no intention of abandoning." This requirement provides a convenient way for consular officers—especially those who are terrified that they will be the one who let a terrorist in—to deny visas. But it contradicts the American economic interest in luring the best and brightest, on whom we depend to remain competitive, which is essential to ensuring more jobs for Americans as well. The United States is not the only country that depends on our allowing bright young scholars and entrepreneurs to study and work here. When they develop skills that they can take back to their home countries, they help the rest of the world to grow. The repatriation of skills learned in the United States also, in the long run, has the potential to decrease the kind of migration that happens because people see no options at home for bettering themselves and feeding their families.

The long-standing policy of requiring students to prove that they will return to their home countries illustrates America's ambivalence about whether we should encourage immigrants to stay or to go. Sometimes critics complain that today's immigrants are not assimilating fast enough; yet they also often oppose letting guest workers stay. The first version of President Bush's guest worker proposal, for example, would have required workers to go home after three or six years, which would have given them little incentive to put down roots in this country and work on their English, and no chance of applying for citizenship. The question of whether guest workers would be allowed to naturalize remains a central sticking point in the debate.

Yet setting up a system that prohibits guest workers from ever naturalizing will give them absolutely no incentive to learn English or to integrate into American society—a recipe for ensuring that these migrants will remain marginalized and segregated. At the same time, if migrant-sending countries are to develop their own economies and reduce the pressure on their citizens to emigrate, they will need their ablest workers to return home. The solution to this dilemma is not to dictate what immigrant workers should do but to tailor a menu of options that lets each

worker's individual circumstances guide his or her decision. America needs skilled workers, but these are the people who arguably could contribute more to the greater good if they eventually return to their home countries after building their skills in the United States—like many of the MIT graduate students I met, who intended to work here for a few years after earning their degrees and then to return home. In these cases, we could require immigrants who decide to stay in America longer than ten years to pay a premium; some of that money could be redirected to the immigrant's homeland and/or to job training for U.S. workers.

Similarly, instead of paying astronomical amounts to criminals to smuggle them across borders, lower-skilled immigrants could pay a fee if they decide to stay after their guest worker status ran out. These fees—which should be lower than those paid by higher-skilled, better-paid workers—would help fund English courses as well as the increase in immigration staff needed to process the corresponding increase in paperwork as these workers come out of the shadows. Another possibility could be to ask guest workers or their employers to pay a deposit to be held in an escrow account; if the worker decided to stay in America, the money would be forfeited to a development bank for use in the home country.

~·~

Immigrants and foreign-born workers make a convenient scapegoat when the real problem facing America is that we have not invested in preparing Americans for the new global age of competition. A near-monopoly firm that uses its dominance of the market as an excuse to become complacent and sluggish and shies away from fair competition winds up squelching innovation and becoming the architect of its own demise unless a crisis forces it to change direction in time to avoid disaster.

The United States faces a choice: We can let ourselves slide, or we can figure out what is wrong and come up with ways to fix things and hold on to our leadership. Closing the gates and retreating from the world once again would be to abdicate America's global responsibility as a leader. Where is our national pride in what we have accomplished, with the

creation of one nation, however imperfect, out of all the peoples of the world? Where is our faith that American can-do optimism and hard work will prevail? We can renew our belief in the power of America, or we can capitulate and pursue policies that increase local and global inequality and lead to instability and economic and social disruption.

We no longer can take for granted that we are the country of choice for the world's best and brightest. Yet instead of taking the steps we need in order to keep them coming, we are making it harder for the world's hardest-working people to come here, depriving our own businesses of the hands and minds they need to innovate and grow even as we make it easier for unscrupulous employers to abuse workers. In the process, we are gumming up the engine of worldwide growth. Instead of focusing on productive tasks, businesses and workers waste tremendous amounts of energy navigating a dysfunctional immigration bureaucracy. Shortsighted measures ostensibly created for the sake of national security have alienated whole groups of foreigners in America and wasted precious resources, when targeted intelligence and outreach to foreign-born communities could have yielded better results. In an ultimately counterproductive attitude, America sees the world in terms of an us-versus-them battle, not a source of opportunities for mutual profit.

Instead of closing our doors, we need to recognize that the idea of America does not stop at our borders. This means we must immediately make it a priority to keep this country as competitive as it needs to be in a world that has followed our own urging to learn to compete.

To do this, we need to restore Americans' faith in ourselves. This involves investing in the public good, most importantly by bringing American education back up to where it needs to be so that we need not rely so heavily on foreigners to provide the brainpower and sweat equity that our economy needs.

Following through on a renewed commitment to government investment in research and development will support a culture of innovation and make it more attractive for U.S. students to pursue careers in science and technology. We also need to fund and promote studies of foreign languages, cultures, and politics, in order to make sure that Americans have

the tools to succeed in a global economy. Above all, America needs to stop acting like we are holed up in a bunker and instead show some pride and self-confidence.

Thanks to our long history of investment and innovation, America remains the world leader in artificial intelligence, medicine, and information technology. We need to recognize our strengths and build on them. By restoring our education system so that it once again is the best in the world, we will bolster the homegrown workforce that will make our companies less dependent on foreign skills. The American Electronics Association, for example, calls for a "son of Sputnik" national program to improve math and engineering, along the lines of the concerted Cold War effort, to make sure that our math, science, and engineering capabilities remain the best in the world.

Investing in America also means helping American workers cope with the changes that the reshaping of the global economy brings, both through immigration to this country and through the growth of jobs abroad. This means providing not only education but also job skills training and health and child care for the low-skilled Americans whose wages are affected most by immigration and outsourcing.

◡•◡

There are many reasons to believe that Americans will make the right choices. For one thing, we have shown that we can learn from past mistakes. When Congress voted to intern citizens and noncitizens of Japanese, German, and Italian descent in World War II, there was not a single dissenting vote, and hardly any Americans spoke out against the decision. By contrast, the USA Patriot Act has met with heated opposition. Many lawsuits have challenged the detention and deportation of noncitizens during the "war on terror," and the courts have not given the government carte blanche.

Time and again, Americans have stood up to defend immigrants whom they felt were being unfairly targeted. In one example, four high school students in a national science competition were arrested near Niagara

Falls in the summer of 2005 because immigration officials targeted them for inspection because they looked Mexican, and the students discovered that they did not have papers, although they had lived in the United States since they were small children. The story became national news because it was obvious that deporting such star students because of a situation that was not their fault would be wrong; a judge dismissed the case.

Thoughtful Americans recognize what's at stake, and universities, business leaders, community members, and cultural and arts organizations have made sure that their elected officials know it.

American students themselves are aware that global education is important; in a 2002 American Council on Education study, three out of ten college students did not believe that their education prepared them to understand the complexities of world events. From 2002 to 2003, the number of Americans studying abroad rose by 8.5 percent. Although most of the students went to Europe, the number of American students in Latin America, Africa, Australia, and New Zealand rose by 14 percent to 16 percent.

If a March 2005 poll of 800 registered voters is any guide, Americans see the need for change in our immigration policies. When asked whether they would support a proposal that would require undocumented workers living here to register as temporary guest workers, provide temporary work visas for those not currently here, provide newly registered workers with a path to legality and citizenship with no preferential treatment over legal immigrants, institute tougher penalties for workers and employers who violate laws, and prioritize uniting close family members, a solid 75 percent supported the proposal, including 38 percent who supported it intensely. Only 22 percent opposed it, 13 percent intensely. Still, there are deep divisions about what should be considered appropriate levels of immigration. In the same poll, some 48 percent felt that immigration should stay at the same level or increase, while 46 percent thought it should be decreased or stopped altogether. Indeed, poll after poll has shown that Americans see solving the illegal immigration problem as a national priority, and that they favor legalization over an approach that would criminalize the more than 10 million people on whom our economy depends.

This is the sort of reasonable, can-do attitude that has made this country what it is today.

◝•◞

One of the contestants in the 2005 Intel Science Talent Search, Yingqiuqi Lei, became "Chelsea" Lei when she came to America in May 2001 with her mother, a Chinese journalist. (Her father stayed in China, where he works for the government as a science historian.) A schoolmate heard her Chinese name and, despairing of pronouncing it, announced that it sounded like "Chelsea," and the name stuck. In just three years, she went from speaking limited English to being one of the top forty science students in the country.

Before she left China in 2001, Chelsea Lei designed an Eightfold Maze—a labyrinth made of circular concentric walls that move—that will be installed in Kunming, the City of Spring. The maze will be large enough to drive a car or ride a horse through. "Ordinary labyrinths are boring," she says.

Once she arrived in the United States, she worked on analyzing what geological conditions must have been like when fossils were buried 30,000 to 40,000 years ago. Through a Williams College program with loose ties to her high school, she worked with the only electron spin resonance (ESR) lab in the United States, receiving summer high school credit for research that was accepted by a peer-reviewed journal. Using ESR and neutron activation analyses, she analyzed fourteen elements in 1,560 fossil teeth and sediment samples from fifty-seven sites around the world. Among her discoveries was that the Tsagaan Agui site in what now is the Mongolian desert once was lush and teeming with diverse wildlife.

Chelsea sees problems with both the Chinese and U.S. approaches to science education: both focus too much on textbooks and do not encourage students to get into laboratories and think in real-life terms about the ideas they are learning. Too few are shown compelling examples of why they should care about science. The difference is that America makes it easier for the students who do care about science to pursue opportunities

to learn: "One thing that is wonderful about the United States is that if you want to do something, there is always a way."

Chelsea shows the combination of determination, flexibility, and the kind of creative "thinking big" attitude that America needs. We are lucky to have her to appreciate what is best about our great country and to remind us that we have many reasons to hope for America.

Notes

The Governator and the Wetback

3   **Tens of millions of short-term visitors:** Elizabeth M. Grieco, "Temporary Admissions of Nonimmigrants to the United States in 2004." Annual Flow Report, Department of Homeland Security, Office of Immigration Statistics, May 2005.

4   **By some estimates, more than half:** Alice P. Gast, "The Impact of Restricting Information Access on Science and Technology." Paper. Cambridge, Mass.: Massachusetts Institute of Technology, 2003.

4   **The Industrial Research Institute:** "R&D Trends Forecast for 2004." Washington, D.C.: Industrial Research Institute, 2004.

7   **As Robert C. Richardson, a Nobel laureate:** Claudia Dreifus, "The Chilling of American Science: A Conversation with Robert C. Richardson." *New York Times Magazine*, July 6, 2004.

7   **U.S. authorities detained Ian McEwan:** John Marshall, "British Author Detained 24 Hours at Border." *Seattle Post-Intelligencer*, April 1, 2004.

8   **Microsoft chairman Bill Gates:** "Gates Laments Visa-Related Brain Drain." *Hispanic Business*, January 31, 2005. Gates was speaking at the World Economic Forum in Davos, Switzerland.

9   **Federal Reserve Board chairman Alan Greenspan:** U.S. Senate, Committee on Banking, Housing, and Urban Affairs, February 24, 2000.

9   **A 1995 survey polled a group of economists:** Economist survey by Stephen Moore, cited in Julian L. Simon, *Immigration: The Demographic and Economic Facts*. Washington, D.C.: Cato Institute and the National Immigration Forum, 1995, 47–48.

10   **"The jobs that Americans won't do":** Jim Edgar, Doris Meissner, Alejandro Silva, "Keeping the Promise: Immigration Proposals from the Heartland." Report of an Independent Task Force. Chicago: Chicago Council on Foreign Relations, 2004.

10   **Although they are spread across occupations:** Gianmarco I.P. Ottaviano and Giovanni Peri, "Rethinking the Gains from Immigration: Theory and Evidence from the U.S." NBER Working Paper No. 11672. Cambridge, Mass.: National Bureau of Economic Research, September 2005.

16   **Roughly a million immigrants come:** United Nations, *World Migration 2005*, citing *Trends in Total Migrant Stock: The 2003 Revision* (POP/DB/MIG/2003/1 and ESA/P/WP.188).

16   **"In my book, anyone who comes here and gives an honest day's work":** Rupert Murdoch, "Commentary: Let Us Give Thanks to Our Immigrants." *Wall Street Journal*, November 24, 2004, A12.

Patriots

19   **One of the newcomers:** "Collinsville Mob Leaders Expected to Be Put on Trial." *St. Louis Globe-Democrat*, April 6, 1918. The most comprehensive account of the Prager lynching is Donald R. Hickey's "The Prager Affair: A Study in Wartime Hysteria," *Journal of the Illinois State Historical Society* 62 (Summer 1969). For a broader account of the context of the killing, see Christopher Cappozzola, "The Only Badge Needed Is Your Patriotic Fervor: Vigilance, Coercion, and the Law in World War I America." *Journal of American History* 88, no. 4 (March 2002).

20   **"It was a drunken mob":** "Sherman Calls Prager Slayers 'A Drunken Mob'," *Chicago Daily Tribune*, April 9, 1918.

21   **When Prager was buried:** "Lynched Man Is Interred in U.S. Flag." *St. Louis Globe-Democrat*, April 11, 1918.

21   **Members of the International Order of Odd Fellows:** Chas. Specht, letter to the editor, "Was in St. Louis." *Edwardsville Intelligencer*, May 24, 1918.

22   **The *Washington Post*:** "Stamping Out Treason." *Washington Post*, April 12, 1918.

22   **Congressmen:** "Spy Law Wanted Now." *Washington Post*, April 6, 1918.

22   **"There was a peculiar coincidence":** "Jury Finds Prager Defendants Not Guilty and Others Are Free." *Edwardsville Intelligencer*, June 8, 1918.

24 **Many of the immigrants:** Mark Wyman, *Round-Trip to America: The Immigrants Return to Europe, 1880–1930*. Ithaca, N.Y.: Cornell University Press, 1993.

25 **Adding insult to injury:** Wyman, *Round-Trip to America*.

26 **"As a jingo":** John Higham, *Strangers in the Land: Patterns of American Nativism, 1860–1925*. New York: Atheneum, 1963 (1955).

30 **The good commissioners' first order:** John M. Lund, "Boundaries of Restriction: The Dillingham Commission." *University of Vermont History Review* 6 (December 1994).

30 **"Instead of the tall":** Lund, "Boundaries of Restriction."

31 **Boas's work would continue:** See, for example, Claudia Roth Pierpont, "The Measure of America: How a Rebel Anthropologist Waged War on Racism." *New Yorker*, March 8, 2004.

31 **Most of the researchers:** Lund, "Boundaries of Restriction."

33 **Patrick Buchanan warned:** Patrick J. Buchanan, *The Death of the West: How Dying Populations and Immigrant Invasions Imperil Our Country and Civilization*. New York: St. Martin's Press, 2002.

33 **In reality, the United States:** United Nations, *Trends in Total Migrant Stock: The 2003 Revision* (POP/DB/MIG/2003/1 and ESA/P/WP.188), data in digital form.

33 **Columnist Michelle Malkin:** Michelle Malkin, *In Defense of Internment: The Case for "Racial Profiling" in World War II and the War on Terror*. Washington, D.C.: Regnery Publishing, 2004.

35 **Ruffians stoned the delivery wagons:** See, for example, Mark Sonntag, "Fighting Everything German in Texas, 1917–1919," *Historian* 56, no. 4 (Summer 1994).

36 **German Americans themselves:** Richard O' Connor, *The German Americans*. New York: Little, Brown, 1968.

39 **In some cases:** Mark Sonntag, "Fighting Everything German in Texas, 1917–1919." *Historian* 56, no. 4 (Summer 1994).

43 **According to Raymond K. Cunningham:** Raymond K. Cunningham Jr., "Prisoners at Fort Douglas: War Barracks Three and the Enemy Aliens, 1917–1920." Salt Lake City: Fort Douglas Military Museum, 1983.

45 **The camps did not close until:** In addition to Cunningham's account, see William B. Glidden, "Internment Camps in America, 1917–1920," *Military Affairs* 37, no. 4 (December 1973), and Mitchell Yockelson, "The War Department: Keeper of Our Nation's Enemy Aliens During World War I," paper presented at the annual meeting of the Society for Military History, April 1998.

Becoming American

49   **Indeed, American voluntarism:** Theda Skocpol, "How Americans Became Civic," in *Civic Engagement in American Democracy*, edited by Theda Skocpol and Morris P. Fiorina. Washington, D.C.: Brookings Institution Press, 1999.

51   **From 1901 to 1920:** Nancy Foner, *From Ellis Island to JFK: Two Great Waves of Immigration.* New Haven, Conn.: Yale University Press and Russell Sage Foundation, 2000; Michael Jones-Correa, *Between Two Nations: The Political Predicament of Latinos in New York.* Ithaca, N.Y.: Cornell University Press, 1998; Mark Wyman, *Round-Trip America: The Immigrants Return to Europe, 1880–1930.* Ithaca, N.Y.: Cornell University Press, 1993.

51   **Then, as today:** Wyman, *Round-Trip America.*

52   **"To many, the impact":** Wyman, *Round-Trip America.*

52   **The United States harbored:** David Montgomery, "Racism, Immigrants, and Political Reform." *Journal of American History* 87 (March 2001).

52   **Eamon de Valera:** Ronald H. Bayor and Timothy J. Meagher, editors, *The New York Irish.* Baltimore: Johns Hopkins University Press, 1996.

53   **It was becoming clearer:** For an excellent overview of Americanization and pluralism during the Progressive Era, see Noah Pickus, *True Faith and Allegiance: Immigration and American Civic Nationalism.* Princeton, N.J.: Princeton University Press, 2005. For a discussion of the peculiarly American relationship between ethnicity and class, see Werner Sollors, "Theory of American Ethnicity, or: '? S Ethnic?/TI and American/TI, DE or United (W) States S S1 and Theor?'" *American Quarterly* 33 (1981).

53   **Frances Kellor:** See John J. Miller. "Miss Americanizer: Frances Kellor," *Policy Review* 83 (May–June 1997), and "The Naturalizers," *Policy Review* 78 (July–August 1996). On Jane Addams's work with immigrants at Hull House, see Jean Bethke Elshtain, *Jane Addams and the Dream of American Democracy.* New York, Basic Books, 2001.

54   **Among the businessmen:** Stephen Meyer, "Adapting the Immigrant to the Line: Americanization in the Ford Factory, 1914–1921." *Journal of Social History* 14 (Fall 1980).

56   **Americanization thus completed:** John Taylor Gatto, *The Underground History of Education in America.* New York: Pathway Books, 2000.

58   **The National German-American Alliance:** Gerhard Becker, "German-American Community in Milwaukee During World War I." Master's thesis, University of Wisconsin–Milwaukee, May 1988.

58   **The group promoted:** Frederick C. Luebke, *Bonds of Loyalty: German-Americans and World War I.* DeKalb: Northern Illinois University Press, 1974.

59 **Berger had become:** Joseph A. Ranney, "Aliens and 'Real Americans': Law and Ethnic Assimilation in Wisconsin, 1846–1920." *Wisconsin Lawyer* (December 1, 1994). Available at www.wisbar.org/AM/Template .cfm?Section=Search&template=/CM/HTMLDisplay.cfm& ContentID=35855.

60 **"All of us":** Jane Addams, *Peace and Bread in Time of War*. New York: Macmillan, 1922.

60 **The nation had abandoned:** Jamin Raskin, "Legal Aliens, Local Citizens: The Historical, Constitutional, and Theoretical Meanings of Alien Suffrage," *University of Pennsylvania Law Review* 141 (1993).

61 **America's ethnic fraternal organizations:** Eric Foner, *The Story of American Freedom*. New York: Norton, 1999.

61 **In the aftermath of the war:** Theda Skocpol, Ziad Munson, Andrew Karch, and Bayliss Camp, "Patriotic Partnerships: Why Great Wars Nourished American Civic Voluntarism." In *Shaped by War and Trade: International Influences on American Political Development*. Edited by Ira Katznelson and Martin Shefter. Princeton, N.J.: Princeton University Press, 2001.

61 **"Suddenly, German churches":** Skocpol et al., "Patriotic Partnerships."

62 **The American Legion's message:** Jacobus Ten Broek, E.H. Barnhart, and F.W. Matson, *Prejudice, War, and the Constitution*. Berkeley: University of California Press, 1968.

65 **Joseph Yenowsky:** "The Most Brainiest Man," *Nation*, April 17, 1920.

65 **As Jane Addams wrote:** Jane Addams to [*Chicago Tribune* editor] Edward S. Beck, February 23, 1920, in JAMC (reel 12-1376-1377), Special Collections, University Library, University of Illinois at Chicago.

66 **"A nation conceived in antonyms":** Daniel T. Rodgers. *Atlantic Crossings: Social Politics in a Progressive Age*. Cambridge, Mass.: Belknap/Harvard University Press, 1998.

66 **J. Hector St. John de Crèvecoeur:** J. Hector St. John de Crèvecoeur, *Letters from an American Farmer*. New York: Penguin Classics, 1981 (1782).

67 **Few thinkers:** Gunnar Myrdal, *An American Dilemma: The Negro Problem and Modern Democracy*. New York: Harper, 1944.

The Eagle and the Ostrich

69 **Before World War I:** Harold James, *The End of Globalization: Lessons from the Great Depression*. Cambridge, Mass.: Harvard University Press, 2001.

69   **By comparison:** World Bank, *World Development Index 2000*; data in digital form at devdata.worldbank.org/data-query/.

69   **"By 1914":** Kevin O'Rourke and Jeffrey Williamson, *Globalization in History: The Evolution of a Nineteenth-Century Global Economy*. Cambridge, Mass.: MIT Press, 1999.

70   **Immigration was a pillar:** Peter H. Lindert and Jeffrey G. Williamson, "Does Globalization Make the World More Unequal?" NBER Working Paper No. 8228. Cambridge, Mass.: National Bureau of Economic Research, April 2001. See also Claudia Goldin, "The Political Economy of Immigration Restriction in the United States, 1890 to 1921," NBER Working Paper No. 4345, April 1993.

70   **The increasing numbers:** Jeffrey G. Williamson, "The Economics of Mass Migrations." Cambridge, Mass.: National Bureau of Economic Research, Summer 1998. See also A. Timmer and J.G. Williamson, "Racism, Xenophobia, or Markets? The Political Economy of Immigration Policy Prior to the Thirties." NBER Working Paper No. 5867, January 1997; and A. Timmer and J.G. Williamson, "Immigration Policy Prior to the Thirties: Labor Markets, Policy Interactions, and Globalization Backlash," Department of Economics, Harvard University, March 1997.

70   **This ambivalence:** James, *The End of Globalization.*

71   **Although the business community:** Daniel Tichenor, *Dividing Lines: The Politics of Immigration Control in America*. Princeton, N.J.: University Press, 2002.

71   **In May 1924:** Roger Daniels, *Guarding the Golden Door*. New York: Hill & Wang, 2004.

72   **Ironically, it is more than likely:** O'Rourke and Williamson, *Globalization in History.*

73   **"In the nineteenth century":** James, *The End of Globalization.*

74   **Elsewhere in the economy:** W. Elliott Brownlee, *Dynamics of Ascent: A History of the American Economy*, 2nd edition. New York: Alfred A. Knopf, 1979 (1974).

74   **Raising tariffs to their highest levels ever:** For more on the economic consequences of Depression-era protectionism, see Barry Eichengreen, "The Political Economy of the Smoot-Hawley Tariff," *Research in Economic History* 12 (1989), 1–43; Douglas A. Irwin, "From Smoot-Hawley to Reciprocal Trade Agreements: Changing the Course of U.S. Trade Policy in the 1930s," in *The Defining Moment: The Great Depression and the American Economy in the Twentieth Century*, edited by Michael D. Bordo, Claudia Goldin, and Eugene N. White. Chicago: University of Chicago Press, 1998; and Charles P. Kindleberger, *The World in Depression, 1929–1939*. Berkeley: University of California Press, 1973.

75　**By the early 1930s:** George McDaniel, "Madison Grant and the Racialist Movement: The Distinguished Origins of Racial Activism." *American Renaissance* (December 1997).

76　**Nevertheless, clear efforts:** Eric Foner, *The Story of American Freedom.* New York: Norton, 1999.

76　**By various estimates:** Alfred McClung Lee, "Subversive Individuals of Minority Status," *Annals of the American Academy of Political and Social Sciences* (September 1942), 164.

76　**"The queerest birds":** Louis De Jong, *The German Fifth Column in the Second World War*, Chicago: University of Chicago Press, 1973 (1956), citing Nikolaus Ritter quote in *Der Stern* (Hamburg), VI, 11 (March 15, 1953), 11–12.

77　**In this case:** Arnold Krammer, *Undue Process: The Untold Story of America's German Alien Internees.* Boulder: Rowman and Littlefield, 1997.

77　**The Bund, however:** Letter, January 7, 1938, to Auswärtige Amt. Doc. German Foreign Policy, D, Vol 1 at 670, cited in De Jong, *The German Fifth Column*, 219.

78　**Italian Americans:** John P. Diggins, "The Italo-American Anti-Fascist Opposition." *Journal of American History* 54, no. 3 (December 1967), 579–598.

79　**Presaging the post-9/11 argument:** Congressional Record, May 5, 1935, cited in John Christgau, *Enemies: World War II Alien Internment.* Lincoln, Neb.: Authors Choice Press, 2001.

79　**J. Edgar Hoover:** Krammer, *Undue Process.*

79　**Reminiscent of:** Athan Theoharis and John Stuart Cox, *The Boss: J. Edgar Hoover and the Great American Inquisition.* Philadelphia: Temple University Press, 1988.

80　**On a single day:** Shepardson and Scroggs, *The United States in World Affairs, 1940* (New York 1941) cited in DeJong, *The German Fifth Column*, 106.

80　**Life magazine:** *Life*, July 1, 1940, cited in DeJong, *The German Fifth Column*, 107.

80　**The public responded:** Krammer, *Undue Process.*

82　**Attorney General Francis Biddle:** Francis Biddle, *In Brief Authority.* Garden City, N.Y.: Doubleday, 1962.

82　**Within the first three weeks:** Jacobus ten Broek, Edward N. Barnhart, and Floyd Watson, *Prejudice, War, and the Constitution: Causes and Consequences of the Evacuation of the Japanese Americans in World War II.* Berkeley: University of California Press: 1975 (1984).

82　**Newspaper columnist Henry McLemore:** Ten Broek et al., *Prejudice, War, and the Constitution.*

84   **While still a senator:** John F. Kennedy, *A Nation of Immigrants.* New York: Harper & Row, 1964.

84   **Kennedy's thoughts:** Roger Daniels, *Guarding the Golden Door: American Immigration Policy and Immigrants since 1882.* New York: Hill & Wang, 2004.

86   **The problem was:** Arthur Mann, *The One and the Many: Reflections on the American Identity.* Chicago: University of Chicago Press, 1979.

87   **A simple "American" identity:** Nathan Glazer and Daniel Patrick Moynihan, *Beyond the Melting Pot.* Cambridge, Mass.: MIT Press, 1963; revised 1970.

87   **One in eight:** Jean-Christophe Dumont and Georges Lemaître, "Counting Immigrants and Expatriates in OECD Countries: New Perspectives." Paris: Organization for Economic Cooperation and Development, 2004.

American Jobs

90   **The personal computer market in India:** "The Insidious Charms of Foreign Investment." *Economist,* March 5, 2005.

90   **America's economic strength:** Computer Systems Policy Project, "Choose to Compete: How Innovation, Investment, and Productivity Can Grow U.S. Jobs and Ensure American Competitiveness in the 21st Century." Washington, D.C.: Computer Systems Policy Project, January 2004.

91   **Paul Grieco, Gary Hufbauer, and Scott Bradford:** Gary Clyde Hufbauer and Paul L.E. Grieco, "The Payoff from Globalization." *Washington Post,* June 7, 2005; Scott Bradford, Paul Grieco, and Gary Hufbauer, "The Payoff to America of Global Integration," in C. Fred Bergsten, editor, *The United States and the World Economy: Foreign Economic Policy for the Next Decade.* Washington, D.C.: Institute for International Economics, 2005.

92   **U.S. Census Bureau director Kenneth Prewitt:** "Census Finds Immigrants Blending in Faster, Easier" (Q&A with Kenneth Prewitt), *USA Today,* December 27, 2000.

93   **In the United States:** Elizabeth Grieco, "The Foreign-Born in the U.S. Labor Force: Numbers and Trends." Migration Policy Institute Fact Sheet No. 4. Washington, D.C., January 2004.

95   **The other side:** Tom Lochner, "San Pablo City Leader Criticized for Poem." *Contra Costa Times,* May 19, 2005.

96   **In Alabama:** Samira Jafari, "Survey: Most Alabamans Believe Immigrants Taking Away Jobs." Associated Press, January 12, 2004. Survey available at www.askalabama.org.

96   **Similarly, a 2004 Minnesota:** Stan Greenberg, Anna Greenberg, Julie Hootkin, "The Changing Shape of Minnesota: Reinvigorating Community and Government in the New Minnesota." Minneapolis: Hubert H. Humphrey Institute of Public Affairs, University of Minnesota, December 14, 2004. Available at www.hhh.umn.edu/projects/mcp/final_report.pdf.

96   **Studies documenting the positive effects:** Andrew Sum, Paul Harrington, and Ishwar Khatiwada, "New Foreign Immigrants and U.S. Labor Markets in the U.S.: The Unprecedented Effects of New Foreign Immigration on the Growth of the Nation's Labor Force and Its Employed Population, 2000 to 2004." Boston: Center for Labor Market Studies, Northeastern University, January 2005.

97   **Urban Institute researchers:** Jeffrey S. Passel and Michael Fix, "Immigration and Immigrants: Setting the Record Straight." Washington, D.C.: Urban Institute, May 1994; Jeffrey S. Passel, "Immigrants and Taxes: A Reappraisal of Huddle's 'The Cost of Immigrants,'" Washington, D.C.: Urban Institute, January 1994.

97   **In 2004, the Center for Immigration Studies:** Steven A. Camarota, "A Jobless Recovery? Immigrant Gains and Native Losses." Center for Immigration Studies Backgrounder. Washington, D.C.: Center for Immigration Studies, October 2004.

97   **In testimony:** Testimony Before U.S. House of Representatives Subcommittee on Immigration, Border Security and Claims, hearing on "New Jobs in Recession and Recovery: Who Are Getting Them and Who Are Not?" May 4, 2005.

98   **Opponents of immigration:** George J. Borjas, *Heaven's Door: Immigration and the American Economy.* Princeton, N.J.: Princeton University Press, 1999.

98   **More recent work:** Gianmarco I.P. Ottaviano and Giovanni Peri, "Rethinking the Gains from Immigration: Theory and Evidence from the U.S." NBER Working Paper No. 11672. Cambridge, Mass.: National Bureau of Economic Research, September 2005. For a summary of the paper, which is quite technical, see Virginia Postrel, "Yes, Immigration May Lift Wages," *New York Times*, November 3, 2005.

99   **The other important assumption:** David Card, "Is the New Immigration Really So Bad?" NBER Working Paper No. 11547. Cambridge, Mass.: National Bureau of Economic Research, August 2005.

99   **The evidence:** A. Dianne Schmidley, "Profile of the Foreign-Born Population in the United States: 2000." U.S. Census Bureau, Current Population Reports, Series P23-206. Washington, D.C.: U.S. Census Bureau, December 2001.

100   **The bulk of that assistance:** Steven Camarota, "Back Where We Started: An Examination of Trends in Immigrant Welfare Use Since Welfare Reform." Washington, D.C.: Center for Immigration Studies, March 2003.

100   **In a 1997 study:** National Research Council, "The New Americans: Economic, Demographic, and Fiscal Effects of Immigration." Washington, D.C.: National Academy of Sciences, 1997.

100   **Over the long run:** Stuart Anderson, "The Contribution of Legal Immigration to the Social Security System." Arlington, Va.: National Foundation for American Policy, revised and updated March 2005 (February 2005).

101   **Each year:** Eduardo Porter, "Illegal Immigrants Are Bolstering Social Security with Billions." *New York Times*, April 5, 2005.

102   **Refugees were streaming:** Roger Daniels, *Guarding the Golden Door.* New York: Hill & Wang, 2004.

103   **The conservative writer:** Peter Brimelow, *Alien Nation: Common Sense About America's Immigration Disaster.* New York: Harper Perennial, 1996.

107   **In response to:** U.S. Citizenship and Naturalization Service, *Statistical Yearbook 2003.* See also Michael Fix and Jeffrey Passel, "Trends in Naturalization." Washington, D.C.: Urban Institute, 2004; Hans P. Johnson, Belinda I. Reyes, Laura Mameesh, and Elisa Barbour, "Taking the Oath: An Analysis of Naturalization in California and the United States." San Francisco: Public Policy Institute of California, 1999.

107   **In September 2000, however:** Gallup Poll News Service Poll Analysis, July 18, 2001, cited in Daniels, *Guarding the Golden Gates.*

109   **On October 1, 2004:** U.S. Citizenship and Immigration Services, press release, dated February 17, 2004 (revised February 19, 2004).

109   **In a small concession:** Christina Hoag, "Visas Allow More High-Tech Workers to Come." *Miami Herald*, April 6, 2005.

110   **This is about reforming:** Sona Shah, Testimony to the Committee on International Relations, U.S. House of Representatives, February 4, 2004.

110   **Using the slang:** N. Sivakumar, *Debugging Indian Computer Programmers: Dude, Did I Steal Your Job?* Bridgewater, N.J.: Divine Tree, 2004.

111   **A survey and analysis:** Patrick Thibodeau, "The H-1B Equation: Salary Data Shows Split With Wages of U.S. Workers." *Computerworld*, February 28, 2005.

111   **The economic slowdown:** "A Jobless Recovery?" Washington, D.C.: Center for Immigration Studies, October 2004.

112   **Immigrants filled 86 percent:** Jeffrey Sparshott, "Bay Firms Depend on Foreign Workers." *Washington Times*, June 1, 2005.

113   **Indeed, workplace abuses:** Lori Nessel, "Undocumented Immigrants in the Workplace: The Fallacy of Labor Protection and the Need for

Reform." *Harvard Civil Rights–Civil Liberties Law Review* 36, Summer 2001.

113 **This is not an isolated case:** "Immigration Judge Rules INS Agents Are Bound by Former OI 287.3a Regarding Enforcement Actions During Labor Disputes." *Immigrants' Rights Update* 17, no. 5 (September 4, 2003). Available at www.nilc.org/immsemplymnt/wkplce_enfrcmnt/wkplcenfrc018.htm.

113 **In the late 1990s:** Louis Uchitelle, "I.N.S. Is Looking the Other Way as Illegal Immigrants Fill Jobs." *New York Times*, March 9, 2000.

114 **As immigration authorities:** Statement of Richard M. Stana, Director, Homeland Security and Justice; Testimony Before the Subcommittee on Immigration, Border Security, and Claims, Committee on the Judiciary, House of Representatives, "Immigration Enforcement: Preliminary Observations on Employment Verification and Worksite Enforcement Efforts" (report GAO-05-822T). Washington, D.C.: U.S. Government Accountability Office, June 21, 2005.

114 **The high-profile Wal-Mart case:** "Wal-Mart Pays $11M over Illegal Labor." CNN/Money, March 18, 2005.

115 **This point was driven home:** Hoffman Plastic Compounds, Inc. v. National Labor Relations Board, 535 U.S. 137 (2002).

115 **A 1999 study:** Gregory Rodriguez, "From Newcomers to Americans: The Successful Integration of Immigrants into American Society." Washington, D.C.: National Immigration Forum, 1999.

115 **After dipping during:** Michael Fix, Jeffrey S. Passel, and Kenneth Sucher, "Trends in Naturalization." Washington, D.C.: Urban Institute, 2003.

115 **Far below the high:** Peter Salins, "The Assimilation Contract." In *Reinventing the Melting Pot: The New Immigrants and What It Means to Be American*, edited by Tamar Jacoby. New York: Basic Books, 2004.

115 **Yet not all immigrants:** Rakesh Kochhar, "Latino Labor Report, 2004: More Jobs for New Immigrants but at Lower Wages." Washington, D.C.: Pew Hispanic Center, 2005.

117 **Two out of five Latinos:** Matthew Josefowicz and Sang Lee, "Ethnic Minorities, Financial Services, and the Web." Boston: Celent Communications, January 28, 2003.

The Best and the Brightest

119 **Of the Nobel Prizes:** Rob Paral and Benjamin Johnson, "Maintaining a Competitive Edge: The Role of the Foreign-Born and U.S. Immigration Policies in Science and Engineering." Washington, D.C.: Immigration Policy Center, *Immigration Policy In Focus* 3, no. 3 (August 2004).

120   **In 2000, Chinese or Indian:** Louise Auerhahn, Bob Brownstein, "The Economic Effects of Immigration in Santa Clara County and California." San Jose, Calif.: Working Parnerships USA, September 2004. Available at www.wpusa.org/publications/complete/wpusa_immig.pdf.

120   **The flying ace:** "Major James Jabara: First American Jet Ace, USAF F-86 Sabre Pilot." Association of Patriotic Arab Americans in the Military. Available at www.apaam.org/jamesjabara2.htm.

121   **Our economic dependence:** Jeanne Batalova, "College-Educated Foreign Born in the U.S. Labor Source." Washington, D.C.: Migration Information Source, February 1, 2005. Available at www.migration information.org/USfocus/print.cfm?ID=285.

121   **The foreign-born population:** Jean-Christophe Dumont and Georges Lemaître, "Counting Immigrants and Expatriates in OECD Countries: A New Perspective." OECD Social, Employment, and Migration Working Papers DELSA/ELSA/WD/SEM(2005)4. Paris: Organization for Economic Cooperation and Development, 2004.

121   **Nearly half of the National Institutes of Health's:** Bernard Wysocki Jr., "Under a Microscope: Foreign Scientists Are Being Stranded by War on Terror." *Wall Street Journal*, January 20, 2003.

121   **In 1966:** National Science Foundation, Science and Engineering Indicators, 2004.

122   **One in five college and university:** B. Lindsey Lowell, "State of Knowledge on the Flow of Foreign Science and Technology Workers in the United States." Paper prepared for the Task Force on National Workforce Policies. Cited in National Science Board, "The Science and Engineering Workforce: Realizing America's Potential." Washington, D.C.: National Science Foundation, August 14, 2003.

122   **At the University of Maryland:** Testimony of C.D. Mote Jr., President, University of Maryland, College Park. Subcommittees on 21st Century Competitiveness and Select Education Committee on Education and the Workforce, Hearing on "Tracking International Students in Higher Education: A Progress Report," March 17, 2005.

122   *Time* **magazine:** "The Coming Job Boom." *Time*, May 6, 2002.

122   **The other part:** National Science Foundation, *Science and Engineering Indicators 2004*, Appendix, Tables 2-25, 2-27, 2-33, 2-38, and 2-39.

122   **Similarly, European universities:** Richard Freeman, "Does Globalization of the Scientific/Engineering Workforce Threaten U.S. Economic Leadership?" NBER Working Paper No. 11457. Cambridge, Mass.: National Bureau of Economic Research, June 2005.

123   **Richard Freeman:** Freeman, "Does Globalization of the Scientific/ Engineering Workforce Threaten U.S. Economic Leadership?"

129   **The outperformance of immigrant students:** Stuart Anderson, "The Multiplier Effect." *International Educator*, Summer 2004.

129   **America is the economic engine:** J.P. Morgan and NTC Research, "JP-Morgan Global PMI Report on Manufacturing and Services." New York and London, August 3, 2005.

131   **National Bureau of Economic Research economists:** Laura Bottazzi and Giovanni Peri, "The International Dynamics of R&D and Innovation in the Short and in the Long Run." NBER Working Paper No. 11524. Cambridge, Mass.: National Bureau of Economic Research, August 2005.

131   **"International science":** "International Science: What's in It for the United States?" Statement of Bruce Alberts, President, National Academy of Sciences, and Chairman, National Research Council, before the Committee on Science, U.S. House of Representatives, March 25, 1998.

133   **An Indian-born entrepreneur:** "An American in Bangalore." *Economist*, February 8, 2003.

133   **A Public Policy Institute of California study:** AnnaLee Saxenian, "Local and Global Networks of Immigrant Professionals in Silicon Valley." San Francisco: Public Policy Institute of California, 2002.

133   **Thus, a growing number of patents:** "I Spy Spies." *Economist*, February 5, 2005.

137   **B. Lindsay Lowell:** B. Lindsay Lowell, "Some Developmental Effects of the International Migration of Highly Skilled Persons." International Migration Paper 46. Geneva: International Labour Office, 2002.

137   **Madhu Yaskhi Goud:** Sujeet Rajan, "New Jersey Businessman Swept into Office in Indian Elections." *Indian Express*, May 14, 2004.

138   **Hometown associations can:** Carol Zabin, "Mexican Hometown Associations and Mexican Immigrant Political Empowerment in Los Angeles." Washington, D.C.: Nonprofit Sector Research Fund, Aspen Foundation, 1998.

Homeland Insecurity

140   **Every year:** Elizabeth M. Grieco, "Temporary Admissions of Nonimmigrants to the United States in 2004." Washington, D.C.: Department of Homeland Security Office of Immigration Statistics, May 2005.

144   **In March 2004:** "Repeated Arrests of American-Bangladeshi Nuclear Scientist Has the Community in an Uproar." Translated by Moinuddin Nasser. *Voices That Must Be Heard,* March 8, 2005; originally published in *Bangla Patrika,* February 25, 2005.

145   **Three members of Congress:** Immigration.com, "Members of Congress Protest Special Registration." December 23, 2002. Available at www .immigration.com/newsletter1/memcongreg.html.

146   **Mohammad Sarfaraz Hussain:** Gary Ackerman, "Commending Edward J. McElroy of the Bureau of Immigration and Customs Enforcement." *Congressional Record,* May 1, 2003; Corey Kilgannon, "Pakistani, 18, Wins Fight Against Order to Leave U.S." *New York Times,* April 30, 2003.

146   **When the Department of Homeland Security:** Nancy Lofholm, "Ridgway Rallies Around Armenians." *Denver Post,* August 20, 2004; Kirk Johnson, "Deportation Case Riles Colorado Town." *New York Times,* December 13, 2004.

147   **A May 2003 congressional study:** "Homeland Security–Justice Department's Project to Interview Aliens After September 11, 2001." Report to Congressional Committees GAO–03–459. Washington, D.C.: U.S. General Accountability Office, April 2003.

147   **According to a report:** "The September 11 Detainees: A Review of the Treatment of Aliens Held on Immigration Charges in Connection with the Investigation of the September 11 Attacks," Department of Justice, Office of the Inspector General, April 2003, available at www.usdoj .gov/oig/special/0306/full.pdf; and Dan Eggen, "Tapes Show Abuse of 9/11 Detainees," *Washington Post,* December 19, 2003.

147   **The Cato Institute:** Charles V. Peña, *TIA Redux: Still Bad Math.* Washington, D.C.: Cato Institute, June 12, 2003. Available at www.masnet .org/articleinterest.asp?id=156.

148   **Carla Freeman:** Blaine Harden, "Widows Face U.S. Deportation." *Washington Post,* December 2, 2004.

148   **In March 2005:** "Anti-Immigration Billboard Gets Complaints from Residents." Las Vegas, Nev.: www.kvbc.com, March 14, 2005.

149   **Some Americans:** Michael Marizco, "Border-Watch Group: All Talk?" *Arizona Daily Star* (Tucson), February 22, 2005.

149   **The Minutemen took care:** Jerry Seper, "Border Project Declared Success." *Washington Times,* April 13, 2005.

150   **Other groups:** Jonathan Athens, "Patriots Go on Patrol at Border." *Yuma Sun,* April 12, 2005.

150   **Others who resent:** Ted McDonough, "Homeland Insecurity." *Salt Lake City Weekly*, July 21, 2005.

150   **Idaho's Canyon County:** Rebecca Boone, "Idaho County Sues Over Immigrant Workers." Associated Press, July 17, 2005.

150   **New Ipswich, New Hampshire:** Pam Belluck, "Town Uses Trespass Law to Fight Illegal Immigrants." Associated Press, July 13, 2005.

152   **Not long after:** "U.S. Army Recruiter Crosses Mexico Border." Associated Press, May 9, 2003.

153   **Rafed al Janabi:** Mary Beth Sheridan, "Some Would-Be Citizens Languish for Years in Security-Check Limbo." *Washington Post*, February 7, 2005.

Lockout

155   **As Fareed Zakaria:** Fareed Zakaria, "Rejecting the Next Bill Gates." *Newsweek*, November 29, 2004.

156   **The Department of Homeland Security:** Alice P. Gast, "The Impact of Restricting Information Access on Science and Technology." Paper. Cambridge, Mass.: Massachusetts Institute of Technology, 2003.

156   **Around the time:** Stephen A. Edson, Managing Director, U.S. State Department Office of Visa Services, Testimony Before House Committee on Education and the Workforce Subcommittees on 21st Century Competitiveness and Select Education, March 17, 2005.

156   **Even as the government:** David A. Martin, "Immigration Policy and the Homeland Security Act Reorganization: An Early Agenda for Practical Improvements." Washington, D.C.: Migration Policy Institute, *MPI Insight*, April 2003.

157   **In a 2004 report:** "Border Security: Improvements Needed to Reduce Time Taken to Adjudicate Visas for Science Students and Scholars" (GAO-04-443T). Washington, D.C.: Government Accountability Office, February 25, 2004.

157   **Business applications:** Greenberg Traurig LLP, "Rejection Rates for U.S. Visa Applications," April 2004, based on data from the U.S. State Department Bureau of Consular Affairs, "Report of the Visa Office 2003," Washington, D.C., 2004.

158   **"Far too many scarce resources":** Marlene M. Johnson, "Addressing the New Reality of Current Visa Policy on International Students and Researchers." Testimony Before U.S. Senate Foreign Relations Committee, October 6, 2004.

158   **Business associations:** See, for example, National Association of Man-
        ufacturers, Manufacturing Institute, and Deloitte & Touche, "Keeping
        America Competitive: How a Talent Shortage Threatens U.S. Manu-
        facturing." Washington, D.C.: National Association of Manufacturers,
        2003; National Science Board, "The Science and Engineering Work-
        force: Realizing America's Potential." Washington, D.C.: National Sci-
        ence Foundation, August 14, 2003; American Electronics Association,
        "Losing the Competitive Advantage?" Washington, D.C.: American
        Electronics Association, February 2005; Computer Systems Policy
        Project, "Choose to Compete." Washington, D.C.: Computer Systems
        Policy Project, 2004; Council on Competitiveness, "Innovate Amer-
        ica." Washington, D.C.: Council on Competitiveness, 2004.

158   **"If action is not taken soon":** "Statement and Recommendations on
        Visa Problems Harming America's Scientific, Economic, and Security
        Interests." May 12, 2004. Available at www.aau.edu/homeland/Joint
        VisaStatement.pdf.

160   **Transcription errors:** Joint Statement of Randolph C. Hite, Director,
        Information Technology Architecture and Systems Issues, and Jess T.
        Ford, Director, International Affairs and Trade, "Homeland Security:
        Performance of Foreign Student and Exchange Visitor Information Sys-
        tem Continues to Improve, But Issues Remain" (GAO–05–440T).
        Washington, D.C.: Government Accountability Office, March 17,
        2005.

160   **"Backlogs and protracted delays":** Lawrence H. Bell, Testimony to the
        House Committee on Education and the Workforce Subcommittee on
        21st Century Competitiveness and Select Education, March 17, 2005.
        Available at http://edworkforce.house.gov/hearings/109th/21st/joint
        hea031705/bell.htm.

161   **SEVIS produces:** Victor X. Cerda, "Tracking International Students in
        Higher Education: A Progress Report." Testimony at House Subcom-
        mittee on 21st Century Competitiveness and Select Education Com-
        mittee on Education and the Workforce, March 17, 2005.

161   **Institute of International Education:** Institute for International Edu-
        cation, *Open Doors 2003.* New York: Institute for International Educa-
        tion, 2003.

161   **The Council of Graduate Schools:** Heath Brown and Maria Doulis,
        "Findings from 2005 CGS International Graduate Admissions Survey
        1." Washington, D.C.: Council of Graduate Schools, March 2005.

162   **In 2003, 20 percent:** Cited in Rob Paral and Benjamin Johnson,
        "Maintaining a Competitive Edge: The Role of the Foreign-Born and

U.S. Immigration Policies in Science and Engineering." Washington, D.C.: Immigration Policy Center, *Immigration Policy In Focus* 3, no. 3 (August 2004).

162   **Lijun Zhu, a physics graduate student:** Eric Berger, "Science Seen as Slipping in U.S.; Visa Hurdles Are Turning Away Foreign Talent, Experts Argue." *Houston Chronicle*, August 22, 2004.

162   **University of Utah physicist:** Michael Stroh, "Tougher Visa Rules to Stop Terrorism Hamper Research." *Baltimore Sun*, July 13, 2003; Yilu Zhao, "The Visa Trap." *New York Times*, January 18, 2004.

163   **Yang Wang, a 26-year-old:** Yilu Zhao, "The Visa Trap." *New York Times*, January 18, 2004.

163   **Late in 2003:** Doug Payne, "Students Blocked from U.S. Meeting." *Scientist*, February 2, 2004.

163   **"Is this a temporary blip":** Lawrence Bell, Testimony to the House Committee on Education and the Workforce Subcommittee on 21st Century Competitiveness and Select Education, March 17, 2005.

168   **According to the U.S. Department of Health and Human Services:** Lee Hockstader, "Post-9/11 Visa Rules Keep Thousands from Coming to the U.S." *Washington Post*, November 11, 2003.

169   **A rule change mandated by Congress:** Paral and Johnson, "Maintaining a Competitive Edge."

169   **The supply of nurses:** Paul Harasim, "Nursing Source at Risk: Influx of Health-Care Workers from Philippines Might Fall with Rule Change." *Las Vegas Review-Journal*, December 26, 2004.

169   **In the past:** Ann M. Simmons, "New Visa Process for Foreign Nurses May Affect Hospitals." *Los Angeles Times*, March 9, 2005.

169   **The visa restrictions:** Keith Muller, principal author, "The Immediate and Future Role of the J-1 Visa Waiver Program for Physicians: The Consequences of Change for Rural Health Care Service Delivery." Columbia, Mo.: Rural Policy Research Institute, April 2002. Available at www.rupri.org/publications/archive/reports/P2002-3/index.html.

170   **Just one example:** Statement of Palma R. Yanni, American Immigration Lawyers Association, Before the House Committee on Small Business, June 4, 2003.

171   **Eight major U.S. business groups:** "Do Visa Delays Hurt U.S. Businesses?" Santangelo Group, June 2004; a survey of 734 members of eight major industry groups, commissioned by Aerospace Industries Association, American Council on International Personnel, Association for Manufacturing Technology, Coalition for Employment Through Exports, National Foreign Trade Council, U.S.-China Business Council,

U.S.-Russia Business Council, U.S.-Vietnam Trade Council, prepared by the Santangelo Group.

174   **"Long delays and increased denials":** Testimony of Dr. Paul Freedenberg, Vice President for Government Relations, on Behalf of the Association For Manufacturing Technology, Before the U.S.-China Economic and Security Review Commission, June 21, 2005.

175   **Kanawha Scales and Systems, Inc.:** William J. McHale, Vice President of Sales, Kanawha Scales and Systems, Inc., Prepared Statement to the House Committee on Small Business, June 4, 2003.

176   **The International Consumer Electronics Show:** Teresa Borden, "Businesses Feel Pinch on Visas: Security Delays Hit Tech Sector Hardest." *Atlanta Journal-Constitution,* July 29, 2004.

177   **Anticipating the new biometric passport:** David Hackett, "Terrorism Will Have Consequences that Impact on C&I Travel." *Conference and Incentive Travel* (London), February 2004.

178   **In 2003, visa delays:** Gast, "The Impact of Restricting Information Access."

178   **The International Astronomical Union:** Sam Dillon, "Foreign Enrollment Declines at Universities, Surveys Say." *New York Times,* November 10, 2004.

181   **The United States deals with massive numbers:** U.S. Citizenship and Immigration Services (USCIS), "Fact Sheet: A Day in the Life of USCIS." June 29, 2005.

182   **According to a report in August 2005:** Sam Coates, "A Help Line in Need of Help." *Washington Post,* August 3, 2005; USCIS, "Fact Sheet."

If Not Here, Then Where?

185   **"The obvious advantage":** John Harker and William Archey, "Foreword," in "Losing the Competitive Advantage: The Challenge for Science and Technology in the United States." Washington, D.C.: American Electronics Association, February 2005.

185   **The U.S. Council on Competitiveness:** Michael E. Porter and Scott Stern, "The New Challenge to America's Prosperity: Findings from the Innovation Index." Washington, D.C.: Council on Competitiveness, 1999.

186   **What they are reading:** Thomas Friedman, *The World Is Flat: A Brief History of the Twenty-first Century.* New York: Farrar, Straus, Giroux, 2005; Clyde Prestowitz, *Three Billion New Capitalists: The Great Shift of Wealth and Power to the East.* New York: Basic Books, 2005; Ted Fish-

man, *China Inc.: How the Rise of the Next Superpower Challenges America and the World.* New York: Scribner, 2005; Richard Florida, *The Flight of the Creative Class: The New Global Competition for Talent.* New York: HarperCollins, 2005.

187 **In 1989, Japan:** United Nations, World Economic and Social Report, 2004.

187 **The European Union has set:** "New Expat Policy 'A Good Step, But EU Must Do More.'" *Expatica News,* October 1, 2004.

187 **Other wealthy countries:** Jean-Christophe Dumont and Georges Lemaître, "Counting Immigrants and Expatriates in OECD Countries: A New Perspective." Paris: Organization for Economic Cooperation and Development, Directorate for Employment Labor and Social Affairs, 2004.

188 **China's government has worked hard:** Jonathan Kaufman, "Seeking Fortunes, Chinese Return Home." *Wall Street Journal Europe,* March 10, 2003.

188 **Since 2003, more foreign direct investment:** A.T. Kearney, news release, "China and India Jockey for the Top Most Attractive Foreign Direct Investment Destination Globally While the U.S. Is Challenged by These Rapidly Evolving Economies." October 12, 2004.

188 **South Korea, for example:** "Ranking Economies by Broadband Penetration." International Telecommunication Union, Strategy and Policy Unit Newslog, September 15, 2004. Available at www.itu.int/osg/spu/newslog/categories/indicatorsAndStatistics/2004/09/15.html.

188 **"While we continue to believe":** American Electronics Association, "Losing the Competitive Advantage: The Challenge for Science and Technology in the United States." Washington, D.C.: American Electronics Association, February 2005. See also Michael Kanellos, "South Korea's Digital Dynasty." *CNet,* June 25, 2004; and John Borland and Michael Kanellos, "South Korea leads the way." *CNet,* July 28, 2004.

189 **In 1975, the United States was third:** National Science Board, "The Science and Engineering Workforce: Realizing America's Potential." Washington, D.C.: National Science Foundation, August 14, 2003.

189 **Today, the proportion has fallen:** Richard B. Freeman, "The Challenge of Integrating China, India, and the Former Soviet Bloc into the World Economy." Presentation at "Doubling the Global Work Force" conference, Washington, D.C., November 8, 2004.

190 **In 2004, top honors:** Jason Bush, "A Renaissance For Russian Science." *BusinessWeek,* August 9, 2004.

190 **From 1997 to 2003, Australia:** British Council and IDP Education Australia, "Vision 2020: Forecasting International Student Mobility,"

cited in Matthew Thompson, "Unis Attract More Students." *Sydney Morning Herald*, July 15, 2004.

190 **Because the policy change increased:** Greg Winter, "Students to Bear More of the Cost of College." *New York Times*, December 23, 2004.

190 **From 2002 to 2003, Chinese enrollment:** Yilu Zhao, "The Visa Trap." *New York Times*, January 18, 2004.

190 **The British Council predicts:** Cited by Marlene Johnson, in Statement of Marlene M. Johnson, Executive Director and CEO, NAFSA: Association of International Educators, Before the Committee on Foreign Relations, United States Senate, "Addressing the New Reality of Current Visa Policy on International Students and Researchers," October 6, 2004.

191 **"The medical school in New Delhi":** Brent Schlender, "Peter Drucker Sets Us Straight." *Fortune*, January 12, 2004.

191 **Seeking to capitalize:** Eric Berger, "Science Seen as Slipping in U.S.; Visa Hurdles Are Turning Away Foreign Talent, Experts Argue." *Houston Chronicle*, August 22, 2004.

192 **In a 2003 survey carried out:** Organization for Economic Cooperation and Development, Program for International Student Assessment 2003. Paris, December 2004. Available at www.oecd.org/document/28/0,2340, en_2649_201185_34010524_1_1_1_1,00.html. See also International Association for the Evaluation of Educational Achievement, Third International Mathematics and Science Study (TIMSS).

193 **Nearly eight in ten respondents:** National Association of Manufacturers, *The Skills Gap 2001: Manufacturers Confront Persistent Skills Shortages in an Uncertain Economy*. Washington, D.C.: National Association of Manufacturers, 2001; and National Association of Manufacturers, Manufacturing Institute, and Deloitte & Touche, "Keeping America Competitive: How a Talent Shortage Threatens U.S. Manufacturing." Washington, D.C.: National Association of Manufacturers, 2003.

193 **From 1990 to 2002, for example, employment in high-tech:** U.S. National Science Foundation and American Electronics Association, *Cyberstates 3.0* and *Cyberstates 2002*.

193 **During the same period:** American Electronics Association, "Losing the Competitive Advantage."

194 **A National Manufacturers Association survey:** National Association of Manufacturers, *The Skills Gap 2001*.

194 **Richard Florida:** Richard Florida, *The Flight of the Creative Class: The New Global Competition for Talent*. New York: HarperBusiness, 2005.

195   **According to the *Economist*:** "Foreign Bosses: Outside In." *Economist*, January 1, 2005.

196   **A December 2004 British poll:** "Out with the New." *Economist*, December 11, 2004.

196   **Among OECD countries:** National Science Board, "Realizing America's Potential."

196   **R&D investment in the United States:** American Electronics Association, "Losing the Competitive Advantage."

197   **Preliminary 2002 data show:** "OECD Countries Spend More on Research and Development, Face New Challenges." Paris: Organization for Economic Cooperation and Development, December 12, 2004.

197   **From 1994 to 2000, for example:** Francisco Moris, "U.S.-China R&D Linkages: Direct Investment and Industrial Alliances in the 1990s." National Science Foundation Info Brief NSF 04-306, February 2004.

198   **Already by 2000:** "Globalizing Through Turbulence: Global Investment Trends of U.S. Manufacturers." Deloitte Consulting and Deloitte & Touche LLP, 2001.

198   **Starting out with call centers:** Narayanan Madhavan, "New Start-Up Breed: Born in the USA, Made in India." Reuters, September 19, 2004.

199   **The list of companies setting up:** Hiawatha Bray, "The White-Collar Job Migration: As Economy Gains, Outsourcing Surges." *Boston Globe*, November 3, 2003.

199   **Thomas Friedman has argued:** Thomas Friedman, *The World Is Flat: A Brief History of the Twenty-first Century*. Farrar, Straus, Giroux, 2005.

200   **A 2004 McKinsey Global Institute study:** Martin N. Baily and Diana Farrell, "Exploding the Myths About Offshoring." McKinsey & Company, April 2004.

201   **A University of California–Berkeley study:** Ashok Deo Bardhan and Cynthia Kroll, "The New Wave of Outsourcing." Fischer Center for Real Estate and Urban Economics, University of California, Berkeley, 2003.

201   **Not surprisingly, the jobs:** National Association of Manufacturers, "Keeping America Competitive."

201   **Yet after companies factor in:** Estimate by Joseph Feman at Gartner Inc., in Steve Lohr, "Jobs in Technology: Opportunity or Threat?" *New York Times*, December 22, 2003.

202   **In 2004, the credit card group:** Katherine Griffiths and Niklin Kumar, "AXA Repatriates Call Centre Jobs from Bangalore." *Independent* (London), April 2, 2004.

202   **In a survey of 100 British companies:** "Over There Can't Compare." *Observer* (London), November 30, 2003.

The Day They Go Away

204   **Look at what happened:** Justin Huggler, "Malaysia Begs Expelled Immigrant Workers to Return." *Independent*, May 27, 2005; John Aglionby, "Clamp on Illegal Migrant Workers Lifted." *Guardian*, May 27, 2005.

205   **A Chesapeake Bay crab picking company:** Sofia Kosmetatos, "Maryland Scrambling for Shore Workers." *Daily Record* (Baltimore), February 14, 2005.

205   **The summer hospitality industry:** John Flesher, "Grand Experiment at Grand Hotel: Michigan Resort Bends with Law on Foreign Staff." Associated Press, March 24, 2005.

206   **A group of 800 manufacturers in a survey:** Deloitte Consulting LLP, National Association of Manufacturers, and Manufacturing Institute, *2005 Skills Gap Report: A Survey of the American Manufacturing Workforce*. Washington, D.C.: National Association of Manufacturers, November 22, 2005.

206   **"If a U.S. company needs":** American Electronics Association, "Losing the Competitive Advantage: The Challenge for Science and Technology in the United States." Washington, D.C.: American Electronics Association, February 2005; and National Association of Manufacturers et al., "Keeping America Competitive."

207   **As Clay Risen reported:** Clay Risen, "Remaindered: The Decline of Brand America." *New Republic*, April 11, 2005.

208   **Shirley Ann Jackson:** Shirley Ann Jackson, "The Perfect Storm: A Weather Forecast." Speech delivered at the annual meeting of the American Association for the Advancement of Science, February 14, 2004.

213   **Researchers in a 2001 study:** Gordon Lafer, Helen Moss, Rachel Kirtner, and Vicki Rees, "Solving the Nursing Shortage." A Report Prepared for the United Nurses of America, American Federation of State, County and Municipal Employees, AFL-CIO. Eugene, Ore.: Labor Education and Research Center, University of Oregon, May 2003.

213   **A 2003 survey of medical school deans:** Rimin Dutt, "H-1B Cap Could Push 1,600 Doctors from U.S." *IndUS Business Journal*, March 15, 2004.

214   **Similarly, the nursing industry:** Jo Anne Chernev Adlerstein, "Brain Drain: Our Immigration Law Isn't Helping Us." *New York Newsday*, December 10, 2004.

214   **In California:** Ann M. Simmons, "New Visa Process for Foreign Nurses May Affect Hospitals." *Los Angeles Times*, March 9, 2005.

214   **Stuart Anderson:** Stuart Anderson, "The Contribution of Legal Immigration to the Social Security System." Arlington, Va.: National Foundation for American Policy, March 2005 (updated and revised from January 2005). Available at www.nfap.net/researchactivities/studies/SocialSecurityStudy2005.pdf.

Getting Immigration Right

227   **John Fonte:** John Fonte, "We Need a Patriotic Assimilation Policy." *American Outlook*, Winter 2003.

228   **As Robert D. Putnam lamented:** Robert D. Putnam, *Bowling Alone: The Collapse and Revival of American Community*. New York: Simon & Schuster, 2000.

229   **Above all, we desperately need:** New York Immigration Coalition, "Eager for English: How and Why New York's Shortage of English Classes Should Be Addressed." New York: New York Immigration Coalition, March 2001; and U.S. Citizenship and Immigration Services, "Helping Immigrants Become New Americans: Communities Discuss the Issues." Washington, D.C., 2004.

234   **According to a 2005 Pew Hispanic Center report:** Jeffrey Passel and Robert Suro, "Rise, Peak, and Decline: Trends in U.S. Immigration 1992–2004." Washington, D.C.: Pew Hispanic Center, September 2005.

234   **This change in numbers:** Passel and Suro, "Rise, Peak, and Decline."

235   **As sociologist Ramona Hernández:** Ramona Hernández, *The Mobility of Workers Under Advanced Capitalism*. New York: Columbia University Press, 2002.

235   **Between 1985 and 2002:** David Dixon and Julia Gelatt, "Immigration Enforcement Spending Since IRCA." Washington, D.C.: Migration Policy Institute, November 2005.

242   **American students themselves:** Jim Lobe, "Foreign Students Enrollment Decline for First Time in Generation." OneWorld US—IIENetwork, November 16, 2004.

242   **If a March 2005 poll:** National Immigration Forum, "A National Survey of Voter Attitudes on Immigration." National poll conducted March 20–22, 2005, by Lake Snell Perry Mermin and the Tarrance Group.

Selective Bibliography

Immigrants in the Early Twentieth Century

The *Journal of American Ethnic History* has an article in nearly every issue covering immigrants in the United States in the first part of the twentieth century.

Jane Addams. *Peace and Bread in Time of War*. New York: Macmillan, 1922.

Saul Alinsky. *Reveille for Radicals*. New York: Vintage, 1969 (1946).

John Bodnar. *The Transplanted: A History of Immigrants in Urban America*. Bloomington: Indiana University Press, 1985.

Jean Bethke Elshtain. *Jane Addams and the Dream of American Democracy*. New York: Basic Books, 2001.

Nancy Foner. *From Ellis Island to JFK: New York's Two Great Waves of Immigration*. New Haven, Conn.: Yale University Press and Russell Sage Foundation, 2000.

_____. *New Immigrants in New York*. New York: Columbia University Press, 1987.

John Higham. *Strangers in the Land: Patterns of American Nativism 1860–1925*. New York: Atheneum, 1963 (1955).

Daniel T. Rodgers. *Atlantic Crossings: Social Politics in a Progressive Age*. Cambridge, Mass.: Belknap/Harvard University Press, 1998.

Mark Wyman. *Round-Trip to America: The Immigrants Return to Europe, 1880–1930*. Ithaca, N.Y.: Cornell University Press, 1993.

Becoming American

Richard D. Alba. *Ethnic Identity: The Transformation of White America*. New Haven, Conn.: Yale University Press, 1990.

Michael Barone. *The New Americans*. Washington, D.C.: Regnery Publishing, 2001.

Peter Brimelow. *Alien Nation: Common Sense About America's Immigration Disaster*. New York: Harper Perennial, 1996.

Randolph Bourne. *Selected Writings, 1911–1918*. Edited by Olaf Hansen, foreword by Christopher Lasch. Berkeley: University of California Press, 1992.

Patrick Buchanan. *The Death of the West: How Dying Populations and Immigrant Invasions Imperil Our Country and Civilization*. New York: St. Martin's Press, 2002.

Héctor St. John de Crèvecoeur. *Letters of an American Farmer*. New York: Penguin Classics, 1981 (1782).

Alexis de Tocqueville. *Democracy in America*. New York: Modern Library, 1981 (1839).

Gerstle, Gary. *American Crucible: Race and Nation in the Twentieth Century*. Princeton, N.J.: Princeton University Press, 1992.

Todd Gitlin. *The Twilight of Common Dreams: Why America Is Wracked by Culture Wars*. New York: Metropolitan Books, 1995.

Nathan Glazer and Daniel P. Moynihan. *Beyond the Melting Pot: The Negroes, Puerto Ricans, Jews, Italians, and Irish of New York City*, 2nd edition. Cambridge, Mass.: MIT Press, 1995 (1970).

Milton Gordon. *Assimilation in American Life: The Role of Race, Religion, and National Origins*. New York: Oxford University Press, 1964.

Oscar Handlin. *The Uprooted: The Epic Story of the Great Migrations that Made the American People*. Boston: Atlantic Monthly Press, 1973 (1951).

Marcus Lee Hansen. *The Immigrant in American History*. New York: Harper Torchbooks, 1964 (1940).

Victor Davis Hanson. *Mexifornia: A State of Becoming*. San Francisco: Encounter Books, 2003.

Samuel Huntington. *Who Are We? The Challenges to America's National Identity*. New York: Simon & Schuster, 2004.

John Isbister. *The Immigration Debate: Remaking America*. West Hartford, Conn.: Kumarian Press, 1996.

Matthew Jacobson. *Whiteness of a Different Color: European Immigrants and the Alchemy of Race*. Cambridge, Mass.: Harvard University Press, 1998.

Tamar Jacoby, editor. *Reinventing the Melting Pot: The New Immigrants and What It Means to Be American*. New York: Basic Books, 2004.

Horace Kallen. *Cultural Pluralism and the American Idea: An Essay in Social Philosphy*. Philadelphia: University of Pennsylvania Press, 1956.

John F. Kennedy. *A Nation of Immigrants*. New York: Harper & Row, 1964.

Arthur Mann. *The One and the Many: Reflections on the American Identity*. Chicago: University of Chicago Press, 1979.

Michael Novak. *Rise of the Unmeltable Ethnics: Politics and Culture in the Seventies*. New York: Macmillan, 1972.

Gunnar Myrdal. *An American Dilemma: The Negro Problem and Modern Democracy*. New Brunswick, N.J.: Transaction Publishers, 1996 (1944).

Noah Pickus. *True Faith and Allegiance: Immigration and American Civic Nationalism*. Princeton, N.J.: Princeton University Press, 2005.

Stanley Renshon. *The 50% American: Immigration and National Identity in an Age of Terror*. Washington, D.C.: Georgetown University Press, 2005.

Ruben G. Rumbaut and Alejandro Portes, editors. *Ethnicities: Children of Immigrants in America*. Berkeley and Los Angeles: University of California Press and Russell Sage Foundation, 2001.

Arthur M. Schlesinger Jr. *The Disuniting of America: Reflections on a Multicultural Society*. New York: W.W. Norton, 1992.

Peter Skerry. *Mexican Americans: The Ambivalent Minority*. Cambridge, Mass.: Harvard University Press, 1995.

Werner Sollors. *Beyond Ethnicity: Consent and Descent in American Culture*. New York: Oxford University Press, 1998. Also see two volumes edited by Sollors, *The Invention of Ethnicity* (Oxford University Press reprint edition, 1991) and *Theories of Ethnicity* (New York University Press, 1996).

Ronald Takaki. *A Different Mirror: A History of Multicultural America*. New York: Little, Brown, 1993.

Immigration Policy and Background

The following books provide a variety of perspectives on immigration law, undocumented migrants, citizenship policies, and other issues that provide a backdrop for discussion of immigration today. In addition, several organizations issue regular publications on these issues: the Center for Immigration Studies, which advocates sharply restricting immigration; the Immigration Policy Center, an arm of the American Immigration Law Foundation, with a particular focus on law and immigrants' rights; the Migration Policy Institute, an independent research institute that does an excellent job of presenting all sides of issues and supporting underlying data; the National Immigration Forum, an advocacy group; and the Center for Comparative Immigration Studies at University of California–San Diego.

Roger Daniels. *Guarding the Golden Door: American Immigration Policy and Immigrants Since 1882.* New York: Hill & Wang, 2004.

John Higham. *Send These to Me: Immigrants in Urban America,* 2nd edition. Baltimore: Johns Hopkins University Press, 1984.

Michelle Malkin. *Invasion: How America Still Welcomes Terrorists, Criminals, and Other Foreign Menaces to Our Shores.* Washington, D.C.: Regnery Publishing, 2004.

Joseph Nevins. *Operation Gatekeeper: The Rise of the "Illegal Alien" and the Making of the U.S.-Mexico Boundary.* New York: Routledge, 2002.

Mae M. Ngai. *Impossible Subjects: Illegal Aliens and the Making of Modern America.* Princeton: N.J.: Princeton University Press, 2004.

Thomas Sowell. *Migrations and Cultures: A World View.* New York: Basic Books, 1996.

Bill Ong Hing. *Defining America Through Immigration Policy.* Philadelphia: Temple University Press, 2004.

David Jacobson. *Rights Across Borders: Immigration and the Decline of Citizenship.* Baltimore: Johns Hopkins University Press, 1997 (1996).

Kevin R. Johnson. *The "Huddled Masses" Myth: Immigration and Civil Rights.* Philadelphia: Temple University Press, 2004.

T. Alexander Aleinikoff and Douglas Klusmeyer, editors. *Citizenship Today: Global Perspectives and Practices.* Washington, D.C.: Carnegie Endowment for Peace, 2001.

Will Kymlicka. *Multicultural Citizenship.* New York: Oxford University Press, 1995.

Daniel Tichenor. *Dividing Lines: The Politics of Immigration Control in America.* Princeton, N.J.: Princeton University Press, 2002.

Immigrants in Wartime

Although the widespread internment and harassment of Germans and Italians during World War II have received relatively little public attention in comparison with the Japanese internments, the body of literature documenting the lesser known internments is growing. Similarly, the World War I internment of approximately 6,000 foreign-born visitors and citizens is little known but has been covered, mainly in works focusing on German Americans.

Frederick C. Luebke, *Bonds of Loyalty: German-Americans and World War I.* DeKalb: Northern Illinois University Press, 1974.

John Christgau. *Enemies: World War II Alien Internment.* Lincoln, Neb.: Authors Choice Press, 2001.

Roger Daniels. *Politics of Prejudice.* Berkeley: University of California Press, 1962.

Louis DeJong. *The German Fifth Column in the Second World War*. Chicago: University of Chicago Press, 1973 (1956).

Stephen Fox. *The Unknown Internment: An Oral History of the Relocation of Italian Americans During World War II*. Boston: Twayne, 1990.

_____. *America's Invisible Gulag: A Biography of German American Internment and Exclusion in World War II*. New York: Peter Lang, 2000.

Lawson Fusao Inada, editor. *Only What We Could Carry: The Japanese American Internment Experience*. Berkeley, Calif.: Heyday Books, 2000.

Commission on Wartime Relocation and the Internment of Citizens. *Personal Justice Denied*. Washington, D.C., and Seattle: Civil Liberties Public Education Fund and University of Washington Press, 1997 (1982).

John Hawgood. *The Tragedy of German-America: The Germans in the United States of America During the Nineteenth Century—and After*. New York: G.P. Putnam's Sons, 1940.

Arnold Krammer. *Undue Process: the Untold Story of America's German Alien Internees*. Boulder: Rowman & Littlefield, 1997.

Michelle Malkin. *In Defense of Internment: The Case for "Racial Profiling" in World War II and the War on Terror*. Washington, D.C.: Regnery Publishing, 2004.

Richard O'Connor. *The German-Americans*. New York: Little, Brown, 1968.

Geoffrey Stone. *Perilous Times: Free Speech in Wartime from the Sedition Act of 1798 to the War on Terrorism*. New York: W.W. Norton, 2004.

William H. Rehnquist. *All the Laws But One: Civil Liberties In Wartime*. New York: Random House, 1998.

Jacobus ten Broek, Edward N. Barnhart, and Floyd Watson. *Prejudice, War, and the Constitution: Causes and Consequences of the Evacuation of the Japanese Americans in World War II*. Berkeley: University of California Press: 1975 (1954).

Michi Weglyn. *Years of Infamy: The Untold Story of America's Concentration Camps*. New York: Morrow, 1976.

Carl Wittke. *German-Americans and the World War*. Columbus: Ohio State Archaeological and Historical Society, 1936.

Immigrants and Their Homelands Today

There is a broad and growing academic literature on immigrants' connections to their homeland today. I have listed just a few titles here, along with some books written for wider audiences. The relationship between immigrants and their homeland is often best portrayed in fiction, so I have included a sampling of notable novels and short stories written by immigrant American writers in recent years.

Edwidge Danticat, editor. *The Butterfly's Way: Voices from the Haitian Dyaspora in the United States*. New York: Soho Press, 2001.

Barbara Fischkin. *Muddy Cup: A Dominican Family Comes of Age in a New America*. New York: Scribner, 1991.

Nina G. Schiller, Linda G. Basch, and Cristina Szanton Blanc, editors. *Towards a Transnational Perspective on Migration: Race, Class, Ethnicity, and Nationalism Reconsidered*. New York: New York Academy of Sciences, 1992.

Sherri Grasmuck and Patricia R. Pessar. *Between Two Islands: Dominican International Migration*. Berkeley: University of California Press, 1991.

Michael Jones-Correa. *Between Two Nations: The Political Predicament of Latinos in New York*. Ithaca, N.Y.: Cornell University Press, 1998.

Peggy Levitt. *The Transnational Villagers*. Berkeley: University of California Press, 2001.

Mira Kamdar. *Motiba's Tattoos: A Granddaughter's Journey from America into her Indian Family's Past*. New York: PublicAffairs Books, 2000.

Frank McCourt. *Angela's Ashes: A Memoir*. New York: Scribner, 1996.

Stacy Sullivan. *Be Not Afraid, For You Have Sons In America: How a Brooklyn Roofer Helped Lure the U.S. into the Kosovo War*. New York: St. Martin's Press, 2004.

Fiction

Julia Alvarez. *How the García Girls Lost Their Accents*. Chapel Hill, N.C.: Algonquin Books, 1991.

Lan Samantha Chang. *Hunger: A Novella and Stories*. New York: W.W. Norton, 1998.

Junot Díaz. *Drown*. New York: Riverhead, 1997.

Cristina García. *Dreaming in Cuban*. New York: Knopf, 1992.

Oscar Hijuelos. *The Mambo Kings Play Songs of Love*. New York: Farrar, Straus and Giroux, 1989. Also *Empress of the Splendid Season*. New York: HarperCollins, 1999.

Gish Jen. *Typical American*. New York: Houghton Mifflin, 1992.

Jhumpa Lahiri. *Interpreter of Maladies*. New York: Mariner Books, 1999.

Gary Shteyngart. *The Russian Debutante's Handbook*. New York: Riverhead, 2002.

Amy Tan. *The Joy Luck Club*. Palo Alto, Calif.: Minerva, 1997.

Immigrants, Globalization, and the American Economy

The following books give historical and contemporary accounts of various aspects of the economics of immigration, the relationship between globalization

and immigration, and the relationship between globalization and prosperity or decline. Several organizations track these issues (from various perspectives), among them the American Institute of Physics, the Center for Immigration Studies, the Council of Graduate Schools, the Institute for International Education, NAFSA: Association of International Educators, the National Association of Manufacturers, the Institute for International Economics, the National Foundation for American Policy, the National Science Board, and the Policy Institute of California. Eight major industry groups commissioned the study "Do Visa Delays Hurt U.S. Businesses?" published in June 2004 by the Santangelo Group.

George J. Borjas. *Heaven's Door: Immigration and the American Economy.* Princeton, N.J.: Princeton University Press, 1999.

Richard Florida. *The Flight of the Creative Class: The New Global Competition for Talent.* New York: HarperCollins, 2005.

Thomas L. Friedman. *The World Is Flat: A Brief History of the Twenty-First Century.* New York: Farrar, Straus and Giroux, 2005.

John Kenneth Galbraith. *The Great Crash, 1929.* New York: Houghton Mifflin, 1997 (1954).

Howard James. *The End of Globalization.* Cambridge, Mass.: Harvard University Press, 2001.

Peter Marber. *Money Changes Everything: How Global Prosperity Is Reshaping Our Needs, Values, and Lifestyles.* New York: Prentice Hall, 2003.

Joel Millman. *The Other Americans: How Immigrants Renew Our Country, Our Economy, and Our Values.* New York: Viking Press, 1997.

Kevin O'Rourke and Jeffrey Williamson. *Globalization in History: The Evolution of a Nineteenth-Century Global Economy.* Cambridge, Mass.: MIT Press, 1999.

N. Sivakumar. *Debugging Indian Computer Programmers: Dude, Did I Steal Your Job?* Bridgewater, N.J.: DivineTree Press, 2004.

G. Paschal Zachary. *The Global Me: New Cosmopolitans and the Competitive Edge: Picking Globalism's Winners and Losers.* New York: PublicAffairs Books, 2000.

Homeland Security After 9/11

A number of organizations track the effectiveness of post-9/11 security measures and their impact on those who cross U.S. borders. These include the American Immigration Law Foundation and Immigration Policy Center (sympathetic to immigrant advocates' concerns), the Center for Immigration Studies (arguing for restrictions to immigration), the General Accountability

Office, the Department of Homeland Security Ombudsman's Office, the Department of Justice, Human Rights First, and the Migration Policy Institute.

David Cole. *Enemy Aliens*. New York: New Press, 2003.

John Tirman, editor. *The Maze of Fear: Security and Migration After 9/11*. A Social Science Research Council book. New York: New Press, 2004.

Tram Nguyen. *We Are All Suspects Now: Untold Stories from Immigrant Communities After 9/11*. Boston: Beacon Press, 2005.

Roberto Suro. "Who Are 'We' Now? The Collateral Damage to Immigration." In *The War on Our Freedoms: Civil Liberties in an Age of Terrorism*. Edited by Richard Leone and Greg Anrig. A Century Foundation Book. New York: PublicAffairs Books, 2003.

Index

PublicAffairs is a publishing house founded in 1997. It is a tribute to the standards, values, and flair of three persons who have served as mentors to countless reporters, writers, editors, and book people of all kinds, including me.

I.F. STONE, proprietor of *I. F. Stone's Weekly*, combined a commitment to the First Amendment with entrepreneurial zeal and reporting skill and became one of the great independent journalists in American history. At the age of eighty, Izzy published *The Trial of Socrates*, which was a national bestseller. He wrote the book after he taught himself ancient Greek.

BENJAMIN C. BRADLEE was for nearly thirty years the charismatic editorial leader of *The Washington Post*. It was Ben who gave the *Post* the range and courage to pursue such historic issues as Watergate. He supported his reporters with a tenacity that made them fearless and it is no accident that so many became authors of influential, best-selling books.

ROBERT L. BERNSTEIN, the chief executive of Random House for more than a quarter century, guided one of the nation's premier publishing houses. Bob was personally responsible for many books of political dissent and argument that challenged tyranny around the globe. He is also the founder and longtime chair of Human Rights Watch, one of the most respected human rights organizations in the world.

For fifty years, the banner of Public Affairs Press was carried by its owner Morris B. Schnapper, who published Gandhi, Nasser, Toynbee, Truman, and about 1,500 other authors. In 1983, Schnapper was described by *The Washington Post* as "a redoubtable gadfly." His legacy will endure in the books to come.

Peter Osnos, *Founder and Editor-at-Large*